TANGLED UP IN TUNES

BALLAD OF A DYLANHEAD

To Kip,

Enjoy!

Howard Weiner

HOWARD F. WEINER

ISBN: 0615555721
ISBN 13: 9780615555720
Library of Congress Control Number: 2011918945
Pencil Hill Publishing New York, New York

Acknowledgements

I received essential help throughout the writing of this book. Here's to the genius of generosity. In particular, I'd like to thank Meghan Pino, Robert Polito, Kimberly Perel, Lauren Cardon, Perry Paletta, Robert Levinson, Stephanie Weiner, and my mother, Fran.

*This book is dedicated to the memory of my father, Lenny,
and also to the future—my oldest nephews, Lucas and Logan.*

Contents

"For me, I think the only danger is being too much in love with guitar playing. The music is the most important thing, and the guitar is only the instrument."

- Jerry Garcia

"I find the religiosity and the philosophy in the music. I don't find it anywhere else...I don't adhere to rabbis, preachers, evangelists, all of that. I've learned more from the songs than I've learned from any of this kind of entity. The songs are my lexicon, I believe the songs."

- Bob Dylan

"The best teacher is experience and not through someone's distorted point of view."

- Jack Kerouac

SHOOTING STAR

*The Lumberjack Incident...Coed Fever...Shooting
Star of the North Country...A spontaneous soiree
for Obama...Democracy strikes again, a Deadhead
elected to the senate...Beer-pong with Dylan...*

I was chilling in Dylan's old crash pad, now part of Loring Pasta Bar, the swankiest joint on the town's modest strip. The beer I had for brunch tickled my brain, so I went down and grabbed another for dessert, and then returned to my throne by the window. Hazy sunshine and sticky seventy-five-degree air flowed in—bizarre North Country weather for mid-autumn. Somewhere in the near distance, orgasmic female screams answered honking horns—a call and response blues jam. Far from an ordinary Tuesday afternoon in Minneapolis, this was November 4, 2008, a historic Election Day for America. It was also my forty-fifth birthday. I was in town to see The Bob Dylan Show later that evening.

I was on a pilgrimage, seeking inspiration in Dylan's old apartment on top of what used to be Grey's Drugstore in Dinkytown, the bohemian enclave of Minneapolis. This was where Dylan was first turned on to Woody Guthrie, and it was here that his passion for Woody's songs became an obsession. Perhaps I'd pick up on some mystical vibe that still lingered in the air forty-eight years after Dylan left for New York City. Unfortunately, there was nothing commemorating Dylan's residency here, and I didn't commune with any ghosts. Dylan's soul and spirit lie within his songs. I played *Highway 61 Revisited* on my CD Walkman and split.

On the way back to the Radisson, I cut through the University of Minnesota campus to preview the concert site, Northrop Auditorium. I couldn't spot a billboard or marquee with Dylan's name or image. Was I in the right place? This was Obama nation. Dazzling posters of Obama cluttered message boards, garbage cans, thick-rooted trees, bus stop shelters and lampposts. The portraits of Barack made him seem even more handsome and charismatic than he already was—the American Idolization of his image. Campus was calm, but I continued to hear outbursts of cheering and horns honking back and forth in rhyme—a piercing prelude to Obama's ascension.

I'd arrived from New York City the night before and checked into the Radisson around midnight. I set up my portable JBL speakers and played *Tell Tale Signs*, a scintillating collection of outtakes that captures the haunting tone of Dylan's recent albums. I had just begun to sing along with Bob on an acoustic version of "Mississippi" when I heard thunderous pounding against the wall. *Bam! Bam! Bam!* Startled by this barbaric outburst, I lowered the volume of the music and concluded that my neighbor was either Barney Rubble's son or a lumberjack with hands of stone. I further determined he wasn't going to appreciate the way I harmonized with Dylan on "The Girl from the Red River Shore." Instead of confronting my big-fisted foe, I went to the front desk and begged for a room change. Fortuitously, I met the manager, a Dylan and Grateful Dead fan. He understood my needs and upgraded me to a room where my only neighbor was an ice machine. I sang myself to sleep without incident.

The following afternoon, I dropped by the manager's office for a chat.

"Hey bro. I just wanted to thank you for the hospitality last night. After delays at JFK and a bumpy plane ride, I needed to kick back and enjoy some tunes," I said.

"Great, Howie. I'm glad we were able to accommodate you," said the manager. "If you gotta a few minutes to spare, I got an amazing Grateful Dead DVD you should check out."

"Sure," I said. "For live Dead, time's not an issue."

The manager angled his computer so we both could see it. The Dead broke into "All Along the Watchtower." Jerry Garcia's guitar boiled, Bob Weir's falsetto voice shrieked, and the crowd was manic. I could name that concert. "9-18-87 MSG," I yelled, like a crazed contestant solving the puzzle on *Wheel of Fortune*.

"Say what?" asked the manager.

"I was there! Madison Square Garden on Friday, September 18, 1987. It was one year after Jerry's coma. And wait 'til you hear 'Morning Dew,' the Garden goes ballistic," I said.

The Radisson Manager was mystified by my ability to identify this bootleg DVD after only hearing a few notes. He also might have thought I was partially deranged, but that gig has a tight connection to my heart. I'd experienced many Grateful Dead shows, but I never heard a crowd roar like that before. Jerry laid his soul on the line for New York City. That "Morning Dew" was one of my last transcendent moments with Jerry Garcia. After that night, watching Jerry struggle in concert was like watching Don Mattingly fade away at the plate during his final years in pinstripes. Anyway, my knowledge impressed my gracious host. He handed me a twenty-dollar comp for the hotel bar and said, "Enjoy, brother. I'll probably see you inside the Dylan show." I finally got compensated for my lunacy.

As showtime neared, anticipation and expectation swelled inside Northrop Auditorium. The Prodigal Son had returned. This was Dylan's debut concert on the campus of the college he had dropped out of to claim fame in New York. Dylan's past was present: folks from his hometown of Hibbing, Minnesota, who knew him as Bobby Zimmerman; peers from his Dinkytown days; academics and professors who scrutinized his oeuvre. The poet laureate of American music, our Jewish homeboy from the Iron Range, was serenading the faithful on the evening that an African American born in Hawaii would break the ultimate color barrier.

I settled into my twentieth-row seat. Right behind me were two affable young ladies in Minnesota Gopher attire. They were studying biophysics, and I was studying them. Their approach to this concert was simple: they didn't know any of Dylan's tunes, but they were psyched to see a legend. I told them I was from Manhattan, and I was writing a book on Dylan. They just might be impressed by a mystery man on a scholarly quest. How else could I smoothly explain why I'd traveled cross-country to see one Dylan concert when I've already seen ninety-two? I was thrilled these girls were my friends for the evening. They looked like cast members from the Real World: one a natural California blonde; the other a sultry Asian beauty. One smelled like magnolias, and the other banana bread. My scalp was bare, but with my baby face and rugged physique, I hoped to pass for thirty-five.

The sultry Asian student with jeans torn at the knees placed her dainty fingers on my shoulder, leaned over my neck, and whispered, "We're, like, so excited for the concert, and that's, like—ah, so cool that you're a writer and you live in Manhattan. We don't have any ID. If we give you money, can you buy us beers?"

I refused the money with a nonchalant wave of my hand and returned with three jumbo beers as the lights dimmed.

Dressed in black with a wide-brimmed, white top hat, Dylan exuded alpha maleness despite his slender frame. His bandmates wore fine tailored suits, Obama pins, and serious expressions. The audience cheered lustily when they identified "The Times They Are-A-Changin'" and "Masters of War." Playing keyboards most of the night, Dylan aroused the crowd whenever he grabbed his harmonica and blasted away, tiptoeing across the stage. Rapturous applause erupted at the beginning and ending of Dylan's idiosyncratic harp solos.

The reality girls yahooed and shook their hips as Dylan twisted away behind his keyboards to the electrified swing of "Summer Days."

The blonde one tapped me on the shoulder, cupped her hand to my ear and said, "This is sooooo amazing." Her tongue ever so slightly grazed my earlobe. Good vibrations surrounded me. I was relieved that these college cookies were digging the groove because Dylan's voice was gruff like an old carnival barker at the end of a double shift. Either you were drawn to the rumbling or you were repulsed, but everyone listened. Dylan's mysterious web of charisma hypnotized the audience.

Dylan muffed some lyrics and his vocals were more jagged than usual, but the audacious fifteen-song set made up for any performance hiccups. Hopscotching across his canon, Dylan offered sketches of America that represented all five decades of his career. When Bob grunted, "Even the President of the United States must sometimes have to stand naked," it sounded more like a warning shot for Obama than a eulogy for Bush. Revolution was in the air. It was the sentimental "Shooting Star," however, that jingle-jangled indelibly in my mind.

A backdrop of a star-cluttered sky unfurled behind the band as they glided into the opening chords. "Shooting Star" is a sacred song that Dylan only breaks out once or twice a tour. Dylan sang with a gentle caress: "Seen a shooting star tonight, and I thought of me. If I was still the same. If I ever became what you wanted me to be." If ever a singer became his words, Dylan did that night. He was Minnesota's shooting star. Trekking down memory lane, Dylan moseyed from the organ and snatched an electric guitar. The crowd showered their North Star with love as he stood like a toy soldier and plucked an awkwardly authentic solo.

My mind left the action in Minneapolis when Dylan crooned, "Seen a shooting star tonight, and I thought of you. You were trying to break into another world; a world I never knew." I reflected back on my twenty-one-year fascination with Dylan's music. "Shooting Star" is the final tune on *Oh Mercy,* Dylan's gloomy 1989 masterpiece. I skipped all my college classes at SUNY New Paltz that semester and held daily *Oh Mercy* listening parties in my ground floor crash pad. The baby blue house I rented bore a striking resemblance to Dylan's childhood home in Hibbing. Some folks settle down, but some of us are shooting stars, restless strangers, in a constant state of becoming—lonesome and a long way from home.

New Paltz was my first home away from my parent's house, but I'll always remember that town as the place where I was seduced by *Blood on the Tracks* while driving north on Route 32. After hearing that tape, my brain went berserk. I scored every Dylan album and felt immediate connection to a level of experience that could only be accessed through his songs. I'd seen the Promised Land, and I tried sharing my vision with everybody in town. Time spent studying Dylan played a part in my academic dismissal from SUNY New Paltz. Also factoring into my "downfall" was a predilection for debauchery and hedonism. Many years later, my interest in Dylan's lyrics brought me back to the classroom. I finally earned an undergraduate degree, and I was now working on my Master's in creative writing. "Shooting Star" slipped away—nothing left but an illusionary sparkle. Dylan rolled on to his next performance, preaching, "He not busy being born, is busy dying."

Jimmy Carter quoted that line when he accepted the Democratic Party nomination for President. It's a daily struggle: either you're living or you're dying. Many days you're on a treadmill, vacillating between the two, no matter how hard you strive. Dylan then warned, "Money doesn't talk; it swears." In the midst of a vicious recession, the relevance of Dylan's poetry was uncanny.

After introducing his band, Dylan offered a rare comment: "I was born the year Pearl Harbor was attacked, and I've seen some pretty dark days since then. It looks like things are going to change now."

Dylan's declaration was a nod to Obama, even though the statement was vague. When you're Bob Dylan, every statement you make can and will be scrutinized for eternity. I suppose that's why Bob lets his songs do all the yapping. However, there was nothing ambiguous about his final entrée of the evening, "Blowin' in the Wind."

Inspiration can strike in the strangest of places. I respect this anthem, but I've never before detected an emotional connection between the singer and his iconic song. Like so many times before, Dylan asked, "How many roads must a man walk down before you call him a man?" On this momentous night for America, Dylan answered with a resounding, "The answer my friend is blowing in the wind. The answer is blowing in the wiiiiindd!" The answer seemed tangible, at least for now. There was boundless optimism rippling through this rendition—a sense that this song, which has meant so much to so many, had finally resonated with its creator. The crowd was frenzied when Dylan came out for his final ovation. With a wild smile, the Prodigal Son opened his arms to the faithful as if to say, "How about that? What a night!" Tears of triumph slid down my cheeks.

I was lured into a photo shoot with my fabulous reality girls. They hooted and danced all night while I double-shuffled and plucked air-guitar. One of our neighbors took a snapshot of us. I then posed with each girl individually as they snapped away on their iPhones. Ahhhh, the sensuous smell of magnolias and banana bread. It had been a while since I'd practiced the art of seduction on a twenty-year-old coed, but I had an early flight back to New York. I teetered on the ledge of temptation. I wondered if they lived off campus.

My musings were interrupted by lusty screams and a rumbling roar from the halls. Jumping Jesus! Bob Dylan must be outside greeting fans. As I stepped into the lobby, the hollering and cheering felt biblical. I looked up at the big screen, and there was the face I'd seen all day— honest and promising. The scoreboard read: Obama 297, McCain 188. NBC News had just projected that Barack Obama would be the 44th President of the United States.

Delirious students flocked from the dorms to the front of the auditorium, joining revelers who had just seen Dylan. The tribe chanted and danced as one: "O-ba-ma, O-ba-ma, O-ba-ma, O-ba-ma." I floated into the surging celebration and soaked in the primal exhilaration. It was unlike any group euphoria I'd experienced. It was as is if the crowd had given collective birth. I knew Obama was going to win, but I never envisioned this.

Separating myself from the spontaneous soirée, and forever ending my chances with the co-eds, I walked to the far end of the courtyard and peered in at the ruckus through the tall feather reed grass. The students bounced and howled as one in the warm North Country night. Choked up with emotion, I watched in silence. This was their glory. I shared it from a distance. *This land is your land, this land is my land.* I'm skeptical of politicians, especially those who reside in the White House. I liked Obama and enjoyed the rush of historical significance, but I didn't share the unbridled optimism of the students. I lurked in the background until the surreal scene dissipated into the evening haze.

When Dylan stood on the stage on Election Day 2008, the announcer's intro had reminded us that Bob was "The voice of the promise of the '60s counterculture." Seconds after Dylan took his final bow and disappeared into the darkness, a slice of that promise had been realized.

You might think that traveling from Manhattan to Minneapolis for one Dylan concert is extreme, but as I devoured chicken wings at a Dinkytown dive, I was glad I'd followed my musical instincts again. In the midst of analytical commentary on Obama's decisive victory, a news agency had projected that Republican Norm Coleman was re-elected to the senate in the tightest race of the night. I was following this contest because Norm's opponent, Al Franken, of Saturday Night Live fame, was a Deadhead. Chalk it up as another Election Day media blunder. But, after a recount which included absentee ballots, Minnesota elected Franken, a Deadhead Democrat, to represent them in the U.S. Senate. *Well, well, well, you can never tell.*

My mind raged on after I passed out in my hotel room. I dreamt I was in the back of a dimly lit tavern with a filthy floor. Bob Dylan and his bassist, Tony Garnier, entered the room through the swinging wooden doors of the kitchen. Bob approached me and said, "Heyyyy, Catfish. You want to play beer-pong?" I said, "Sure, Bob," even though I don't play beer-pong. How could I refuse? Dylan was wearing a rather tall black pillbox hat and a shiny black leather jacket with white gloves. I took my place behind the ping-pong table facing the swinging doors. Bob began pulling ping-pong balls from inside his jacket and sinking them into the beer cups. Dylan aced every serve, and I kept chugging beer. Tony Garnier, also dressed in black leather, disappeared into the kitchen and returned with a tray full of fresh brew. Replacing the empties and grinning like Satan, Tony said, "It seems like you've got yourself in quite a pickle here, Catfish." Dylan's expression was stoic as he continued to loft ping-pong balls into the cups before me.

I said, "There must be some way out of here." Tony chuckled as he exited through the swinging doors. Dylan's focus was upon our game, which remained one-sided.

Early the next morning the sun was shining, and I awoke with a slight hangover. I placed the JBLs in my backpack and pondered my strange odyssey as I headed to the airport. I had seen the Grateful Dead 152 times, the Jerry Garcia Band 51 times, and now I'd seen 93 Dylan shows. These are impressive numbers, which might sparkle on a résumé if I was applying for the position of chief guru with an alternative life-style firm. But, as Jerry used to sing, "I love the life I live, and I'm gonna live the life I love. I'm a roadrunner, baby." I said so long to the manager and headed to the airport.

Somewhere above the clouds, between Minneapolis and *JFK* Airport, I read the opening line of D.H. Lawrence's *Sea and Sardinia*: "Comes over one an absolute necessity to move." If my body isn't on the move, then my mind is rambling to the sound. Inspirational music equals transcendence. Great performances can stop time in its tracks. Thanks to gigabytes, more music than we can ever listen to lies at our fingertips, but a restless fever still burns inside me. I must chase lightning and hunt for fresh experience. It is only in music and motion that I trust.

Northrop Auditorium, November 4, 2008

IT'S ALRIGHT MA
(It's My Life Only)

Walton Avenue Blues...A girl named Maria...Mr. Magoo
discovers the Beatles...Ode to Columbia House and 77
WABC...The Bar Mitzvah Boy commits a petty crime...
Bong hits and Dewar's...Paradise in the backseat
as Van Halen wails...An unspeakable tragedy...

I sat cross-legged on the shredded red carpet in the pocket-sized living room of my Grandma Tilly's apartment, hypnotized by sound. *Fiddler on the Roof* played on the turntable in the center compartment of an aged mahogany cabinet. Tattered album jackets and scuffed vinyl discs, in and out of their sleeves, were spread out on the floor around me. Scratching and shuffling records on and off the phonograph, I was a natural-born DJ. There was a black and white TV on the other side of the room showing a man walking on the moon. But, even as a five-year-old, I clung to the music.

I'd been born eighteen days prior to JFK's assassination and given up for adoption immediately. My new parents, Lenny and Doris Weiner, picked me up in Cheverly, Maryland, and drove me back to Brooklyn— my first road trip. By the time I was three, my adopted mother had died of an illness on December 31, 1966, and my father and I moved into my grandmother's shoebox apartment on Walton Avenue in the Bronx. My earliest memories, however, are not of grief or longing for my mother, but of the sounds of my father's records. The harmonies and melodies danced inside in my mind—a dreamer's paradise.

Infatuated by the soundtrack of *West Side Story,* I could see the Jets and Sharks rumbling on a city playground, and I dreamed of a girl named Maria. I developed an attachment to the Latin-tinged instrumentation of Herb Albert & the Tijuana Brass, and The Weaver's live rendition of the "The Sinking of the Ruben James." I preferred tragic tales over fairy tales. Dad didn't listen to his records much, but I wore out the grooves. *When you're a Jet, you're a Jet all the way, from your first cigarette till your last dying day...Tell me, what were their names? Tell me, what were their names? Did you have a friend on the old Ruben James?*

Music was medication for my lonesome childhood. I never saw a picture of my adopted mother, nor would I ever meet anyone from her side of the family. I didn't have siblings or friends, and my father was a workaholic. Because the public school system was deemed unsafe, I was sent to a Yeshiva for kindergarten and first grade. For years, I only knew two females—one real, Grandma Tilly, and one imagined, Maria. *Say it loud, and there's music playing. Say it soft, and it's almost like praying. Maria. I'll never stop saying Maria.*

I was turned on to The Beatles by my teenage cousins, the Baskin boys—Jeffery, Seth and Keith. They lived with my Uncle Murray and Aunt Ruth in a yellow house surrounded by a healthy yard with enormous trees. It was the last home on a dead-end street in Deer Park— an unpretentious high-rise by Long Island standards. But with cars and bikes clogging the driveway, their house was a holiday camp to me. Uncle Murray called me Mr. Magoo. I fancied the idea of being somebody else. When I was six, my father began dropping me off in Deer Park for one-week stays during the summers. It was there that I finally experienced family.

My cousins were clean-cut Jewish teens who loved Yankee Baseball, and though I was eight years the junior of the youngest brother, they enjoyed having me around as a young protégé. I was amazed that they each had their own bedrooms—I was holed up in a single bedroom with Dad and Grandma. Though the Baskins weren't the Gatsbys, I was envious of the possessions piling-up in my cousins' rooms: bedraggled baseball gloves reeking of leather and oil; fuzzy Wilson tennis balls freshly sprung from canisters; stickball bats with sticky black tape spiraling around the handles; stacks of bubblegum-scented baseball cards; Beatles photos and album art smothering every nook and cranny of wall space; Beatles records lying on mattresses and desks.

While your typical six year-old might sing, "Yankee Doodle went to town riding on a pony," I harmonized to the Beatles' "I Dig a Pony." I nagged Dad until he bought me my first two Beatles records: *Let It Be* and a 45rpm single of "All You Need is Love" with "Baby You're a Rich Man" on the flipside. The plastic inserts that had to be placed in the record holes of 45s were funky. Yellow, red, and green, the inserts resembled flattened ship steering wheels with gaps on the outer rim. It was as if their sole purpose was to forever lodge themselves in our memories so we would never forget 45s after they were passé.

My imagination was aroused by the cover of *Let it Be,* which featured close-up mug shots of the band laid out tic-tac-toe style. The cover was cohesive—long-haired hippies sprouting shaggy facial growth (with the exception of the clean-shaven John Lennon), and there was self-assured solitude in their expressions. Although George Harrison was smiling, his eyes were shifted to the extreme right, seemingly scared to look at the camera lens because it would reveal what he was feeling inside. With songs titled "I Got a Feeling" and "I Me Mine" and Lennon singing, "Nothing's gonna change my world," I identified with their isolation. I stared at the cover, thinking Lennon was Ringo and Ringo was Lennon. Those four hippies were my best friends, and those twelve songs fueled my fantasies.

Dad remarried, and we relocated. I was pulled from the Yeshiva and promptly plunked into P.S. 26 in Yonkers for second grade. With my first exposure to females on a massive scale, second grade was socially awkward, but a marked improvement over the drab existence of the Yeshiva, where the rabbi routinely disciplined by whacking knuckles with a thick wooden ruler. Authority figures already equaled disillusionment for me. Music never let me down; it was more than continuity, it was hope and perseverance in the face of adversity. *I wake up to the sound of music, Mother Mary comes to me, speaking words of wisdom, let it be.*

My new mother was a thirty-two-year-old elementary school teacher from Parkchester, in the Bronx. Fran gave up teaching to take care of me and start a new family with Dad. She tried to instill some discipline into my life, but I shut the bedroom door and turned up the tunes. I was an adorable kid, there's irrefutable photographic proof of that, but Mr. Congeniality I wasn't.

Nothing but *Let it Be* blasted from my room when we first moved into Crestwood Lake apartments—garden dwellings without adequate sound insulation. My parents quickly found out there weren't many Beatles fans in our unit at 8 Nassau Drive. Mr. Rizzi, a glum widower who lived below, was the chief antagonist complaining to my parents about having to hear "Dose hippy bums." Another habit of mine that made the natives restless was my fondness for replaying the same song. If I was in a "Get Back" kind of mood, I would play it over and over again. I could listen to a song forty times in a row and dig it more each time. I was skilled at dropping the needle, but my neighbors were not impressed.

My folks were seemingly ambivalent to my Beatles fixation. I thought they were bizarre because they expressed no interest in the awesome music piping out from behind my bedroom door. How was it that these rhythms were not speaking to them like they spoke to me? As a youngster, Bob Dylan had similar feelings of disconnect from his folks when he listened to Bill Monroe records in his parents' house. In the documentary, *No Direction Home*, Dylan said, "The sound of the record ("Drifting Too Far From the Shore") made me feel like I was somebody else. I was maybe not even born to the right parents or something."

I gravitated to the eccentricity of *Let It Be*. Odd snippets of Beatles conversation appeared before most tracks: *"I dig a pigmy by Charles*

Hawtry on the deaf aids...Phase one in which Doris gets her oats...That was Can You Dig It by Georgie Wood. Now we'd like to do Ark the Angels Come...Oh Danny boy, the Isles of Ken are calling...The Queen says 'No' to pot smoking F.B.I. member...Thanks Mo. I'd like to say thank you on behalf of the group and ourselves and I hope we pass the audition."

These British voices leaped into my imagination—high-pitched, moody, silly, authoritative, and hypnotic. The spoken declarations of *Let it Be* were buffers between ballads soaked in sentimentality and songs that mocked in anger. With whistling, cat calls and false starts, *Let it Be* had the suspense and herky-jerky flow of an American football game with the weirdness of a Labor Day pig roast at your wicked Uncle Ernie's house. I'd tapped into a liberated hip spirit that reinforced my bullheaded individuality. *Nothing's gonna change my world.*

When I was eight, my brother Michael was born. I loved the hairy headed peanut-faced infant in the candy-cane jump suit, but the age difference kept us from having a meaningful sibling relationship. My brother's arrival also increased financial pressure on my father. He worked zealously, developing his accounting practice to provide us with a better home and fancier cars. I was thankful we were able to ditch that hideous Ford station wagon with the wood paneling, but I would have preferred my father's company. I used to beg him to play catch, and occasionally he acquiesced. He'd pound the pocket of his mitt and yell out, "Whaddaya say there, Howid? Chuck 'em in there babe." I never wanted our catches to end.

My father's pork chop sideburns framed an illuminating smile. If he was an alcoholic, gambler, child abuser, or wife beater, that might have worked out better for me. I would have despised and feared him, rendering his absence less painful. On the rare occasions when Dad was there for me, he was fantastic. He didn't have any vices or a secret life—just pencil, paper and an adding machine. I wondered what his father, Abe, was like, but my Grandpa Herman "Abe" Weiner died before I was born, and Dad never talked about him.

Soon after my brother's birth, my Aunt Ruth, a habitual smoker, was diagnosed with throat cancer that hastily ended her life. Ruth was my father's only sibling. Dad put up an unaffected front through it all, digging deeper into his mounds of paperwork, so I matched my old man's detachment. I didn't mourn; I just kept playing records.

In third grade, I was a freckle-faced boy with dirty blonde hair and hanging bangs who often dressed in funky-looking plaid pants or queer-colored corduroys. I obviously had no interest in becoming a fashion designer, nor did I want to be a fireman, policeman, scientist or doctor. I wanted to be a lead singer, or possibly wail on an instrument in a rock and roll band. I also dreamed of growing up to have amazing athletic prowess, smacking homeruns like Johnny Bench or draining jump shots like "Clyde the Glide," Walt Frazier. With one swing of the bat, or one jump shot, I could become a hero, loved by millions. Unfortunately, I was an undersized kid who never competed against anybody. A weird aptitude for numbers made me a wiz at memorizing stats, but I never rose above mediocrity on the playing field. I was a perennial dreamer.

My parents suggested I join the P.S. 26 school band. Like most kids who pick up a trumpet, my playing produced a wretched racket. I lacked the desire to practice, and nobody offered me a pep talk. *Son, if you stick with the trumpet and diligently play those scales, you will harvest the fruits of your labor. By participating in a band, you will learn the thrill of group collaboration—how the sum is greater than the parts. Then, and only then, will you be able to fulfill your dreams and inspire people with your artistic vision, so get your lazy ass back in your room and keep disturbing the peace.* Those were the words I longed to hear, but nope. After a couple of weeks of listening to me butcher and blast my way through "When the Saints Come Marching In," my parents were relieved to be hearing *Let it Be* again, which was soon followed by my next addiction, AM radio.

The first station I tuned into was 66 WNBC New York. Some of the jingles that made an indelible impression upon me were: "Indian

Reservation," "Love Train," "Crocodile Rock," "Song Sung Blue," and a song sung nasally—"Lay, lady, lay; lay across my big brass bed." I was drawn to Dylan's nasally twang, but he didn't receive much exposure on the AM dial. I began to dig more of Zimmy's stuff after receiving an eight-track tape of *Dylan's Greatest Hits Volume II* as part of a larger shipment from Columbia House. Cost? Only 99 cents! Enrollment was a breeze and membership was bliss. Busting open a piggybank? Unnecessary. However, due to a seemingly innocuous stipulation in my relations with Casa De Columbia, I had to purchase seven new albums or tapes at inflated club prices over the next three years. Gotcha, cha-ching! Welcome to the American Dream—fantasize now, pay later, or defer forever. And enjoy those groovy tunes.

77AM WABC, New York was tops in pop—more hit music with less talk was their motto. Roberta Flack was the diva, and "Killing Me Softly with His Song" sizzled. Roberta's sultry singing was my earliest taste of sensuality. When this Flack gem was the reigning queen of the charts in 1973, I spun the dial back and forth between WABC and WNBC, hoping to catch her lovely lullaby time after time. Sometimes a song was so hot, WABC would play it twice in a row. I first experienced instant replay with Vicky Lawrence's "The Night the Lights Went Out in Georgia." Tunes about Georgia equaled Billboard success. *I'm leaving on a midnight train to Georgia...Now the devil went down to Georgia; he was looking for a soul to steal...My father was a gambler down in Georgia.* The country was a-jonesin' for Georgia.

I used to switch stations at the slightest hint of commercials or news—with one exception. On WABC, an authoritative New Yawk voice blasted through clogged sinuses and demanded to be heard: "Dis is Howid Cosell spee-king of spawts" Suddenly, any game or event he was talking about was colossal, and Cosell's spin was definitive. He even had the audacity to verbally spar with Muhammad Ali. You were either absolutely sucked into Howard's world, or you tried to tune him out. Cosell was one authority figure I listened to. He was "Telling it like it is."

TV tubes provided some visual fantasy. I was hot for Marcia Brady, and traveling gig to gig on the Partridge Family bus would have been groovy. The catchy theme songs of these shows reinforced the mystical power of music in my mind; it was the glue keeping these untraditional families unified. For pure drama and exotic location, I dug *Hawaii Five-O* and *Streets of San Francisco.* TV was an amusing diversion, but I had to get back to the radio to hear about "The Night Chicago Died," "Bad Bad Leroy Brown," and "The Wreck of the Edmund Fitzgerald."

The hits of the '70s also coughed up some of the corniest classics. Let's all break out our pet rocks and stroke them as we sing: "Whoa oh whoa feelings, nothing more than feelings, trying to forget my feelings of love…We had joy we had fun we had seasons in the sun…Billy, don't be a hero! Don't be a fool with your life." And who can forget Paul Anka's regurgitated hairball, "Having My Baby."

My mom got pregnant again and had her second child, Risa, when I was ten. We moved into a new high-rise house with brown cedar shingles on Carnation Drive in Nanuet, New York. Our home stood out from the rest of the cookie cutter development, thanks to the brick posts with roaring lion busts at the foot of our driveway. These sculptures earned my father the nickname "Lenny the Lion" amongst the kids in the neighborhood. Lenny filled the driveway with a new Cadillac Cimarron and a basketball court for me. His fiscal success drove him to work even harder. I vowed to never toil like that. There had to be a simpler stairway to satisfaction.

I was desperate for role models or someone to confide in. Life lessons were dispersed to me from my friends on WABC: *Nothing from nothing leaves nothing, you got have something if you wanna be with me…Smoking in the boys room. Now teacher don't you fill me up with your rules, but everybody knows that smoking ain't allowed in school.*

Every morning before school I'd grab a bowl of Apple Jacks, and then feed my head with tunes—enough music to keep me daydreaming until I got home. Following the life cycle of WABC'S top hits was my top priority. I rooted for songs as they burst their way into the Top

Ten, surfing a wave of popularity. I didn't care if the artist was Paul McCartney, Elton John, Chicago, The Carpenters or Redbone. My allegiance was with the song as I listened to it climb and climb until it peaked on the charts and then heroically tried to hang in the Top Ten, struggling for survival on a weekly basis. I savored the songs as they slowly faded and made room for the hungry newcomers. Darwinism on the airwaves.

Weekend road trips with the family became frequent. I didn't ask my parents for much, but I demanded respect; the radio must be playing. Sometimes I successfully negotiated sitting shotgun so I could scan the dial. Music and motion became an intoxicating combo I could never shake. The names of the bridges and roads sang sweetly like a rhapsody: the expressways—Major Deegan, Bruckner, Kosciusko; the parkways— Palisades, Taconic, Sprain Brook; the bridges—Throgs Neck, Tappan Zee, Verrazano. We rambled steadily on the New York State Thruway, twisted round the bends of the Harlem River and FDR Drives, headed West on 287, East on 17, North on 95, South on 87, crawled on the GW Bridge and stalled on the Cross Bronx. Even the signposts were compelling: New York 37 Bear Mt. 6—just like a football score. Emergency Parking 1000 feet, Falling Rock Zone, Deer Crossing, Scenic Lookout Ahead, Rest Area 2.5 miles. Who needed to rest? I craved to feel the wheel and hear the tires squeal along endless highways with the tunes a-thundering.

Yonkers was a drag; it never felt like a home. The only worthwhile place was Nathan's Famous on Central Avenue. The aroma of the burnt weenies smothered in sauerkraut is tattooed in my memory. Oh, those scrumptious weenies, lazily lounging in their buns until they were drizzled with tangy golden mustard! And those freshly fried crinkle-cut potatoes that sizzled and smoked in oil. Lightly browned, the crammed fries waited in paper cups to be cooled off by blobs of thick ketchup dispensed from the push-down stainless steel tubes at the condiment station. Pinballs bashed into bumpers, and bells clanged in the game room—a place where those with supple wrists ruled. Luckily, there was a Nathan's near my new home, on Route 59 between the Nanuet Mall and the store where I would buy almost every album I owned: Tapesville USA.

My new bedroom was downstairs next to my father's accounting office, which he used on weekends and in the evening. Lenny had some wild clients, especially the jazz cats. Because they were musicians, my father was always excited to introduce them to me. "Hey, Howid. I want you to meet Jack DeJohnette and his wife, Lydia. They're coming over tomorrow. Jack's a drummer. He does very well in Europe." Europe? It sounded like a place that you were banished to if you couldn't make it in America.

Jack had an Afro and looked like Link from The Mod Squad. Lydia was white. They dressed in jeans and ponchos. These were the most laid back adults I'd ever met. Jack often collaborated with bassist Dave Holland, who was also my father's client. Dave had a thick English accent that reminded me of *Let it Be* hipness. Guitarist Larry Coryell was also part of the famous jazz posse who had their taxes done by my old man.

The jazz cats took a liking to Lenny. Though my father was solidly square, he was charming, especially when he talked business. DeJohnette, Holland, and Coryell used to autograph their albums for me. My father never had time to listen to their records, and the whacky fusion jazz was too weird for my inexperienced tastes. About fifteen years later, I became a huge Miles Davis fan and discovered that Jack and Dave had played on *Bitches Brew*. If only I had known I was in the presence of jazz royalty, I could have been listening to tales of what it was like to jam with Miles in his prime. Damn. I wish I could relive this part of my childhood again.

One of my father's clients owned a hopping Mexican joint in Yonkers called Pancho Villa's. Lenny decided to go into business with him, and they opened up El Bandido, the first Mexican Restaurant in Rockland County. Free fajitas were fantastic, and the restaurant brought more wealth to our family, but El Bandido completely robbed me of my father. Between Bandido and taxes, my old man worked over 100 hours a week.

A year before my Bar Mitzvah, Grandma Tilly was diagnosed with breast cancer. She moved into our house. Cancer turned her yellow and sucked the life out of her. She prayed for one thing: that, for all her suffering, God would let her see my Bar Mitzvah. She died two months before. Thankfully, her painful ordeal was over. I should have felt a great sense of loss for this woman, who provided me with unconditional love. But, like my father, I was a master of avoiding emotional pain. My mantra became "Carry on, Wayward Son," the progressive rock anthem by Kansas.

When I was thirteen, I must confess, I fell for Kiss. I wasn't impressed by their costumes or makeup; I actually tapped into the energy of their thrashing vibrations. That phase didn't last long, as Boston became my muse, and "More Than a Feeling" went gonzo on AM and FM. Boston's debut album featured a sterile, yet sophisticated, studio sound that was more than appealing. One autumn afternoon in E.J. Korvette department store, my friend Jay and I slipped *Boston* eight-track tapes inside of our jackets and exited center stage, side-stepping the cashiers. Our decision to pilfer was spontaneous, but before we neared the sliding glass doors and parking lot freedom, we were apprehended by security. To sour matters further, we were traveling with my Mama, who was in aisle eight, tossing pantyhose into a shopping cart.

I wish I'd been busted for swiping something more manly, like Johnny Cash's *Live at Folsom Prison*, but there I was, a thief seated at a rectangular table with Jay across from two pot-bellied guards. The evidence, two crumpled cartons containing *Boston*, was splayed out in front of us. A booming aristocratic voice blasted over the intercom: "Mrs. Weiner, Mrs. Weiner. Please report to the security office. Mrs. Weiner, please report to security." I'll never forget that look. My mother's face was contorted with rage and embarrassment. A simple errand like picking up thermal underwear for the family had turned into a fiasco. The Bar Mitzvah boy was *mashugana*. Six weeks earlier, I had been the pride of the local Jewish Community, flawlessly chanting the Haftorah and taking a giant step towards manhood. And now this! I was grounded indefinitely, although that didn't stick past a week. The Korvette's debacle helped steer me away from a life of petty crime and thievery from retail stores, but I'd taken my first step on the rocky road of raucous rebellion.

I acquired *Boston* legally and lost interest in it rapidly. It was a gateway album leading to harder stuff like *The Song Remains the Same*. Sucked into the teenage Led Zeppelin vortex, I had to own all their albums yesterday. I pawned half of my stamp collection at a shop by the Nanuet Mall and completed my Led collection with a massive purchase at Tapesville USA. Collectively, the seven albums were a rock and roll tsunami accented by shrieking "oh, baby babies" from the bare-chested singer with the girly blonde hair. Now I was in crazed pursuit of albums from the mighty FM rock gods of the day, and my cravings could only be satisfied when I owned everything by that artist or group. I frantically needed cash, so I shoveled snow, mowed lawns, and begged my parents for allowance raises. Actually, I did more begging than working. I never saved a cent; all my assets were invested in vinyl.

I wasn't a lone wolf, but I'd yet to have a friend who was a kindred spirit. I competed and connected with neighborhood kids on the playing fields, but these acquaintances were always interchangeable. Somehow, I managed to stay one rung above the putz who got bullied every day.

That all changed when I met Doug Schmell by my locker after homeroom in eighth grade. His striking presence set him apart from our peers—flush cheeks, black wavy hair, peering eyes scanning his surroundings for the next thrill. His tall, agile frame was sculpted for competition. Doug's effervescent personality matched his vibrant physicality. I wanted to befriend him immediately. He looked like a friendly version of Jim Morrison. His sly smile balanced a compassionate glance that made You feel important. Doug was popular amongst the cool kids, yet he seemed oblivious to cliques and social status.

Raised in the neighboring town of Spring Valley, Doug was the middle son of a middle-class family that educated its boys in a Yeshiva before turning them loose on the Clarkstown Public School System. Though Doug and I didn't cross paths until junior high school, our interests were in sync. We were fanatical about the same TV shows—*Get Smart*, *Monty Python's Flying Circus*, and the *Twilight Zone*—and, in a region dominated by New York Rangers fans, our favorite hockey team was the Islanders. But our strongest bond of all was music.

It was not uncommon for fourteen-year-old white males to be digging on The Beatles, The Rolling Stones, The Who, The Doors, Pink Floyd, Led Zeppelin, Lynyrd Skynyrd, Steely Dan and Jethro Tull, but we went berserk, scrutinizing their every album and rapidly absorbing every lyrical and instrumental intricacy. We derived scholarly gratification from listening to progressive concept-based albums like Jethro Tull's *Thick as a Brick* and Emerson Lake & Palmer's *Brain Salad Surgery.*

Neither one of us had any serious musical training, so we improvised a language to discuss and dissect guitar jams. In lieu of using musical terms, we measured time with whammies, rounds, loops, phases, and segments. Jams could tease, build, redirect, explode, go off, come off, and shift gears. We processed guitar jams by taking mental snapshots of them which enabled us to analyze the musical interludes and talk about them in our invented tongue.

For physical activity, we spent precious hours shooting, rebounding, and dribbling our afternoons away on various hoop courts in the neighborhood. Doug usually was on the winning team; nobody competed with more tenacity or enjoyed victory more than he. But all these hobbies were not enough. Many of our peers began experimenting with marijuana. The temptation was irresistible.

Our first ganja get-together commenced at twilight by a shallow creek near our local hangout, Tennyson Park. Doug arrived with his brother's bong and a tiny ziplocked pouch containing potent green herb. My contribution was a bottle of dusty Dewar's that I pilfered from my house. My parents rarely drank, but because my father owned El Bandido, he stockpiled booze in a closet which happened to be conveniently located between my bedroom and the garage. Instead of pouring water in the bong to cool off the harsh smoke, I poured a quarter-bottle of Dewar's into the two-foot red tube, turning this into a science and biology project. Firing up bong hits, we coughed violently as smoke bubbled through the scotch and scorched our lungs. After the coughing ceased, unhinged laughter exploded from deep within us. And then it was decided that drinking the dirty Dewar's from the bong was the prudent thing to do.

On the leaves of the trees, under the cover of darkness, the insects of the night harmonized—a flickering orchestra in surround sound. The moon appeared brilliantly, glowing like a wobbling egg. Hovering over stepping stones, a shallow stream flowed below—the invisible force of Mother Earth leading the way. The liberating promise of spring lingered in the air—wild summer nights beckoned. Stoned to the brim, Doug and I stumbled back to my downstairs pad and listened to *Dark Side of the Moon* and *The White Album*. I was closer to the artistic vision than ever before.

Getting high linked me up with a social network of stoners. In this rebellious realm, my musical wisdom gave me instant credibility and a touch of shaky confidence. Girls started to show some interest in me. This was a spectacular development for an awkward kid who never had any dates or girlfriends, even though he had always been mesmerized by female beauty. Music had kept hope alive for me as a child, but now it was opening doors and, possibly, thighs.

Almost every essential recollection of my existence is part of the never ending soundtrack that plays in my brain. I first pleasured myself to a picture of a busty woman in a one-piece green bathing suit from the pages of *Cosmopolitan* as "Fifty Ways to Leave Your Lover" filled the air. My first adventurous make-out session with a girl was set to the sounds of George Harrison's guitar gently weeping. Her name was, of course, Maria, and her breasts were impressive, bordering on spectacular. I must not have handled them with proper care because

I wasn't invited back for an encore. However, I was thankful for this exploration and was ready to go beyond.

On New Year's Eve, 1979, I bid farewell to the 70s at El Bandido. I was only sixteen, but I'd set my sights on Cecilia, a more experienced senior with whom I was celebrating. We stepped out of the boozy soirée and into the arctic night to smoke a doobie in her Oldsmobile Cutlass Supreme. I barely knew this uninhibited chic with the flowing blonde hair and snug-tight Jordache jeans, but that was all right because I hadn't attached romantic fantasies to my first time, and she bore a slight resemblance to Marcia Brady. We got stoned, put on *Van Halen,* and moved into the back seat. Our sultry session began to the rumbling beat of "Runnin' with the Devil." The frosty chill and street lamps illuminated our heated breath through fogged-up windows as Van Halen wailed on. Our lusty tango came to a pleasant ending during "Ain't Talkin' 'Bout Love."

The '80s were here and I was ready for anything—except this:

> *Remember, this is just a football game, no matter who wins or loses. An unspeakable tragedy confirmed to us by ABC News in New York City. John Lennon, outside of his apartment building on the West Side of New York City. The most famous of perhaps all the Beatles, was shot twice in the back and rushed to Roosevelt Hospital. Dead on arrival. Hard to go back to the game after that news flash.*

Howard Cosell, Monday Night Football, December 8, 1980.

My fantasy brother, John Lennon, murdered while I was watching the Miami Dolphins and New England Patriots close in on halftime. Bereaving fans gathered in Central Park. I preferred to stay home. I chose revolution, declaring a peaceful war against everything society deemed significant—religion, education, and family. I stopped attending classes as a sophomore and just showed up at school to purchase and smoke marijuana. I was a free man.

In the years prior to Lennon's murder, the American Dream had turned into a series of night terrors. Son of Sam was shooting lovers in parked cars, Jim Jones wiped out his followers with killer Kool-Aid, and the mayor of San Francisco was assassinated. On November 4, 1979, Iranian students seized hostages during a hostile takeover of the American Embassy. It was my sixteenth birthday, and Nightline with Ted Koppel was born. While America was humiliated in Iran, Soviet tanks stormed Afghanistan. Foreign policy shifted from the weakness of Jimmy Carter to the madness of Ronald Reagan. The economy was in a state of decay: inflation, stagnation, recession. American cities were crumbling—fear and loathing on the rise. Everything was breaking down, and I escaped deeper into my musical cocoon. I smoked massive amounts of marijuana and dabbled with booze, bennies, greenies, mescaline, mushrooms, LSD, coke, caffeine, Quaaludes, hash, valiums, whippets and yellow jackets. Times were crazy. Bob Dylan found Jesus. I found Jerry.

THE GOLDEN ROAD
(To Unlimited Devotion)

The Gospel of Garcia...Hockey immortality and the discovery of Europe '72...The Englishtown Half Step, collective genius...Road revelations on Rorer 714s... High School misfit to campus hipster...The Grateful Dead Movie...April blizzard blues...Morning Dew in Philly, oh the humanity!...Grateful Glossary...

My predilection for aggressive guitarists and thunderous sounds didn't logically lead to the Grateful Dead, but I couldn't avoid cosmic fate.

While I had a hot and heavy affair with Lady Jane during the summer of '80, Doug Schmell went off to a predominantly Jewish sleep away camp like he had the year before, except this time he returned preaching the Gospel of Jerry Garcia. Yes, that bearded cat from the Grateful Dead, a marginal lead guitarist with a name that was as generic as it was bizarre. Suddenly, Doug was trying to convince me that Señor Garcia was king of the guitar universe. Ho, ho, ho!

"Howie, you gotta get into Garcia, bro. This guy has moved more men than Mao Tse Tung. I'll play you some jams that will blow your mind. I promise you," pleaded Doug. "I swear. Jerry blows away Hendrix, Clapton, Richards, Van Halen and Santana. I gotta turn you on to live Dead. That's where it's at, my friend." Everything else about

Doug seemed normal, but obviously somebody from the notorious Deadhead cult had brainwashed him.

Doug's charming powers of persuasion were hard to resist. If you went to a Chinese restaurant with Doug, and Sesame Beef was his favorite dish, it became your favorite dish, and he usually felt obliged to share his culinary expertise with other diners:

"Excuse me, madam, sir...I noticed you were about to order. Me and my friend Howie eat here at Fortune Garden all the time. You really should try the Sesame Beef. The cook's a certified genius. He gathers ancient Chinese secrets from the tiny shacks of Canton and imports them here to America's shores. Wait 'til you get a whiff of the sesame oil smoking off those plump meat cubes. The beef is lightly fried in a crispy breading, drenched in a pungent red sauce, and seeds are sprinkled on top. Then, the chef strategically, and liberally, surrounds the beef with a ring of steamed broccoli. You're gonna love it."

Doug's passion could dominate a room full of strangers whether he was pushing General Tso's chicken or describing the majesty of a Dr. J (Julius Erving) slam dunk. I wanted to share in his exuberance for the Grateful Dead, but I couldn't grasp the premise.

Hip to FM ditties like "Casey Jones" and "Ripple," I used to think of the Grateful Dead as just another good-time group with a Grate name. I ranked them as about my 40th favorite band, tucked in somewhere between ELP and ELO. The band's imagery and artwork was happening. I wore a jean jacket with a red, white and blue grinning Grateful Dead skull tattooed on the back, but it wasn't an assertion of musical loyalty. That jacket was my declaration of weirdness. I owned two Grateful Dead albums: *American Beauty* and *Skeletons in the Closet*. The tunes on these records were clever and catchy, but they offered me little evidence that Jerry Garcia could wail like the new God, Eddie Van Halen.

Doug turned me on to an assortment of live Dead bootlegs. Supposedly, this was where Garcia's guitar virtuosity shined. The songs were slow and slower, spacey and never ending. I zoned out by the time Garcia started to jam, and then it seemed like an eternity until Jerry hit his stride and unleashed anything impressive. Doug's Grateful Dead fixation was puzzling. Where was the defining masterpiece like "Stairway to Heaven" or "Free Bird?" It didn't seem like I'd be paying homage to Señor Garcia any time soon.

An inconspicuous white Honda Civic hatchback, purchased by Lou Zlottlow, would become the vehicle that finally delivered my Grateful Destiny. As most teens in upper-middle-class Nanuet, Seymour Zlottlow inherited the hand-me-down family car. Seymour enjoyed badgering his younger sibling, Scott. I was better friends with Scott, but Seymour always had the stash of hooch manure, the redness in his eyes fluctuated by varying degrees depending on how many bowls he'd smoked. Seymour had several nicknames: "Sea Mower," "Sea Monster," "Monzie." Scott was simply known as "Z." Seymour was a Deadhead, but he deemed his baby brother unworthy of the same status. It was his private province of coolness. On January 24, 1981, I went to an Islander game with the Zlottlow boys. History was hanging in the balance for my favorite Islander, Michael Bossy. An electrifying evening seemed inevitable.

The Nassau Coliseum was a mausoleum until Bossy flipped a backhander past Quebec goalie Ron Grahame with four minutes remaining in the game. The crowd went nuts. If Bossy could score one more goal before the final buzzer, he would become the second NHL player to score fifty goals in the first fifty games of a season. With less than two minutes left, the crowd was on its feet and raising a ruckus. Uniondale, Long Island, trembled in anticipation. We believed we could will Bossy on to hockey immortality.

Bossy, the lanky French-Canadian wearing number twenty-five, stepped onto the ice and peered in at his target—a predator prepared to pounce. The ref dropped the puck. Bryan Trottier won the faceoff and shuffled a precise pass to Bossy, who unleashed a lightning slap shot that whistled past the hapless goaltender and ripped into the back of the net, triggering the flashing red light. "Goal, Islander goal.

I—lan-derrr-goalll!" screamed John Sterling from the radio announcer's booth. Bossy's heroics were the most thrilling sports spectacle that I'd ever been a part of, but it paled in comparison to the ride home.

Buzzing from hockey hysterics, revelers honked their horns as we exited the parking lot and crept along the Jericho Turnpike. Sequestered in the back seat of Seymour's pillbox Honda, I sparked one of his joints, inhaled deeply, and passed it up front to Z. Our brains rewired. Sea Monster's beady eyes glanced my way in the rearview mirror as he slipped a cassette in the deck. With a cocky chuckle, he exclaimed, "Check this out, motha fuckhas. Exhibit A, the Grateful Dead."

A blend of voices harmonized: *We can share the women. We can share the wine. We can share what we got of yours 'cause we done shared all of mine.* The singing was gorgeous and the melody was fine. Suddenly, the tempo intensified, and the lyrics became darker, advancing into scenes of robbery, revenge and murder. Outlaws on the run hopped aboard trains that rambled across America coast to coast. With two tight instrumental passages tucked in, "Jack Straw" came full circle, ending as it began: *We can share the women. We can share the wine*—lovely, yet deceptive. From song structure to plot, "Jack Straw" from Wichita was bizarre. I loved it.

Gripped by *Europe '72*, the Grateful Dead's triple album, I surrendered my mind to the mysterious sounds. The Dead garnered country, bluegrass, jazz and Delta blues, tossed it in a psychedelic blender, and served it with rock and roll sensibility. These songs exuded a strange American presence. No simple label could do them justice. I'd cracked a musical language barrier. There's something about music and motion— the audio dynamics inside a car intensify once that vehicle is rolling on down the highway.

Charging north on the Palisades Parkway, Nanuet-bound, "Ramble on Rose" levied the knockout blow. It must have been my favorite ballad from a past life. Garcia's angelic voice balanced weird history with hip presence. Jerry's piercing solo soared with imagination, like the heroes and villains, real or imagined: Billy Sunday, Mary Shelley,

Frankenstein, Crazy Otto, Wolfman Jack. I had to acquire *Europe '72*. The following morning, I showed up at Tapesville USA and cleared out the Grateful Dead bin. I wasn't prepared to accept Garcia as a deity, but I was digging the Dead.

A few weeks after my epiphany, I paid seven beans for my first Dead bootleg, a ninety minute BASF cassette tape featuring various tunes from the Dead's performance on September 3, 1977, at Englishtown Raceway, New Jersey. The deal went down in front of Clarkstown South High School in West Nyack, prior to homeroom. My enterprising sophomore salesman, Tommy, stood about 6' 3", wore a torn and faded jeans jacket, had a shrub of auburn hair, and sold pregnant dollar doobies out of a Marlboro pack that he casually flicked open with his thumb. In Grateful Dead circles, it's taboo to charge a Deadhead money for a GD tape. Brother must share with brother, but Tommy was no Deadhead. It didn't matter, though. Englishtown is still the best seven-dollar investment I've ever made.

Englishtown was the crème de la crème, a revered bootleg. It was an act of pure luck that I selected this tape from Tommy's list. The Englishtown versions of "Eyes of the World" and "Mississippi Half Step Uptown Toodeloo" opened my ears to the recognition that Garcia was indeed an innovative force on guitar with no equal. The studio versions of these Hunter/ Garcia compositions from *Wake of the Flood* were truncated sketches of what the band was doing with them live. The recording studio was kryptonite to the Grateful Dead—stripping them of their improvisational mojo.

Englishtown's "Mississippi Half Step" contains the most spectacular group interaction that I've ever heard. "Half Step" is a plush live number featuring five separate instrumentals, the fourth one being the longest. During the king jam, Jerry peaked on two lightning runs, enough to make any "Half Step" proud. However, Keith Godchaux extended the adventure, introducing twinkling piano licks, graceful as a butterfly—the rainbow after a drenching storm. Jerry thought it was pretty. Tweeting like a robin, Jerry mimicked Keith's sound. Phil joined the conversation, his bass rumbling—elephants stampeding in the distance. Things heated up again, but the band wisely decided to wallow in their serene space. An intense outburst like the earlier crescendo would have lessened the moment. The jam faded without resistance into the song's bridge: "Across the Rio Grande; across the lazy river." Englishtown roared, 100,000 strong. Transcendence achieved—the ultimate reward of improvisation that goes beyond anything previously conceived by the artists. Collective genius.

Tickled by my acceptance of Jerry as the supreme musical sage, Doug rewarded me with the second set of the infamous Cornell show, 5-8-77. This was the tape that pushed me over the edge. Of my own free will, I would spend the next six years listening to nothing but Jerry.

The day after receiving 5-8-77, My Dad and I listened to that cassette in his Chevy Caprice Classic during a thirty-minute jaunt to see our dentist in Yonkers. "Scarlet Begonias" kicked off the festivities. I was transfixed by Robert Hunter's lyrics as they flowed through Jerry: *Once in a while you get shown the light in the strangest of places if you look at it right.*

I wasn't seeking transcendence; I didn't even know what that word meant, but I was on my way, setting sail with the Grateful Dead. Donna Godchaux's voice cried, "ooh and ahh" as Jerry responded with feathery notes that morphed into piercing flurries. Drifting into no man's land, half the band was playing "Scarlet Begonias" and the other half was igniting "Fire on the Mountain." The transition between songs was positively hypnotic. I occupied time and space with the Dead in Cornell until "Fire on the Mountain" reached its smoldering conclusion.

I wondered what my father thought about that *Scarlet -> Fire*? How did this stack up in his mind compared to *West Side Story*, or *Let it Be*? Did it stack up at all? The world will never know because we didn't communicate once during the entire trip, although my father listened to Cornell without flinching, and he never asked me to turn the volume down.

My light-headed state during that car ride was aided by a Quaalude I'd popped the night before. There was an abundance of Rorer 714s in circulation in the early '80s. They usually ran four dollars a tablet and came in various strengths. You never knew how potent your tablet was until it was being absorbed into your bloodstream. I was still reeling from a dose that would have knocked a Clydesdale on its ass. Chemicals aside, the right Grateful Dead jam led to a mind out of time phenomena—transcendence. And, once again, a moving vehicle enhanced my experience.

Prior to the Grateful Dead, my musical comprehension was black and white. Pink Floyd was *The Wall* and *Dark Side of the Moon*, and the Beatles were simple, "Love Me Do," and complex, "Strawberry Fields Forever." The Grateful Dead were not their albums or what people heard on FM. Their greatest works were hidden in a secret world of bootlegs. Deadheads were taping every concert, and the band was winging it every night. There were vast chunks of improvisational brilliance all over the place: Englishtown 9-3-77, Cornell 5-8-77, Des Moines 6-16-74, UCLA 11-11-73, Roosevelt Stadium 7-18-72 (Bob Dylan was in the audience for this show), Fillmore East 4-29-71. This was a roadmap with its own timeline of inspiration—history, chemistry, geography, sociology, philosophy, and musical theory, all rolled into one.

I was in tenth grade at the time, but not really. I chronically cut classes. Letters, lectures, threats, detentions and suspensions from school officials were futile in altering my incorrigible behavior. After my sophomore year of 1980, I was left back and Jimmy crack corn, I didn't care. The spring of 1981 was like déjà vu all over again. Someone looking for me during school hours would find me outside blasting my massive boombox. I conducted weed-huffing and music appreciation seminars in the bountiful West Nyack woods surrounding Clarkstown South. I simply preferred not to go to class. I was a sixteen-year-old Bartleby.

Clarkstown South's Vice-Principal Longo emerged as a sympathetic soul and fleeting heroic figure in my life. A slender gentleman in his fifties, Mr. Longo wore drab gray suits and had a few wisps of gray hair clinging to his scalp. We got to know each other over time because I was often sent to his office for disciplinary action. In a meeting with my parents, Mr. Longo suggested that I drop out of high school and pursue a GED at Rockland Community College. He was confident I would thrive in a different academic environment with a more mature crowd. This solution sounded brilliant—a permanent get out of jail free card.

Adios, Clarkstown South! I had no desire to conjugate Spanish verbs, balance mathematical equations, cheer on jocks, join peculiar clubs, cram for SATs, or seek dates for awkward school dances. The idea of going to college was improbable, far off in another galaxy. Finishing three more years of high school was a ludicrous concept. I hadn't even conceived of life as a college student until Mr. Longo stepped in and waved his wand.

Country club living awaited me at Rockland Community College, aka "The Rock." I began my GED studies in the summer of '81 and earned a diploma in a year. Taking advantage of the sprawling campus facilities in Suffern, I played hoops and tennis in the RCC Field House, bulked-up in the state-of-the-art weight room, smoked Marlboros in the cafeteria and doobies in the outdoor amphitheatre. Amped up on either coffee or yellow jackets, I dominated the ping-pong tables in the student activity room. I had the freedom to rebel at "The Rock," but there was nothing to rebel against.

There was an easily accessible bus that ran from Nanuet to RCC, but I preferred the funky adventure of hitchhiking. The array of drivers willing to pull over boggled my mind: car-pooling moms, gangsters from "The Hill," attractive solo females, Hassidic Jews, truck drivers, senior citizens, members of the clergy, bikers. I even thumbed a ride with a Spring Valley cop on patrol. He dropped me off on campus without a lecture. Despite the rash of violence plaguing society, those were salad days for hitchhikers on Viola Road heading to and from "The Rock."

Ah, the sweet summer of '81. I met Cheryl, a curvaceous nineteen-year-old blonde, in my Psychology 101 class. We shared a fondness for popping Quaaludes, watching *The Rocky Horror Picture Show* at the midnight matinee, and making love beneath moonlight on a nearby golf course. Our fling ended when she returned home to Cherry Hill, New Jersey, after staying in Rockland with a friend for that summer. I never saw Cheryl again, but at age seventeen, my metamorphosis from high school misfit to confident campus hipster was complete. Even my parents were happy with me—for a while. I pulled As in thought-provoking classes like European History, Music Appreciation, and Philosophy. *I think, therefore I scam* became my mantra. Fate was kind. Not many high school dropouts get to reinvent themselves in such an idyllic place.

In the fall, a few days away from my seventeenth birthday, I went to see *The Grateful Dead Movie* on RCC's weekly film night in the student's activity lounge. I brought along Doug Schmell and his friend, "The Wah," Larry Wassermann. The Wah had a great nickname for everybody. Doug was "Schmedley," his best friend, Steve Goldberg, was "Froggy," and Jerry Garcia was "Beard." I was dubbed "Catfish" after The Wah saw me jamming air guitar to "Catfish John."

I snuck refreshments into the film room in my Puma gym bag. I forgot the popcorn, but my black bag had a pint of Southern Comfort, a few grams of Thai Weed and a mini bong. We each dropped a hit of purple microdot mescaline an hour before the movie. In comparison to acid, mescaline's effects are less hallucinatory, but it tends to crank your body up to full voltage.

When the flick began, The Wah, a curly-haired tree trunk of an adolescent, flashed an electrified grin and said, "Catfish, I'm getting off, kid." So was I. Anticipation socked my senses, yet I felt porous, like a floating sponge. The movie's opening animation segment was hard to handle. Skeletons, motorcycles, and roses glistened and gleamed off the big screen. I took a robust swig of Southern Comfort to soothe my swirling head.

An insight into the belly of the San Francisco Dead scene circa 1974, *The Grateful Dead Movie* stars wiry misfits with beards and pony-tails, braless ladies twirling and flailing their arms like ballerinas, and the musicians who stood their ground on stage at the height of their creative powers. It was a stunning portrait of the unique bond between the Grateful Dead and their fans. The audience respected what the Dead were doing and gave them the artistic space they needed for intergalactic exploration.

Deadheads were captured in their natural habitat—freaks doing and taking what they pleased—a carefree community of brotherhood merrily floating along in altered states of consciousness. These California hippies became the quintessential role models for Deadheads after the film was released in 1977. The flick slowly garnered popularity until it evolved into a midnight matinee classic—the manifesto on how to dig a show. Thanks to what people saw on the big screen, this is what they came to expect when the Grateful Dead came to town, and this was usually what happened.

During the epic jazz-infused ending jam of "Eyes of the World," The Wah proclaimed, "Beard is gorgeous, fuckin' beautiful man. Garcia is our Captain. He won't be denied. Schmedley, Catfish, how can anyone not love Beard?" Crazed spurts of laughter flowed from The Wah. Suddenly, he sprung from his chair and bounced around, kicking his legs like a drunken flapper.

I couldn't speak; my jaw muscles were nailed shut, grin-lock. I leapt to my feet and started dancing my own weird jig. Pretty soon, half of the thirty or so students who were there got out of their seats, fantasizing that they were at the Winterland Theatre in 1974. Get your Beard here! Approximately three-quarters of the crowd at RCC was half as baked as me and my friends. Where and whenever I found out about a screening of *The Grateful Dead Movie*, I was there. It would have to suffice until the Grateful Dead's next East Coast tour.

Beard

As I awoke in my bedroom, I sensed an unseasonable chill in the air on the morning of April 6, 1982. Opening the drapes, I was stunned by what I saw—marshmallow mounds of snow reflecting the amber glare of the sun. A day earlier, the trees were sprouting leaves, but now they sat like flagpoles on an Alpine ski course. Without much warning, Nanuet was blanketed by eighteen inches of powdery precipitation overnight. The freak blizzard may have delayed the arrival of spring, but it would not deter my plans to see the Grateful Dead in Philadelphia.

I called the Zolottlow brothers to ensure we were pressing on. The vote was unanimous: we would rendezvous with the Dead in Philly.

Doug had planned on joining us, but he was stuck in Albany with the April blizzard blues. Waiting at the foot of my driveway with my flannel shirt billowing in the howling Nor'easter winds, I wondered how many hours the 118-mile journey might take. Seymour's tiny white Honda sputtered up Carnation Drive, appearing smaller than ever in the only partially plowed street, glinting against the wintry landscape.

Slip-sliding our way south, Seymour navigated us through a treacherous twenty-mile stretch of the Palisades Parkway. The insanity of traveling in these hazardous conditions was an intense rush. Once we reached the New Jersey Turnpike, all roads ahead were clear. Mother Nature had spared the Garden State—smooth sailing to Philadelphia. I let out a vigorous, "Yeeee-haw!" This was my first road trip anywhere without my parents.

Slicing through the swamps and industrial wastelands of New Jersey, we passed the Oranges (East and West) and the Amboys (Perth and South) on our way to Exit 4, where the Walt Whitman Bridge and the City of Brotherly Love beckoned in the near distance.

The Philly Spectrum parking lot was a drive-through hippie safari. A bivouac of psychedelic clowns had claimed their turf. An intoxicating cloud of marijuana and opium smoke floated skywards, mixing with the scent of burnt pretzels and sizzling cheese steaks. As the blue-collar grind of another Philly Tuesday faded into twilight, the freak parade surrounding the Spectrum swelled.

Scott, Seymour, and I seamlessly slipped into this caravan of screwballs. I belonged to this arcane scene, though I wasn't fond of hippie regalia or the stench of Patchouli Oil. However, Deadheads functioned as an extended family, providing unconditional support for each other, regardless of appearances. The spirit and promise of the tunes bound us together. *We can share the women; we can share the wine.*

Escaping the chilly Philly winds, we found our seats, dead center, twelve rows of separation between us and the Grateful Dead. After a day of hard traveling, Jerry and the boys rewarded us with a beloved opener, "Cold Rain & Snow." I loaded a bullet of blow—blast away—one for the right nostril, one for the left. Scott, the fair-skinned sibling with the Dutch haircut and wholesome schoolboy looks, passed the marble bowl. I inhaled deeply and handed the bowl to Seymour, a bedraggled sight with disheveled hair and ragged clothing. Sweet smoke from the sticky green bud burst inside my lungs, causing me to cough in ecstasy. Gripped by euphoria, I double-shuffled to the easy groove—my senses locked in on Jerry.

Norfolk, Raleigh, Charlotte, Birmingham, New Orleans, Houston, Albuquerque, Los Angeles; America blitzed by as Bob Weir strummed Chuck Berry's "Promised Land." With his eyes afire and his head a-snapping at the microphone, driblets of Weir's saliva sailed into the front row during the serenade. Bob and Jerry were the rock and roll odd couple. Weir, the fit, animated hipster in a collared purple shirt with a green alligator patch planted above his left nipple, charged around the stage with energized precision, while Garcia, wearing gold-rimmed glasses, jeans, sneakers and a black t-shirt came off like Buddha, channeling inspiration and wisdom from a stationary stance.

Bob and Jerry alternately handled lead vocals on a society of songs that depended upon each other. Weir shared timeless tales of debauchery and desire during "Mama Tried," "Mexicali Blues," and "It's All Over Now." Garcia boasted of gambling, bootlegging, and living in-the-moment during "Candyman," "Brown Eyed Women" and "Might As Well." A depiction of Old-Time America, the twelve-song set wetted my palate, a satisfying prelude to the main course.

Most folks rolled with the flow of the show. The second set song choices weren't going to make or break their night. I was different. My degree of happiness depended upon song selection and performance. I wanted to experience a legendary concert along the lines of Englishtown or Cornell. Everything was on the line.

After a half-hour break, the band resurfaced. Jerry stepped on the wah-wah pedal, tuning his Tiger in a recognizable language. The duck-like quacking gave away the opener, "Shakedown Street." A sonic bass blast unleashed waves of Grateful Funk. "Don't tell me this town ain't got no hear-art-art," growled Jerry Bear, emerging from hibernation. "Well, well, well, you can never tell," responded Bob, Brent and Deadhead Nation. Cross one tune off my wish list; the second set was raging.

With blues-infused leads, Jerry unleashed the first monster jam of the evening. The silky smooth sounds from Brent Mydland's B3 Hammond organ mimicked Jerry. After this fiddle-faddle, the band shifted into overdrive. I was a dancing fool, shuffling like Sugar Ray Leonard and plucking air guitar note for note with Jerry. All around me, Deadheads danced on air. Harnessing the vast energy in the house, Garcia's guitar sang in rapturous elation. This was exactly what I was looking for—an onslaught of emotionally-charged playing highlighted by unique phrasing—something that spoke directly to this audience on this night.

The next sublime moment arrived as the smoldering remains of "Saint of Circumstance" crystallized into the familiar chord riff of "Terrapin Station." Jerry's voice lightly touched down: "Let my inspiration flow in token rhyme suggesting rhythm that will not forsake me 'til my tale is told and done." The Spectrum softly swayed to the poetic musings of Robert Hunter. Line after lyrical line, verse after vivacious verse, we listened in reverence as if Garcia were delivering Holy Scripture. Everybody was getting off on the spiritual powers of music in a communal setting.

Terrapin's instrumental refrain crashed down upon us like a royal symphony. It had an air of significance about it, like the theme song from the opening ceremony to the Olympics. Actually, a Terrapin Refrain would make a satisfactory replacement for the playing of national anthems:

"Ladies and gentleman, we will now honor the gold medalist of the 1500-meter steeple-chase, from the nation of Kenya, Abadu Runjucan. In the true spirit of athletic sportsmanship and international goodwill, we ask that you stand as we raise the flag with the Grateful Dead skeleton and pay homage to a 1977 Terrapin Refrain. Peace on Earth. Thank you."

Back at the Philly Spectrum, Billy Kreutzman and Mickey Hart pounded their drum duet. I scored a brew as the spinners kept twirling in the halls. A long line of hippies in dresses (men and women), were squatting Indian-style, massaging the shoulders of the person in front of them and chanting, "ommm, ommm, ommm." Bemused Spectrum employees looked on as if they were observing life forms from another galaxy. Feeling at ease amidst the weirdness, my social anxieties had vanished.

The post-drums "Space" sounded like ravens gone mad and seagulls squawking. Deadheads drifted in from the hallways and wiggled to their seats—some squatting, some standing. A brother in front of us passed back a hash pipe. Is there any substance with a more exotic scent than hash? I took a long, luxurious hit. A sensation of weightlessness seized me, yet, thanks to another blast of blow, I felt like juggling bowling balls.

Optimism oozed through my pores. I sought The Holy Grail, "Morning Dew." A rarely-played jewel, The Dead only played the Dew when they had IT going on. A cyclone of psychedelic sound was unleashed in the jam between "Truckin" and "The Other One." I hollered and yodeled approval; the band was ripping. Now I had mental telepathy working: *The Dew, Jerry. For the love of God, please play the Dew.* Weir sang, "Cowboy Neal at the wheel, the bus to never ever land; Coming, coming, coming around; coming around, coming around; coming around." The time had come.

A fractioned second of silence framed the moment. Jerry struck the magic Dew chord.

Oh, the humanity! I grabbed Scott by the waist and proudly hoisted him over my head like he was the Stanley Cup Trophy. A young lady standing in front of me let out two primal, erotic screams. Pandemonium in Philly! Folks were crying, hugging, kissing, and squeezing each other.

Jerry's solitary voice emerged: "Walk me out in the morning dew my honey; walk me out in the morning dew today." The tempo was dirge-like, almost still. Jerry appeared egoless, just standing there in black t-shirt and jeans. He poured his soul into each syllable, seemingly stopping time, freezing the moment, connecting with the raw emotion of the masses: "I thought I heard a baby cry this morning; I thought I heard a baby cry today!"

Jerry compressed a screaming tirade of notes into his solo, punctuated by a resounding blast from Phil's bass. Jerry's solitary voice returned, more solemn than before, repetitiously crying, "I guess it doesn't matter anyway." Silence filled the arena. Deadheads prepared for takeoff.

Garcia began his sermon deliberately, plucking strings with surgeon-like precision. He was immobile nobility—his bearded mug intense, his brain boiling. Each note radiating from his fret board did so with intimacy. Each note was crucial. The band followed in a trance, adding layers and waves of aural sensation. As the foundation solidified, the velocity and volume of Jerry's playing spiraled until the steam valve blew. Each musician was engaged in the spectacular display—they scaled the pyramid of transcendence together. The wall of sound crashed down. Jerry mournfully wailed, "I guess it doesn't matter, anyway ay ay ayyyyy!"

Overwhelmed by the Dew, I didn't care what was next. I let out a lunatic's laugh as the band burst into "Sugar Magnolia." Sweat poured as Deadheads bounced off the Spectrum floor like it was a trampoline. This was the exclamation point for a historic set. The boys delivered my wish list: Shakedown Street, Terrapin Station, Morning Dew, Sugar Magnolia. It was the only time in Grateful Dead history that those four songs appeared together in the same show. Just once in 2,314 concerts. Was it a coincidence, or was my presence part of the equation?

Much like the sports fan who goes to his favorite pub week after week and roots for his favorite football team, and wears the same dingy sweatshirt, and sits in the same wobbly stool, and orders the same pint of beer from the same bartender until his team wins the Super Bowl or flops and he realizes the folly of his ways, I believed my presence in Philly inspired the band.

Returning home, we felt sensational. There was something heroic about it all. I was an active participant in the musical process. I knew I'd soon land a bootleg tape of the show and, if I listened close enough, I might even hear myself howling. Musical recordings are breathing snapshots of life and emotion that pass through time and endure in a way that no other art form can.

Cruising along the Palisades Parkway, fifteen minutes from my twin mattress, Seymour suddenly lost control of the wheel. His pillbox Honda hit an ice patch and went spinning like a sock in a dryer. When the whirling ceased, we were ensconced in a snow drift, a few feet from the towering pines that might have mangled the car. A tragedy was narrowly averted. Miraculously, there wasn't a scratch on the car or anybody in it. I pried the door ajar, looked up at the star-cluttered sky and pumped my fist into the night. Standing knee deep in snow while waiting for help to arrive, I cut loose with a "Yee-haw, yippie yah-hoo, Jerry is God-od-od-od." My crazed voice echoed through the valley.

Thirty minutes later, a tow truck yanked the tiny vehicle from its snowy trap. Three teens were on the road again. Scott and Seymour were subdued and shaken. I was hooked. I'd found my calling, and seeking more days like this would dominate my foreseeable future. I was dropped off at my parents' house, but there was no going home. My heart and soul were on the road with the Grateful Dead.

But, before we go down that path, I'd like to share some buzzwords and phrases. For some readers this will be familiar terrain, but for everybody else, Welcome to Deadhead Nation.

Bomb: bone rattling, sonic blast emanating from Phil Lesh's bass.

Bullet: plastic gadget that conveniently loads substantial blasts of cocaine for easy snorting, eliminating the need for rolled-up dollar bills, razor blades and teaspoons.

Boot: officially unreleased recording of a Dead concert. The band was supportive of fans who taped their shows as long as they didn't sell the music for profit.

Dugout: a wooden contraption that stores a modest stash of marijuana. The weed is scooped into the *one-hitter* before it's set ablaze and sucked through the metal bat. One who sucks too hard shall receive a discharge of hot ashes in his or her throat.

Doses: hits of acid. A Deadhead hungry for psychedelics prior to a show would yell out, "Hey man, who's got doses?" And it wouldn't take him or her long to score. Tiny perforated squares of *Blotter Acid* were the most common form of *doses* and liquid LSD doses, usually dispensed from eye droppers, were the most potent. Those who may have overloaded their brains with one too many trips were referred to as *burnt cookies* or *fried dogs.*

Persian: a refined Iranian opium usually smoked in tinfoil pipes. It cost a whopping $700 a gram and was extremely addictive. This was Jerry's baby; eventually, Persian became Jerry's master.

Peruvian: in addition to having huge succulent shrimp swimming off its coastline, Peru is also famous for its fertile fields, which produce some of the world's finest cocaine.

Tiger: Jerry's custom-built guitar, a ferocious beast.

JGB: Jerry Garcia Band—always featuring bassist John Kahn. *JGB* primarily performed Garcia/ Hunter compositions, slow ballads, R&B standards, and a number of Dylan tunes. When the Dead were in hibernation, JGB was jamming. In 1974 and 1975, Jerry's band was known as *Legion of Mary*, and in 1979 they were briefly called *Reconstruction.*

Captain Trips: a nickname Jerry earned for his propensity to gobble up acid during the Summer of Love.

Private Garcia: the name Jerry answered to during his brief army stint in 1960. Not one for rules and regulations, Garcia was given a general discharge from service.

Noodling: Guitar masturbation without any direction. This could occur before, during, or after songs and was also called *doodling* or *spacing.* When Garcia strummed chords with stunning velocity, he was *fanning.* Jams that really clicked were *steaming, smoking* and *cooking;* this happened when the band was *en fuego.* And when Jerry turned it up a notch beyond that, he was *demented, deranged* or *insane*—Garcia was *coming off as nut.*

Spinners: Freaks who perpetually twirled at Grateful Dead concerts regardless of the tune being performed. Long-haired and wiry, spinners never ran out of steam, and they apparently never got dizzy.

I Need a Miracle: A Dead song sung by Bob Weir. If a hippie was waving an index finger in the air and crying out, *"I need a miracle,"* they were trying to score a free ticket. *"Come on, dude, hook a brother up,"* was a plea for more freebies. *Free Hugs* were what they sound like, but beware—the freak dishing out the hugs was probably soaked in sweat and in dire need of a bar of soap and a warm shower.

Hey now: a universal greeting amongst Deadheads that had elastic connotations similar to the Hebrew word shalom. Either one could mean: hello, goodbye, peace, or simply be a way of saying "What's up, bro?" *Hey now* originated from the popular party song that kicked off many Dead shows, "Iko Iko."

THE MUSIC NEVER STOPPED

*Ode to a Chevy Caprice Classic...Music Mountain
Meltdown...Marching orders from James Brown...The
Tennyson Boys...Bad news for Van Halen fans...Stoned and
suspended over the Chesapeake Bay...Help on the Way...*

I was a peculiar eighteen-year-old male. I had no visions of a dream car, and I harbored no desire to mess with engines, operate stick shifts, keep my ride clean, rotate tires or change oil. Up and down the driveways of Nanuet, teenagers with grimy hands, greasy shirts, and oil-stained jeans were hovering above and below open-hooded cars. I wasn't one of them. However, I loved driving, and fortunately, I inherited my father's Maroon 1978 Chevy Caprice Classic—a virtually maintenance-free marvel of American technology. It was a masculine vehicle, but stepping inside the red interior was like being back inside a womb. With a powerful engine, massive cargo space, and an explosive sound system, my Dad's Chevy Caprice became my beloved mobile home.

On April, 9 1982, three days after Philly, I took my Chevy on her first road trip to see the Dead in Rochester. I zipped up to Route 17 as Doug Schmell fed fresh boots into the tape deck. The Rochester concert was an above average affair; the second set ended with a blazing Goin' Down the Road Feelin' Bad > (I Can't Get No) Satisfaction combo.

We spent the night at our friend Froggy's college crash pad in a cow-town near Rochester.

Rambling home on Route 81 South, somewhere near Oneonta, Doug and I were bopping our heads in unison to "Alabama Getaway." Icy clumps of snow clung to the low-lying farmlands—remnants of the blizzard. My unconscious driving flow was interrupted by an awesome vision. Standing on top of a foothill was a beautiful and rather large creature, proudly posing, antlers erect and stretching towards the skies. The magnificent deer, apparently moved by the sight of my maroon Chevy, bolted towards us.

I stomped on the brakes and hollered, "Holy Shit!" The deer looked at us as we made contact—"Ka-Pung!" Careening off the front grill of my tank, the deer sailed through the air like a shanked punt on a blustery Sunday at Lambeau Field. The carcass landed at least five yards off to the side of the road.

There was no swerving or stopping. Oblivious to what just happened, my Chevy continued to ease on down the road. Every blood vessel and nerve in my body was ready to burst, yet there was no reason to panic. "Alabama Getaway" transitioned smoothly into "Greatest Story Ever Told."

"Whoa, wow-wow-wow! That was incredible!" said Doug.

"I can't believe it. Let's pull over and look at the damage," I said.

There were lots of remarkable things going on here but, most amazingly, neither one of us was injured in this collision. Not a fractured fibula, bruised tibia, or punctured spleen; not even a bloody scratch! A physics expert might be able to explain how the deer didn't fly back through the windshield, or how the car was still functioning, but this was beyond scientific reasoning. This was a miracle and, by definition, it couldn't be logically explained.

On the side of the road, we observed the blood dripping off the squashed car front. Tiny patches of deer hair clung to the bumper.

I looked at Doug and cried, "Oh deer."

All the adrenaline rushing through us exploded into uncontrollable laughter. I felt awful about hitting the deer, but I was overwhelmed by the joyful sensation that follows avoiding an unforeseen, split-second showdown with death.

Doug channeled his thoughts into an animated rant.

"Howie, my friend. Do you rea-a-lize, if we altered our activities in any way this morning, you never would have hit that deer. If you would have raided Froggy's fridge, or if we pulled over at any rest area, any adjustment to our schedule, no matter how meaningless, that deer lives. If you tried to hit it, no way, impossible! By slamming on your brakes, you made the perfect hit. The freakin' deer turned its head and looked right at us! It's as if he was trying to tell us something... *'now now, youuuu fellas, go ahead and enjoy yourselves. Me, I'm doomed. You fellas, though, you all right, you young, witty, shit, you keep smoking them reefers and chasing them pretty girls and knocking yourselves out with that Jerry Garcia fella. And when you get home, order yourselves up a pie from Nanuet Restaurant, half garlic, half pepperonis, I love-uv-uv-uv-uv them ronis, ha ha ha, go to that batting cage ya'll love in Monsey, and knock the hell out of them balls and say hello to Old Man Lou for me. You fellas are really something. Donchaya worry a thing about me. Everything is gonna be allllll-right.'"*

I'd never been in a car accident of any kind. If I threw in the wild auto mishap from three nights earlier, after the Philly show, the statistical improbability of avoiding injury was mind-boggling. Aside from the death of the deer, my eighteen-year-old brain processed all these happenings as thrilling. I could play with fire. A guardian angel had my back.

My bedraggled Chevy rattled and clanged the remaining three hours back to Nanuet. After undergoing radical reconstructive surgery at Manny's Auto Shop in the South Bronx, my Caprice Classic bounced back, becoming an indispensible touring vehicle. A long, rectangular four-door sedan with a 350 V8 engine and the power of 170 Clydesdales, my Chevy could plow through any terrain, endure inclement weather and manhandle any moveable object in its path. Yet, she was also capable of more than anyone working the assembly line at the Chevrolet plant had ever envisioned.

Doug and I shook off the deer incident like it was a minor nuisance. Nothing was going to slow down our crusade. Our four-part mission was clear: 1) follow Jerry Garcia and identify all the great jams; 2) find tapes of these shows; 3) share the jams with other Deadheads; 4) influence friends and infidels.

Jerry Garcia Band played at Music Mountain on June 16, 1982. An outdoor venue located in South Fallsburg, New York, Music Mountain had a majestic ring to it, and the town sounded sleepier than any dark hollow. Even the numerical date, 6-16-82, appeared like a balanced set of digits embedded with mystical qualities. This show was bound for glory.

Behind the wheel of his mom's yellow Coup De Ville Cadillac, Doug blindly passed cars on Bear Mountain heading west on Route 6. Merging on to Route 17 West, Doug pressed on as if he were competing against an imaginary foe, darting from lane to lane and tailgating every driver in his path. We weren't late, but that's the way Doug rolled— beating time was essential. A jamming JGB rendition of After Midnight > Eleanor Rigby > After Midnight challenged our ear drums—almost too loud, exactly the way Doug desired it. Garcia was the matador, and Doug was the charging bull.

Our jaunt through Sullivan County was one of scenic serenity. Gargantuan trees bunched together like broccoli and hovered over sparkling lakes and reservoirs. Sullivan was hopping with plant and animal life, but it didn't seem compatible for human habitation. Maximum security prisons, rural poverty shacks, and abandoned Borscht Belt hotels scarred the lush terrain. This land was ghostly—a graveyard of failed aspirations.

Cruising through the gut of South Fallsburg, we observed a ramshackle Hassidic community on the lam followed by a black ghetto. It's strange how those ethnic groups always end up side by side, co-existing in a peaceful, yet restless, accord. Down around the bend of Route 42, we saw signs of hippie life: pony-tailed mammals in faded jeans, dresses, sandals and tie-dyes—roaming and scuffling roadside in small packs. The sweet twangs of Jerry's guitar were imminent.

Doug's Caddy sailed into the parking lot, a Great Yellow Shark amongst the dilapidated jalopies of Deadville. The early evening sun was tenacious, and the mosquitoes were thirsty for blood in the sticky air. Some lovely long-haired ladies stripped naked and plunged into a nearby pond, and naturally, a few dudes jumped in, turning the pond into a community bathtub. This scene was reminiscent of the original Woodstock Festival which took place fifteen miles due west on Yasgur's Farm in Bethel. Hail, hail, the hippies are all here to awaken the ghosts of 1969 with a day of peace, love and music.

Grinning through his gray beard, Garcia's vocal inflections were giddy during "How Sweet It Is." Doug and I had each dropped a hit of window-pane acid before the show. I was wondering how, and when, the acid would strike. I wasn't all that comfortable with tripping. I was handing my brain over to a force I couldn't control or predict. I preferred recreational drugs at concerts. Acid was a real game changer, a distraction to my intense focus on the music.

Doug and I settled in the middle of the grassy knoll about thirty yards from the stage. The glorious scents of summer rose from the baked land, commingling with the natural smell of the tribe—cannabis, hashish, opium, sweat, patchouli oil. The swampy sounds of Melvin Seal's organ swirled behind Garcia's electrified bluegrass picking on a massive "Catfish John," featuring the song recipe that JGB made famous: two verses of Jerry > three minutes of noodling brought to a simmering boil > 90 seconds of Melvin Seal's soulful keyboard vamps > equal parts guitar, bass, percussion, and keyboard carefully stirred into a funky Jamaican riff > a volley of shooting stars from Jerry's guitar, and the final chorus fortified by female backup singers. Mmm, mmm, good.

Doug's damp face widened as he said, "Howie, boy, this is unbelievable. Jerry's smoking tonight." I heard those words in slowww-motion.

The empty time between songs had me anxious. I was relieved to hear Jerry pierce the twilight air with the opening lick of "That's What Love Will Make You Do." The window pane was hijacking my brain. I was in deep. My thoughts turned chaotic:

Look at Doug go. He's flapping his elbows and bouncing around like a rooster. I never noticed this before, but he looks like a young Captain Kangaroo. Check out those spinners whirling to the music, or are they oblivious to it? Whoa, check out the one with the long gray locks and shades. It's Cousin It. This is a variety show. I must be Flip Wilson. I gotta soft shoe thing going on, keep it slow, keep it balanced, nice and easy, anchored to the ground. Guitar strings crackle in my ears, sweat leaks down my back. Garcia's up there, fingers prancing, piercing twangs bounce off the clouds. Melvin's organ is soothing—the swampy hisses float off the stage, fluffy in texture, almost hilarious. More sweat, the hill is sinking below my feet. There it is again, that crazy JGB calypso riff, a Brazilian coffeehouse jingle. I must be Juan Valdez. The bassist looks like a number two pencil, his head a smudged eraser. Jerry's percolating, notes piling on top of each other and invading the surrounding forests and farmlands. I hoot and holler with everybody else. Yes, we're all in this together. Even Cousin It is yelping. I feel like a Prairie Dog. Go, Jerry go. His voice cries, "No matter how hard I fight it, baby, I'm still in love with you." I'm weightless, a pile of Silly Putty. Sweet Jesus, I hope I've peaked.

Each song was a test of time and sanity, the slower ballads more challenging. There were blissful flirtations, but if I could do it all over again, I would have skipped the trip. Music Mountain swells in my memory, thanks to the plush audience recording I've been enjoying since that night. 6-16-82 is a harmonious brew: the song selection is innovative, every guitar statement glows, and Jerry's voice is sweet and true. Garcia seemingly stops time with his dirge-like cover of The Band's "The Night They Drove Old Dixie Down." Each syllable drips with the heartache of the Civil War. Jerry croons as if he were an eye witness passing on a precious parcel of history.

A few years after 6-16-82, Music Mountain disappeared as mysteriously as it emerged, out of business quicker than any Borscht Belt hotel. Today, banal condominiums stand where Garcia rocked. Probably not one of its current tenants is aware of the hallowed grounds they inhabit.

It's easy for me to forget that Weir's group, Bobby & the Midnites, was the closing act at Music Mountain. On this mini-tour, Bob and Jerry swapped spots as the headliner. Thankfully for Weir, Deadheads are notoriously loyal and supportive of anyone under the Grateful Dead umbrella. Heavy rains commenced when Weir's band hit the stage, turning Music Mountain into a muddy quagmire. Weir's ensemble performed admirably, yet several degrees of greatness separated them from JGB.

Doug and I split swiftly after the festivities. Others weren't as fortunate. Mud-splattered freaks toiled in vain to free their cars from the muck. The yellow Schmell Coupe De Ville parted its way through the muddy mess and then burned rubber on down the highway. We returned to Nanuet faster than we arrived.

After some rejuvenating sleep, I cooked crispy bacon and a stack of flapjacks and brewed a potent pot of Chock Full of Nuts. My siblings were at camp, mom was shopping, and dad was making dough. I lounged poolside for a while, and then grabbed my Marlboros and picked up the birthday boy, Doug, who was turning nineteen. In an hour we were at the New Haven Coliseum waiting for JGB to come out and play—déjà vu all over again.

During the summer of '82 I worked in a seafood warehouse hauling cases of frozen shrimp and lobster tails in and out of a freezer. All my earnings were allocated for personal pleasures: bags of the finest weed, brews at the New City Pub (legal drinking age in New York was still eighteen), Maxell XL II tapes, Grateful Dead tickets, and travel expenses. I was king of all squatters, but not that different from the other three white adolescents employed by Ramapo Seafood.

I worked alongside rugged men like the Haitian truck driver, Balker Lazar—men who fed their families by grinding it out with brawn. Balker wore long-sleeved, button-down silk shirts tucked into tight slacks as he delivered his routes in summer heatwaves. On the days when drivers had physically demanding routes, Ramapo Seafood would send me along as a helper. I loved the mini-road trips. It beat the hell out of sweating in a freezer. Balker was a kind soul. He let me bring along my tape deck and play Jerry. I never converted him into a Deadhead, but I created a jingle about him. He had a very lyrical name:

Walking the dog with Balker Lazar
Just-a-walking the dog with Balker Lazzar
Wherever I wander, near or far,
The children sing for Balkar Lazzar

Norfus was another memorable trucker. He had a fantastic name, gruff disposition, beach ball gut, and a face like a penguin. On his Chinatown route, Norfus was treated like royalty as we unloaded cases of defrosting shrimp in the dingy basements. "Hey, Nofo, you and your friend want an egg roll and pork fried rice? You want Budweiser? Stay here and rest; it's too hot out." During my first outing with Nofo, I drank a six-pack and devoured the equivalent of three pu pu platters. Nofo also turned me on to my first topless bar after we finished a route in Elizabeth, New Jersey. It was a low-budget joint. We were able to touch tuna for a dollar tip.

Lou Green, the Ramapo warehouse manager, wore an army jacket, tan slacks and blue ski hat, every day. He never figured out how to pronounce my name, and he barked out orders like James Brown sang soul: "How-A, put your gloves on and get back in that cooler and stack those cases of Bee Gee shrimp again. That pile is gonna fall over and kill somebody. I don't know what the fuck you're smoking…Hi-E, where the fuck are the lobster tails? Get me twenty-five pounds, and make it quick. Norfus, can't be waiting on your lazy ass all day." Lou was always pissed at me, and I understood. He was supporting an extended family with his modest paycheck. I was just feeding my head and supporting Jerry Garcia's habits.

After a particularly hectic day of schlepping seafood, I met Doug for hoops at our teenage wasteland, Tennyson Park. We ran with a rambunctious crew. The Tennyson Boys believed in competition, hedonism, and a touch of vandalism. Out in these fields we smoked exotic buds, drank Southern Comfort, and popped pills. We regularly mixed sports and medicine. One night, we actually had a boxing tournament on the field adjacent to the basketball court. I had taken a Quaalude that afternoon without realizing I was scheduled to be in one of the main events. I can't recall how well I boxed, but I was impervious to fear and pain.

Doug was waiting for me in the gravelly Tennyson Park lot, leaning against his yellow Caddy and spinning a red, white, and blue ABA basketball on his index finger. The windows were rolled down, and "Casey Jones" was cranking. He said, "Howie, I got a proposition for you. You're gonna love this idea. It's right up your alley. The Dead are in Wisconsin next weekend at the Alpine Valley Music Theatre. We can get tickets from Ticketron. Howie, picture this: We are outdoors with Jerry in the Midwest next Saturday night. I hear this place is amaaaaazing! Can you imagine how hot Garcia will be in the Midwest? It's only a sixteen-hour drive. Let's do it. Whattaya say?"

The time had come for us to leave the Tennyson Boys behind. Our pursuit of Jerry's next transcendent jam was paramount. I informed my parents I'd be heading West with Doug in my Chevy. My parents were fond of Doug. They knew I was crazy, but if Doug was part of my posse, then there might be some merit to it. In the classic tradition of exploration made famous by Lewis and Clark and perpetuated by Kerouac and Cassidy—look out, America—here comes Catfish and Schmell!

I pulled up in front of the Schmell residence before noon on Friday. We wanted to tackle the bulk of our sixteen-hour-trip in one day and cruise into East Troy, Wisconsin, triumphantly on Saturday, August 7, 1982.

Doug emerged from his house with a duffel bag slung across his torso and a box of Maxell cassettes carefully balanced in his right palm like a tray with Dom Perignon. Stepping into my Chevy, he admired his precious cargo and said, "Howie, these tapes are bad news for Van Halen fans." It was a smug remark—one that a Garcia junkie could appreciate. Comparing anybody to Jerry was comical to us. We understood Garcia's virtuosity, and we had to let everybody else know. Despite the fact that the Dead's latest studio efforts were lame, the legend of Garcia was growing, and his cult following was on the rise.

Chuck and Paul, neighborhood Deadheads, joined us on our journey to Wisconsin. Chuck was a serious young man—Fred Flintstone in tie-dye. He was also a person of great interest to us because he had a substantial bootleg collection, but a bad reputation when it came to returning borrowed tapes. Our other passenger, Paul Blatt, was a tiny red-headed cat I met at Rockland Community College. He looked like a mini-Bill Walton, minus athletic prowess. Cordial Paul spoke in soft squeaky tones and was always willing to roll with the flow of the group.

Charging on to 80 West, I claimed the fast lane and refused to budge—left hand steering, right hand juggling java, joints, Marlboros, and boots. Endless Pennsylvania seemed bleak—blue collar town followed blue collar town through Amish Country, insane amounts of highway construction and detours along the way. We ran into three thunder storms, or maybe it was the same one chasing after us. Sheets of precipitation rap-tap-tapped off the windshield as I raced past monster trailers and trucks on the bedraggled two-lane highway. The sky darkened by the time we reached Ohio. Feeling famished, we stopped for food at a place in Youngstown that had a menu boasting of gizzards. A grease-stained bucket of rest area Roy Rogers chicken would have to suffice. One more cup of coffee, a hit of speed and one more '77 Dead tape; I refused to give up the wheel until Cleveland was in the rearview mirror. By 3 A.M., my comrades were snoring as I pulled into a rest area and slipped into a spot between tractor trailers. Four Deadheads and 100 truckers were motionless beneath the stars, but they were still tearing down the road in their dreams.

On Saturday morning, we blew by Chicago, purchased a road map, and found a quaint cabin in Lake Geneva by noon. We had stumbled upon a wonderful Wisconsin resort town, and the weather was perfect—ah-hoooo! Cotton-candy clouds in sapphire skies dangled over a crystal clear lake. This expedition turned up nothing but gold, and the impending jam was still a seed in Jerry's mind.

Our heroes opened with a Music Never Stopped > Sugaree > Music Never Stopped loop. Once again, the band had rewarded me for my dedication with a combination that was never played before and would never be played again. Garcia raged on, peppering away on the set ending "Let It Grow." Weir shouted the lyrics at Jerry, begging him to deliver: "Let it grow, let it grow, greatly yield." And yield, Garcia did. It's a guitar lover's feast offering three separate instrumental segments, with the middle one being the longest and most complex. The band executed flawlessly, setting the stage for Jerry's mid-summer tirade.

I finished out the year seeing the Dead at Landover, Maryland (9-15-82), Madison Square Garden (9-20 + 21-82), New Haven (9-23-82) and Syracuse (9-24-82), as well as catching the Jerry Garcia Band at the Felt Forum (11-11-82 early & late shows) and in the Wilkins Theatre at Keane College, located in Elizabeth, New Jersey (11-15-82 early & late show). In 1983, I got serious about following Jerry around.

Seagulls with massive wingspans glided around us; other seagulls were perched on the rail preparing for takeoff. Brilliant sunshine bounced off the Chesapeake Bay as the Dead thundered in my Chevy. Doug rocked back and forth—a devotee in a contented trance. As the velocity, pitch, and poignancy of Jerry's guitar intensified, Doug's mug glowed in stunned admiration. Pointing at the tape deck as if Garcia was in our presence, Doug said, "This is deranged. How does Jerry think of this stuff?"

I wondered when we might see land again. We'd been on the Chesapeake Bay Bridge for fifteen minutes, and there was just water, road and birds ahead and water, road and birds behind. I was driving straight into an Alfred Hitchcock sequel. It then occurred to me that I was, in fact, driving. I was so stoned I forgot I was captain of the ship.

There were three hipsters in my backseat—Doug's Deadhead companions from SUNY Albany—Stempel, Genowa and Beehaw. They were quiet cats. Their very names seemed to do all the talking for them. Our destination was Hampton, Virginia: Waffle House, Holiday Inn, hippie chicks, Grateful Dead. Paradise Waits.

Hampton was usually the first stop on the Grateful Dead's spring tour. For some people, spring begins when the first pitch is tossed from the mound at Yankee Stadium. For Doug and me, and thousands of other Deadheads, crossing the Chesapeake Bay Bridge signified the commencement of spring.

There are few pleasures commensurate to roaring down the road while the tunes are-a-thundering. Audio transcendence is possible as long as your car can rev up to seventy without rattling, and the windows are rolled up. Yes, the windows must be sealed to bounce the sound around so you eardrums are filled with nothing but rhythm and melody. You breathe in guitar and exhale staccato bursts of air, in an attempt to echo the singers. The bass rattles your bones as the organ sweeps through the pores of your skin. A tiny portion of our brains can handle driving while all this goes down. Accessing that nugget of my stoned mind, I delivered us to the Hampton Coliseum safely on April 9, 1983.

As the boys tuned up for the second set, I identified the sacred twangs from Jerry's guitar. Doug and I grabbed each other and yelled, "Help on the Way!" hugging and jumping in time to Phil's thumping bass. The rest of the band continued to doodle aimlessly. If this turned out not to be "Help on the Way," our premature celebration would have looked pretty silly. Luckily, it was the tune we craved. It had been six long years since the Grateful Dead had played "Help on the Way" on the East Coast. These were glorious times.

THE WHEEL

*Divine intervention at the Bushnell...Dr. J defies
gravity...Romance and violence at the Roseland...
Fear and Loathing in Passaic...Stan the Man...Tar
Heel justice...St. Stephen and another sacrifice to
the Grateful Gods...Do you believe in miracles?...*

During a savage eight-day stretch in the spring of 1983, I saw ten Jerry Garcia Band shows. After rocking past the midnight hour, my companions and I drove back home every night. I was a nineteen-year-old squatter in my folk's house, but they didn't seem to mind. Living on the road is hard traveling. Truckin' back to your parent's house after every gig is pure lunacy.

My descent into JGB madness began at the Bushnell Auditorium in Hartford, Connecticut, on May 29. The following night, we were back at the Bushnell, courtesy of Doug's banana boat. We were joined by a bulky, disheveled Deadhead, "No Name Bob." Bob earned his nickname after he lent Doug a batch of sloppy boots: songs were misidentified and listed out of order, performance dates were incorrect or left blank. "No Name Bob" was born.

The prospects seemed bleak for our ticketless trio. Saturday night, desperation and depression deepened around the Bushnell. There were no scalpers in sight—just Deadheads praying for a miracle. Suddenly, a door on the side of the theatre swung open. There stood a smiling freak and, behind him, a stairway to ecstasy. A bunch of us scampered up the carpeted steps like rats making a late night raid on Taco Bell. Presto! We were dancing in the Bushnell balcony as Jerry whistled a "Mystery Train." Doug charged into a high-stepping, elbow-flapping polka dance. "No Name Bob" was smirking in admiration, for he never had the pleasure of witnessing Doug under Jerry's spell. The Bushnell shows whetted my appetite for the next tour stop— Jerry off-Broadway.

Anticipation boiled inside the Roseland Ballroom. On the last day of May, New York was juiced for a heaping dose of Garcia. Smoke billowed through the ballroom—that sensuously aromatic mix of hash, ganja and cigarettes. Huddled hippies gathered close to the stage. The spacious ballroom floor was surrounded by carpeted lobbies and long, sleek bars from which you could have a golden glimpse of the stage. Wherever you may have lingered or roamed, cocktail access was a cinch.

Jerry appeared on stage in a red t-shirt instead of his customary black—Santa in summertime. Jerry's belly expansion was obvious, bordering on obscene. He seemed to be adding ten pounds of fat per tour. Keyboardist, Melvin Seals, and the JGB'S new gospel singers, Dee Dee Dickerson and Jacklyn La Branch were extra-large, as well. Bassist John Kahn was a twig amongst heavy lumber. Joining JGB for this one tour, former Sly & the Family Stone drummer Greg Enrico pounded the percussions fast and furious. JGB pulsated like never before.

Jerry set sail with "Rhapsody in Red." It had a rhythm and chord structure that was similar to "Let It Rock," but the slick blues lick set it apart—*a deedle dee dee, a deedle dee diedle... a deedle dee dee, a deedle dee diedle*. Jerry bellowed, "I love to hear that Rhapsody in Red; it just knocks me right out of my head." Sonic brightness vibrated from the furious jam—ideas exploding inside a rhythm and blues container.

Fortified by Melvin's funky organ-grinding, "They Love Each Other" playfully bounced in the second spot. Garcia ignited a two-tier jam: round one, a reconnaissance mission; round two, a searing solo that had the cosmopolitan hipsters howling their approval. Garcia was *en fuego*, and his boisterous devotees knew it. Matters of the heart ruled this show. Garcia blew the roof off the Roseland with explosive fret work during "That's What Love Will Make You Do."

The remainder of the gig was easy like Sunday morning, featuring a "Mississippi Moon" that made bikers weep. Jerry's tone was angelic: "Honey, lay down bee-side meeeee; angels rock us to sleeeep."

I reconvened with Doug at the Roseland bar after the show. The NBA Finals were playing on a TV that dangled down by the single malt scotches. Doug's favorite athlete, Philadelphia Seventy-Sixer Dr. J, was ready to bury the Lakers. Dribbling near the right baseline, the doctor charged to the basket and then took off with a mighty leap. Laker defenders guarded the hoop, forcing the airborne doctor behind the basket. Defying the laws of gravity and comprehension, Julius reappeared on the other side of the basket. And, with a casual flip of his left wrist, the ball rolled off his fingertips, kissed the backboard and swished into the net—poetry in motion. Impossible, but true. Philly had won the NBA Championship. Moments after "The Drive," a gaggle of security guards broke up a bloody ruckus between two lanky, but rather violent, hippies. The gladiators left behind a trial of blood that could have restocked a blood bank. It was an ugly conclusion to a beautiful night.

Back in a black t-shirt for the second Roseland rendezvous, Garcia crooned his mission statement: "I'll take a melody and see what I can do about it; I'll take a simple C to G and feel brand new about it." During "The Harder They Come," I felt like I was being checked into the boards of a hockey rink. The tension of the performances mirrored the international chaos of the times. Soviet-American tensions were peaking, Central America was a boiling cauldron of revolution (who can ever forget the Sandinistas?), and the Middle East was the Middle East—no peace.

"Gomorrah," the Hunter/ Garcia adaption of the biblical tale, fit New York City like a glove on this night. In a Hell's Kitchen ballroom, freaks, hopped-up on psychedelics, gyrated to JGB; depravity and debauchery ran wild. Neighborhoods west of The Roseland were being terrorized by vicious mobsters. The Westies instilled fear by ruthlessly chopping up their lifeless victims and stuffing them in hefty bags before depositing them in the East River. Pimps, hustlers, whores and dealers saturated Times Square, and a squadron of desperados loitered around the neon-lit sex shops. When Jerry sang, "Blew the city off the map, nothing left but fire," it sounded like prophecy that could happen. And, to some extent, it did. The West Side of Manhattan circa 1983 has been eviscerated. There's nothing left but clean-cut capitalism and grimy greed.

In the second half of the show, Garcia bullied four epic songs. If there was a gadget that could count guitar notes picked per minute, the device would have blown up. "Don't Let Go" featured a twenty-minute instrumental during which I chain-smoked three Marlboros. It was gripping and terrifying, commensurate to navigating through turbulent waters on a dark ocean night. Edgar Allan Poe would have approved.

The crowd rejoiced during the most uplifting song of the night "Dear Prudence." It came off as a tribute to Lennon because we were only two-and-a-half years, and less than one mile, away from The Dakota, where John inhaled his last earthly breath. Garcia was the transformer, exploring the beauty of Lennon's song by losing himself in it—suspending time by expanding the moment. The set ending "Deal" was a bloodbath. Garcia sang the song as if he was throwing away a rag doll, but the jam was enormous. Guitar notes swarmed like agitated hornets around the Jackhammer bass and raging drums. When the set was over, it felt like the Roseland had experienced a mass exorcism. With two very different performances on successive nights, Jerry mirrored life on the streets of New York City—a snapshot of that moment in history.

Even the Lord needed a day of rest, and so did JGB and the nuts that followed them. The tour resumed in Passaic, New Jersey, on June 3, 1983.

While I was sucking the brew out of a pint in a seedy watering hole by the Capitol Theatre, a vaguely familiar face approached and asked me if I needed doses. I wasn't in the market, but Doug was. This acid guy, who I think I knew from college, looked like the Court Jester of Passaic with his three-pronged joker hat and tie-dye sweatpants. He handed me a vial of LSD and instructed me to dose my buddy in the bathroom, $5 per drop. In the stall, I handed Doug the vial. He proceeded to dispense three or four drops on his outstretched tongue. Things were going to get real weird, real soon.

The healthy crimson hue vanished from Doug's mug, beads of sweat rolled down his pale cheeks. Probing waves of the mega dose zapped his brain. We fled the bar and stood on the street corner. Doug's arms and legs flailed wildly, and he was babbling gibberish. As nightfall descended upon Passaic, we had issues.

How was I going to explain this to Herb Schmell? When Doug jumped into my Chevy that afternoon, he had had a future. He was the pride and joy of the Schmell clan, heir apparent to his father's law practice. I had great respect for Herb and his wife, Gloria. Though Herb never touched a drink or smoked, he had a zany wit and a fiery passion for life, which he passed on to Doug. Herb also had a terrible temper; I could never explain to the old man why his son was being returned home a comatose vegetable, unfit to tie his own shoes.

My other concern was the nature of the environment we found ourselves in. Nighttime in Passaic was not conducive to psychotic episodes. What type of city was Passaic in the early '80s? The summer before, I pulled into Passaic for a JGB gig and found a spot a few blocks from the Capitol. Prior to parallel parking, I discharged two lovely hippie girls from my maroon Caprice and told them I'd meet them in front of the theatre. A cop stopped the ladies, asked me to roll down my window and hollered, "What? Are you fuckin' nuts? Letting theeeese girls walk by themselves, in this neighborhood! Are you fuckin' nuts?!? And if you don't move your car, you'll be lucky to have a fuckin' steering wheel left!"

So, there I was, in downtown Passaic, trying to find a safe sanctuary to nurse Doug back to sanity. I tried to lure Doug into the theatre, but his heart was pounding for the emergency room. After the ER doctor examined Doug, he assured us we had nothing to fear. The doctor went back to treating emergency patients. We went to see the Captain.

There were two shows that night. We missed the early one and were tardy for the late show. My buddy proved to be a resilient son of a bitch. He really seemed to be enjoying himself during "Love in the Afternoon." The acid stroked the sweet part of his brain as the calypso riffs rolled from Jerry's guitar. I was almost jealous.

We twice missed "Cats Under the Stars," the title song from Jerry's best solo project released in 1978. What I missed was irrelevant. I was happy to be rolling up to the Schmell residence with their pride and joy intact. Doug weathered the mega-dosing and, after a few hours of psychotic sleep, we were back on Jerry's track. This time my friend, Perry, joined us.

Perry Paletta was my other major touring accomplice. I met Perry in tenth grade during my brief stint in Mr. Murphy's geometry class. Perry was a soft-spoken, blonde-haired Norwegian who wore a tan corduroy jacket and smoked Parliaments. We crossed paths again a few years later at Rockland Community College. Our new common denominator was the Grateful Dead, and Perry had become the lead guitarist of a band called The Roadrunners. They played a whole lotta Dead and mixed in some Clapton, Hendrix, Stevie Ray Vaughn, Little Feat, and CCR. They didn't have a distinctive voice at first, but inspired by Jerry, Perry's riffs became more creative each time they played. The Roadrunners rapidly found their niche as a roadhouse jam band, becoming popular in the pubs and saloons of New City, Nanuet, and Pearl River.

The day following his showdown with LSD, Doug was tearing north on the curvy Taconic Parkway in his Coup De Ville with Perry lounging in the back. When you're in the thick of a hedonistic marathon like this, the actual day of the week becomes meaningless. Still, it was Saturday night when we were on our way back to see JGB at The Chance in Poughkeepsie. As we drove through the historic town of Poughkeepsie and admired the Hudson River to our west, I sensed the presence of Colonial America. I half expected to see Patrick Henry on horseback galloping through the cobblestone streets.

The Chance was a fantastic gathering nest for a JGB gig. Opened for business as the Dutchess Theatre in 1912, this red brick building resembled a barn and had a 900-person capacity. Closed from 1945–1970, it reopened as Frivolous Sal's Last Chance Saloon before officially being known as The Chance in 1980. The charming Chance was a tiny ballroom, theatre, and bar rolled into one. Such were the allures of a JGB tour. This cozy atmosphere was unattainable at Grateful Dead shows.

With a long night and two shows ahead of us, Doug abstained from anything stronger than a few bong hits. He moved close to the stage and waited for Jerry. Perry and I met up with his older brother Stan and his friend Johnny Bell at the bar. With a can of Budweiser occupying one hand, I kept my other hand free to juggle joints, cigarettes, and bullets. When the red velvet drape was raised, the band was playing "Cats Under The Stars." Jerry was wearing shades and smiling wildly.

"Hey, Howie-baby!" shouted Stan. "Someone forgot to tell Jerry he's at the Chance. He still thinks he's sunbathing." An eruption of laughter followed. The sweet mix of various smokes filled the cozy room. This scene was too good to be a fantasy.

Eight years older than Perry, Stan was built like a harpooner—broad noble shoulders with a sloped stomach solid as granite. Grinning, Stan pivoted towards me and showed me how to wail air guitar left-handed. Knees slightly bent, Stan assumed a sturdy stance, arms opened wide, palms out, like a magician who had just pulled off the grand illusion. His face turned serious as he peeked at his fingers as they slid across an imaginary fret board. Stan strummed away with a bottle of Bud in his right hand. Amused by his own antics, Stan raised his head and trembled in laughter. He suddenly turned towards his best friend, Johnny Bell, and went through the same shtick.

Digging the groove all night long, Johnny Bell was a lumbering figure with thick brown hair compressed like a Brillo pad. Although he had a bouncer's build, Johnny B. Goode had the goofy vibe of a Merry Prankster. He peeled twenties from his wad of cash and kept the Budweiser pipeline rolling. Johnny had recently picked the winning numbers in the New York State Lottery; however, he had the misfortune of having to share the $4,000,000 jackpot with six other winners. After taxes, his cut was about $20,000 a year for twenty years.

When the curtain was hoisted for the late show, JGB rocked "Rhapsody in Red." "Sugaree" was delightful to see; Garcia came off like a thousand terrified turkeys gobbling in unison. Every show had its moments. The "Midnight Moonlight" encore had us prancing about like Russian Cossack dancers.

After partying with reckless abandon for the duration of two shows, Perry and I were sleeping soundly on the ride home. Doug tried to fight off that temptation as he drove south on the Taconic Parkway. We were all awoken by the screeching sound of steel scraping steel. Doug instinctively tugged the wheel to his left, steering us off the guard rail and separating us from a gruesome death in Hopewell Junction.

There was a small dent on the yellow Coup De Ville—not the type of damage that would prevent Doug from driving to Upper Darby, Pennsylvania, for two shows at the Tower Theatre the following night. Enough was never enough—we had to keep on chasing lightning. Garcia rewarded our tenacity with the only "Let It Rock" of the tour, a tremendous version with a pair of furious solos. That one "Let It Rock" made all the sacrifice worthwhile.

As for how Doug explained away the dent on the Coup, I would find that out fifteen years later, at his wedding. During the best man's toast, Doug's younger brother, Eric, asked me to stand up and testify. In front of the entire Schmell clan, I was asked to swear that we actually hit a deer that night coming back from the Garcia show. I proceeded to perjure myself and kept the myth alive. Herb Schmell was laughing so hard his yarmulke almost dislodged from his head.

I ran with the Deadheads at Saratoga Performing Arts Center on June 18th, followed by a pair of shows at the Merriweather Post Pavilion in Columbia, Maryland, and one concert near a nuke plant in Harrisburg, Pennsylvania. Then Doug and I flew out to California to visit Froggy, and it just so happened that The Boys were playing a pair at the Ventura County Fairgrounds. Fabulous shows. We managed to avoid the California Highway Patrol, guard rails, emergency rooms, and deer.

Garcia's solos were long and luxurious in 1983; therefore, I had to travel south of the Mason-Dixon Line for more Dead in October. Autumn was here, and the time was right for this Yankee to be dancing in the land of Dixie.

"Yo mamala, yo mamala!" shouted Stu as he flicked his middle finger at another unsuspecting motorist blocking his progress in the fast lane. Stu gunned my Chevy Caprice in excess of 100 MPH as he drove towards Richmond, the opening destination of the tour. I knew Stu from high school, but he was friendlier with Doug. Stu was the angriest driver I'd ever seen, but he was making good time, so I let him rage on.

Joining us on this expedition was Roger, a ganja dealer who bore a resemblance to Frank Zappa. Richmond was a fine show, but the next night in Greensboro was the real deal. From the spunky Shakedown > Samson opener through "Let it Grow," the first set was loaded, 1980s Power Dead. Considering the lengthy haul home, I let Stu take the wheel again. Stu's abrasive attitude grinded on us all weekend, but he was an alert driver who could turn our nine-hour journey into seven.

Flagrantly disregarding North Carolina's speed limit, Stu's driving rampage was ended by a North Carolina trooper. He was flagged-down for traveling at 105 miles per hour. Stu was handcuffed and carted away to a jailhouse, somewhere in rural North Carolina. Stu would be spending the night in a holding cell for reckless driving. He had to appear before the judge to be released on bail in the morning.

At the jailhouse, Stu whispered, "Hey Catfish, come here…Quick, grab the bag from my poncho pocket." There was no fuzz in sight, so I confiscated the rolled-up baggie containing a quarter-ounce of marijuana, street value: twenty-five bucks.

Stu was done for the night, and Doug was fretting. He said, "Howie, no way, man. We can't wait around here. I gotta get back to Albany. I have an important test tomorrow. We have to leave Stu in Carolina. The kid dug his own grave."

True. He had dug his own grave, but leaving him behind to face Southern Justice? However, there wasn't much we could do on his behalf, and we were running low on cash. Doug and I came from upper-middle-class families, but we toured like peasants. I put Stu's fate to a democratic vote. It was a unanimous verdict. We left him behind. I let Doug break the news to his ex-friend. Stu was headed back to New York on a Greyhound the following afternoon after his parents wired down the necessary ransom.

It was getting late, and we couldn't wait to get out of the Tar Heel State. Without warning, a few minutes after we left Stu behind, there were neon lights in my rearview mirror, and the sirens became louder. I pulled over, rolled down my window and said, "Good evening, officer."

"Sonnn, do y'all know how fast youse was going?" asked the cop.

"Sixty-five, officer." I said.

"Sonnn, I clocked y'all on the radar back there by the side of the road. Youse was doing seventy-one. I want ya'll to gather your driver's license and registration and come with me back to my vehicle. If one of your friends has a valid motor vehicle license, have him follow me to the station. You will be released once you pay the seventy-five-dollar fine for speeding here in North Carolina."

There was no doubt I was the victim of my Yankee plates and bad karma. Maybe this was payback for leaving Stu behind. I knew I wasn't speeding. My cruise control was set on sixty-five. I grabbed my license and said, "Now, Doug and Roger, youse take it easy, you hear? We're running out of drivers pretty darn quickly."

In the backseat of the squad car, I tried to explain things logically. "Officer, I'm positive I was only going sixty-five. I had the cruise control locked on that number."

"Now, Howard. I'd keep my mouth shout if I were-ah you. Y'all're starting to irritate me," said the officer.

I'd seen that movie before: innocent Yankee boy beaten by a Rebel sheriff and sentenced to a hard labor camp on a plantation. I shut my mouth and forked over the seventy-five dollars, which I had to borrow from Roger to pay off the fine. Doug drove us out of North Carolina with one eye on the road and one eye on the speedometer.

The cycle of sacrifice and satisfaction continued two days later at Madison Square Garden. The first set ended with "Hell in a Bucket" and "Day Job," two new songs that pissed me off. In fact, when the lights came on, I yelled, "You guys suck." Perhaps this was a sign that I was taking things too personally.

It didn't have the makings of an extraordinary night, but The Boys electrified the Garden by playing "St. Stephen" for the first time in four years. The excitement of the moment was hard to control or express. Perry and I were slapping each other around—a Three Stooges moment. It was a weird night; the band's performance tailed off again down the homestretch. Returning home, Perry's old warhorse Delta 88 started smoking. On the Palisades Parkway median, it died. The engine was shot—dead from natural causes—a sacrifice to the Grateful Gods. There was no parkway like the Palisades. She was a kind road loaded with personality, and every once in awhile, she liked to twist your fate.

On the way to MSG the following night, I witnessed Doug at the height of his driving prowess. Stalled in horrendous traffic, Doug stepped on the gas and swung his Coup from lane to lane with reckless abandoned. He created lanes where they didn't exist. Doug had a front row seat at MSG, and no GW Bridge standstill was gong make him late for Jerry. The ghost of Neal Cassady was with us. By the slimmest of margins, Doug avoided thirty fender benders and got us to the Garden before the band opened with "Cold Rain & Snow."

Help on the Way > Slipknot! > Franklin's Tower ignited the second set on 10-12-83, and it was perhaps the best thirty minutes of live music I'd ever witnessed. I positioned myself behind the stage and grasped the magnificence of what it's like to perform in Madison Square Garden. I surveyed the floor of Deadheads dancing and swaying as one. The electricity that can be generated in the Garden is undeniable. The atmosphere absolutely fuels greatness.

Garcia's creativity was ceaseless during "Slipknot!"—Coltrane-like riffs took flight, and there was a gritty workingman's quality about it all. Jerry extended time by milking it, constantly in motion, yet relaxed in the moment. The Scarlet Begonias > Fire on the Mountain I witnessed two nights later in Hartford was equally brilliant. Garcia may have appeared detached from those around him, but he was aligned with spirit, speaking through his Tiger. And the East Coast squeezed a little more intensity out of the band, as a whole.

Three days later I frolicked with hippies in the immortal shrine of America's greatest victory since Valley Forge—that little hockey rink in Lake Placid where David slew Goliath. On the day the USA shook up the sports world by beating the Soviet Union in Olympic hockey, I made personal history by debuting as a singer in a rock-and-roll band.

On that star-spangled day in 1980, John Saunders, a guitar player I knew from school, invited me over to his house for a jam. John's brother was a drummer, and I could sing a bit, so we had ourselves a band. We jammed "Brown Sugar," "Can't Explain," and "The Ocean" for two sixteen-year-old girls: Bonnie and Betsy. The highlight of our set came when I called Sports Phone to check on the hockey game. The USSR was leading 3-2 after two periods. I was shocked that the U.S.A had a chance. I went home and watched the stupefying American triumph, during primetime. Our rock trio broke up after that one set, but it was a pretty cool prelude to Al Michaels shouting: "Do you believe in Miracles?"

Naturally, the Grateful Dead played "I Need a Miracle" on 10-17-83. Lake Placid was another killer show with a "Sugaree" opener. The autumn tour ended with a thud in the Carrier Dome in Syracuse—the only uneventful performance of that eleven-show tour. The next morning, I woke up in my maroon Chevy off the side of a road somewhere in the middle of New York State. A cold rain had turned into hail, depositing a sheet of ice on my windshield. I cranked the engine and blasted the heater and defogger. Before I could pop in a Dead tape, I was listening to WCBS News Radio 88 with Doug and Perry. That's when we heard that 200 U.S. Marines were killed in a terrorist attack in Lebanon. Welcome to the age of terrorism.

These were dark days. The Cold War was scary, nobody predicted the easing of tensions. Culturally and politically, America was drifting in a direction that didn't make sense. I clung to the Grateful Dead. That wheel was turning and there was no slowing down.

U.S. BLUES

*Grateful Interventions...A preview of the 1985 NBA
Draft in the style of Moses Malone...The pros and
cons of hitchhikers...Sweating bullets in Cincinnati...
Ominous clouds in Buffalo...The party's over at RFK...*

"I wish Garcia would die already, so I can get on with my life," said Doug, as we crossed the Chesapeake Bay Bridge in the darkness of March 22, 1985.

Doug loved Jerry Garcia's music with purer enthusiasm than anyone I'd ever met, but all the road sacrifice was wearing us down. Garcia was our Dear Mr. Fantasy; it was painful to watch him die before our eyes, and that's what was happening. We couldn't lie to ourselves or each other. Our weekend in Hampton, Virginia was a bust. The opening shows of the tour were insipid. It sounded like a fish taco was lodged in Jerry's windpipe, and the band was paddling through the same muddy river of songs. We'd come to expect brilliance from the Grateful Dead. We were willing to settle for professionalism. Garcia's addiction to Persian was consistently wreaking havoc on his performances. Unfortunately, our minds were hooked on his hypnotic riffs. We couldn't just walk away, a mind-blowing jam might be awaiting us behind door number two.

Three nights after Hampton, Jerry had the right stuff. The Grateful Dead amazed us with a mad dash through Jack Straw > Sugaree in

Springfield, Massachusetts. Here we were at the home of the Basketball Hall of Fame, but the only thing that mattered was Jerry's virtuosity. We had to keep on chasing the tail of the dragon.

Patched up in hippie regalia, the average Deadhead weighed in at around 123 pounds. Jerry Garcia was a gray-bearded whale, tipping the scales at over 300 pounds. Unlike the glorious sea prowling mammal, Jerry was immobile, unkempt, and sullen, especially in 1984. His voice had to burrow through a smoke-scarred larynx to communicate, and when he was successful, our spirits soared.

There were bumper stickers aplenty stating "The Fat Man Rocks." I hated those stickers, although they stated the truth. I saw my usual allotment of shows in 1984—about thirty Grateful Dead and fifteen JGB affairs. On November 18, at Avery Fisher Hall in Lincoln Center, John Kahn and Garcia played acoustic. With his arms fully stretched out in front of his rotund belly, Jerry fingers barely reached his guitar strings.

According to Rock Scully's book *Living With the Dead*, the band and their extended business family arranged an intervention for Jerry—a very Eighties approach to drug dependency. At the band's request, drummer Billy Kreutzmann delivered an ultimatum to Jerry: "Either you gotta quit this Persian shit, or you're fired."

"Promises, promises," said Garcia. "Okay, after careful consideration, I'm afraid I'll have to go with the Persian…Anyway, who you gonna hire? It's a lot easier to find a drummer than it is a lead guitar player."

My parents had their own intervention going with me. Actually, it turned out to be more of a negotiation. They offered to buy me a stereo if I quit smoking cigarettes—a loving gesture that I appreciated, but I had a stereo. What I really needed were tickets to the Grateful Dead's Spring Tour in 1985. Where did I get the balls? My folks offered to buy me tickets for all eleven East Coast tour dates and threw in hotel accommodations in Hampton and Portland. Live Dead was all the leverage I needed to kick my two-pack-a-day Marlboro habit. After dumping nicotine, I was pumping myself up to the exercise routines depicted in Arnold Schwarzenegger's Encyclopedia of Body-Building. Honestly, Captain Trips saved my lungs. I never looked back—habit kicked.

In 1984, the Grateful Dead sanctioned a taping section behind the sound-boards. Since the band wasn't opposed to fans taping their performances as long as they weren't trying to profit from it, organizing the tapers in one section made sense: better-sounding bootlegs, less security hassles for tapers, and less conflict between tapers and fans who liked to yell, "Yee-hah" every twelve seconds.

Doug couldn't resist the temptation of becoming a taper. He loved listening to his master audience recordings on the way home, and he loved the art of taping. Being that my chief touring accomplice would have fresh masters on the spot, I skipped that scene. A taper had to buy tickets for the taping section, lug the equipment in, claim turf, raise the microphones on twenty-foot stands, check batteries and recording levels, flip tapes, guard the area, and break down afterwards. The breakdown was a serious drag after a subpar performance. Tapers had to lug their mobile studios back out to their cars stoned off their gourds.

Immensely enjoying the Schmell masters of the recently played Greek Theatre shows, we made our annual trip to Alpine Valley in July of '85. Paul Blatt was along for the ride again. The new kid in our crew was Phil Hyman, a Dylan/ Deadhead from Boston. I met Phil at Rockland Community College through Paul. Phil had bushy hair, bushy beard, and a mustache. His lanky shrub look blended in well with the Dead scene. You get the rest of the picture—ripped jeans, tie-dyes, sandals, and the smell of patchouli oil marked his presence.

The Dylan fanatic in Phil remained under wraps. We only had ears for Garcia. Our respect for Dylan as a songwriter was immense. The Dead and JGB covered Dylan way more than any other artist, but that didn't mean we had to actually listen to Dylan. For five years now, I had feasted on nothing but Garcia, and with all the boots at our disposal, I didn't anticipate change.

I drove into more trouble than usual on 80 West. Nailed for speeding in New Jersey and Pennsylvania, I talked my way out of a ticket in Ohio and was simply given a friendly warning.

At a service area in the pines of Western Pennsylvania, I grabbed a football from the trunk and started tossing it around with Ragamuffin Phil. In his Guatemalan shorts and tie-dye shirt, he planted his sandals on the pavement and rifled the football like Broadway Joe. Welcome to Namath and Marino country. Spiral after speeding spiral, the pigskin stung my reddened hands. There was more to Phil than met the eye. I learned that he was one of the better players on his high school baseball team in Framingham, Massachusetts. I imagined we'd become good friends, if only he eased off the patchouli oil.

Bolting across Ohio, Doug permanently implanted the 1985 NBA draft in our minds. Bragging about his Seventy-Sixers, Doug started channeling his thoughts on the upcoming season, as if he were Philadelphia's dominating center, Moses Malone.

"Sure, I know it's gonna be a tough-tough year, but we committed to winning the whole thang. It's gonna be Philly's year. I know there's a whole lotta naysayers out there, and also lots of young studs coming into the league, but I'll show those rookies a thing or two. You know, yaw got yaw Pad-trick Ewinggggg, you got the Kri Mull-onnn, coming from St. John'sss, you got the Way-mawn Ti-day-lllll, yaw got the powerful Kete Leeeee, you got yaw Eddie Pick-nkeeeee, you got, you got yaw Deadly Shrimp, the forward from West Germany, you got that tall, lean fella from Africa, the Manu Bowllll, you got, you got, you got yaw X-man, Xavier McDan...yulll, you got yaw Ben-oy Ben-ja-man. I'll be damned if one of these kids is gonna stop us from winning it all!"

For the rest of journey, Moses-talk was the answer to any question.

"What do you think the Dead will open the second set with?"

"Well, we due for de 'Touch of Grey,' but you never know what Jerry's thinking or smoking, you got yaw Cat > Riderrr and ya got yaw Scarlet > Firrre. You got the Half Step > Franklin's...They may even blow us away with da Jack Straw from Witchitawww...Yaw never know."

We lodged in the same place as we had during our initial Alpine foray—that cherished cabin in Lake Geneva. There's something exotic about revisiting a familiar place in a strange land. I'm still an almost complete unknown in Lake Geneva, but I've established a history in this place; I've been down this way before. By the time I stay in certain towns two or three times, I start coming off like the mayor. Lake Geneva was one of those towns.

On the way into the Alpine Music Theatre Parking lot, I was pulled over by the police. I was weary of revisiting these scenes.

The cop said, "Sir, having an open container of alcohol in your car is a $150 fine."

I said, "Officer, I'm not sure what you're talking about."

"Sir, my fellow officer is sitting in that tower over there, with binoculars. You had a Pabst tall boy in your hand. Either you produce that can and pay the fine, or I'll search your entire vehicle and everybody in it right now."

Poker time was over. You got to know when to fold them.

When the Grateful Dead came to town, it was a golden opportunity for cowtowns like East Troy, Wisconsin, to round up cash from the peaceful invaders. They didn't even check my driver's license at the police station. They just fleeced me out of $150 and let me go so they could get on with the business of collecting money from as many Deadheads as possible. It was a shakedown factory. I was now broke, and I was on my way back to Alpine Valley for pre-show festivities, with concerts in Cincinnati and Cayuga Falls on the horizon.

The Alpine shows were tight, welcomed consistency after the Helter Skelter Spring tour. On the second night, the "Saint of Circumstance" jam raged, and The Boys opened the second set with the Derek and the Dominoes classic, "Keep on Growing," featuring Phil Lesh on lead vocals. Lesh had recently emerged from a ten-year singing hiatus. A new Deadhead chant was born: "Let Phil sing." I wanted to chant: "Bad idea." The beloved bassist, who wore tie-dyes and looked like a chemist, had a distinct vocal style—awful as can be. This didn't matter to

Deadheads. Tight-knit crowds crave simplistic mantras to chant. In Yankee Stadium they yell, "Boston sucks," and in the Boston Garden they holler, "Beat L.A." When Phil Lesh sang, I cringed.

June 23, 1985, was a travel day. Our crew fiddled around Lake Geneva all afternoon and then started the journey towards Cincinnati by sundown. We picked up a hitchhiking Deadhead who looked like a young Rodney Dangerfield in a Hawaiian shirt. His name was Steve Miller. His sticky bud made us fly like eagles, and his stinky feet made us roll down the windows. We had an intervention and ordered him to put his boots in the trunk. Doug's Alpine Masters sounded sensational as I pressed on for five hours before pulling over to sleep in an Indiana service area.

Sunshine was beating upon my forehead as I awoke in the front seat. My clothes were heavy with perspiration. I was steaming like a burrito that had been slowly baking all night. Doug was snoring and schvitzing in the back seat. Steve Miller restlessly rolled on the trunk. Phil and Paul had been napping in sleeping bags on the grass, but I found them having coffee in the cafeteria. Their sleeping quarters were invaded by a bivouac of ants at dawn.

The mid-morning heat was relentless, and there wasn't a cloud over the Midwest. Our spirits were bolstered again as we headed down the highway with the AC cranking. We reached the River Bend Music Theatre at noon, way too soon—we had seven hours to kill on a 100-degree day.

"Iko Iko," the righteous party song, commenced the second set in Cincinnati. Behind the stage, a steamboat slowly sailed up the Ohio River. *Look out, mama, there's a white boat coming up the river.* The enormous Grateful Dead twentieth celebration banner dropped down behind the band as they slammed into "Samson & Delilah." River Bend buzzed below the setting sun.

For their Twentieth Anniversary concerts in Berkeley, the Dead broke out "Cryptical Envelopments," an *Anthem of the Sun* beauty that had been sitting on the shelf since 1970. In Cincinnati we were treated to a Cryptical Loop: Cryptical Envelopments > Drums > Space > Come

A Time > The Other One > Cryptical Envelopments. A la 1985, Garcia's voice crackled through this segment, but the loving intent was palpable.

Driving away from River Bend, I gushed about Garcia's nifty fretwork on "Let It Grow." Had I been looking at road signs, I might have been warned about the winding pavement that veered sharply to the right. Without time to stomp on the brakes, I snapped the wheel to my right in a desperate attempt to save myself and my crew from flying off the mountainside. The tires screeched louder than a bullhorn, and my Chevy was airborne—cups, cans, tapes, pipes, and humans in orbit. I stuck the landing on the road like a gold medal skier in the downhill, still cruising at a 60 MPH clip. My crew was silenced with acute shock syndrome.

"Whoa, Catfish. That was nuts; that was incredible," said Doug, breaking the silence. "How, how, how? I say, how the hell did you do that?"

I said, *"Well, You got yaw Pad-trick Ewinggg, you got the Kri Mull-on..."* By now everybody was singing: *"You got the Way-mawn Ti-dale, yaw got the Kete Leeeeee, you got yaw Eddie Pick-nkeeeee, you got yaw Deadly Shrimp."* Even Steve Miller was in on the Moses-talk.

In the taping section, Doug befriended some geeks who were spending the night in a motel outside of Cincinnati. Enticing them with the promise of listening to his masters, Doug elicited an invitation to their room. These guys had no idea that Mr. Schmell would be arriving with four road-weary clowns.

Our hosts were alarmed when they opened the motel door. *Guess who's coming to crash, boys?* Doug took charge right away: "Joe, Denny, you and your friends are not going to believe the quality of these masters. Good Lord! Wait 'til you hear this smoking "Samson." We almost didn't make it here alive. Catfish over here almost drove us off a cliff. Yeah, this is my boy Howie. This is Boston Phil, this is Paul, and this young man is Steve. He has unbelievable smoke. Joe and Denny, I didn't get to meet your other friends. Are you guys ready to hear some ripping Jerry?"

Joe and Denny didn't have much to say. They already had five people in their standard-size room with two double beds, and none of these guys were burning with desire to hear Doug's masters, but Doug got us in, and with the AC cranking, we had no plans on leaving. The idea of camping in and around my Chevy Caprice again was horrific on this frying pan June eve. Before anyone asked if we could spend the night, I assumed crash position on the carpet and was snoring by the time the masters were spinning. I sincerely thanked Joe, Denny, and the boys when I woke up in the morning. Cayuga Falls, here we come!

Gripped by restless fever, I decided to shuffle up to Buffalo solo on July 4th. Doug was doing the summer '86 tour, taping his way across America. My father, concerned with the health of my Chevy, offered to buy me a round-trip plane ticket to Buffalo. I accepted. Times were good for Lenny, who now had four El Bandido Restaurants under his wings in addition to his thriving CPA practice. My touring habit was still thriving. A few months earlier I'd seen my 100th show at the Philly Spectrum.

I landed in Buffalo the night before the show and attached myself to the first group of wacky and loveable Deadheads I saw at the airport. I was seeking a place where I could lay my head, and I knew my brothers and sisters wouldn't let me down, even though I looked like a cop. My enthusiasm for musical detail convinced others, beyond a shadow of a doubt, that I was one of them—perhaps even weirder:

"Hey now, you guys psyched for the show tomorrow? I'm Howie; some of my friends call me Catfish. Hey, did any of you guys catch the Gimme Some Lovin > Deal opener in Philly last tour? No, well it was a smoking Deal. Jerry's gonna tear Buffalo apart tomorrow. Can't wait. I just flew in from New York, and I need to find a place to crash. I got money, smoke, and some hot boots…"

These wafer-thin dudes and giggling flower girls accepted me into their good graces and offered me some floor at the Super 8. They freaked out on acid as I drifted in and out of dreamless sleep, tossing and turning on the rug burnt carpet. I wasn't one of these people, but it beat the hell out of trying to sleep in a seat at Buffalo Niagara International Airport.

Bob Dylan and his back-up band, Tom Petty & the Heartbreakers, were the closing act, but the revelry surrounding Rich Stadium was like any other Dead show. Twirlers, peddlers and wizards in second-hand vehicles were sending out waves of music and smoke over the Great Lakes.

In between sets, I ran into Scott Zlottlow and his girl, Donna. I hadn't seen Z at a show since Philly '82. The first set was anemic, so seeing Z was a positive omen. He had the aura of a leprechaun.

Ominous clouds appeared and briefly splattered thick rain drops upon us. The rain suddenly stopped as skies darkened and howling winds swept over Rich Stadium. The entertainment began with "Cold Rain and Snow." Garcia's gray mane was flying in the wind. To my extreme delight, the band hustled into an up-tempo "Fire on the Mountain." Jerry channeled chaotic energy into each solo. The onslaught continued with "Samson and Delilah." I grabbed Z and shook him like a rag doll. It was Philly '82 all over again—for a little while.

Weir welcomed a national TV audience as the Grateful Dead performed their next segment for the first Farm Aid benefit via satellite. The Boys sang and played magnificently during The Wheel > I Need A Miracle > Uncle John's Band for the folks in TV land. It was all down-hill after the TV cameras stopped rolling.

I didn't get to stay for much of the Dylan/ Petty performance on 7-4-86, but I liked what I heard. I had to hitch a ride to the airport to catch my flight back to Newark International.

Traveling with two small gym bags, I was dropped off at the airport by a van of hippies heading to Toronto. Walking towards the security gate, it occurred to me that there was only one bag in my hand; the other bag was bound for the Canadian border. I unzipped the Adidas bag in my hand: car keys, plane ticket, ID, Walkman cassette player, and forty dollars. Thank you merciful Jesus. Hallelujah! It was my lucky day.

The red Converse bag heading north with the hippies contained a toothbrush, dirty laundry, and Right Guard deodorant. Well, it wasn't a total bust for the hippies. The bag was sturdy, and they could probably put the underarm deodorant to use. I boarded my flight with seconds to spare.

I trekked down to Washington, D.C., with Phil and his friend, Laurie, two days after Buffalo. It was as hot as Cincinnati the year before, except the D.C. humidity was lethal. RFK Stadium security was spraying Deadheads with hoses to cool them off. Dylan was on the bill again, and this time he appeared on stage with the Dead. They jointly massacred "Desolation Row."

The night before, we saw fisticuffs between Deadheads in the motel parking lot. Two men in dresses actually traded punches. The dude with the hair down to his ass landed an impressive flurry—left jab, right cross, left hook, jab, jab, right cross. The police arrived to break it up.

Sarge, we've contained the brawl outside the motel. The suspects are under arrest. We got two male Caucasians, one long-haired, the other pony-tailed with earrings. The pony-tailed guy is gonna need stitches, and the other guy's knees are scuffed up pretty good. It appears the altercation started over 78 Red Rocks. I think their dealer's name is Garcia.

Those RFK Stadium shows were pure hell. My enthusiasm for the Grateful Dead hit rock bottom—the salt had lost its taste. Dehydrated and exhausted from the D.C. debacle, Jerry Garcia fell into a diabetic coma three days later.

Jerry's health situation was dire, but he was back out on the road with JGB less than two months after the coma. My lifestyle needed a major overhaul. If only I could find a college that would accept me as a half-assed student, I could move out of my parent's house. That would be a start. I'd improvise from there.

SIMPLE TWIST OF FATE

Blood on the Tracks 101...Welcome to New Paltz:
escapist's paradise since 1678...Busted for roaches
in Mt. Laurel...Buddha from the skies...Seeing the
Real Dylan at last...9-18-87 MSG...Bill Graham taunts
a schoolboy outside the Lunt Fontaine Theatre...

There was something peculiar about stepping into the driver's seat of Phil's light brown Chevy Impala. I felt like I was cheating on my beloved Chevy, which was in the shop receiving an overdue tune-up. The seat and mirror of Phil's car were aligned out of my comfort zone. I also forgot to bring a Dead tape along for the ride. Oh mercy! Heading towards the village of New Paltz for my morning caffeine fix, I pushed in Phil's tape, hoping I'd hear some Jerry. The tune was familiar. Dylan was singing "Tangled Up in Blue." I pulled into the lot of McPeady's, the local ma and pa shop, and scored a pint of dirty java that should have been served in a cup with a skull and crossbones warning label. Two sips could make you want to start training for a decathlon. At the time, I was masquerading as a student at SUNY-New Paltz. I had lots of spare time.

Heading home on Route 32 North, a familiar chord riff flowed gently to my ears. Dylan's voice interrupted the serenity, "We sat together in the park, as the evening sky grew dark." Oh my. This was my first rendezvous with the real "Simple Twist of Fate." Up to this point, I'd only heard JGB's unhurried cover. Dylan's singing was sharp. The words were delivered with an intense poetic cadence. The acoustic accompaniment was spacious and lush at the same time—absolutely hypnotic, like leaves floating from trees. Dylan's essence filled the car. This version was superior to the JGB version that I was fond of.

The next song had the same mesmerizing qualities of the first two. Dylan's voice was filled with sorrow: "Oh, I know where I can find you, in somebody's room. It's a price I have to pay. You're a big girl all the way." Nothing had struck me like this since I discovered the Grateful Dead. I'd been down this way before. I knew an epiphany when I was in the middle of one.

I wanted to rewind the tape and absorb what I'd heard so far, but a wounded Dylan attacked: "Someone's got it in for me; they're planting stories in the press." Each succeeding thought swallowed the previous one in magnitude until the final chorus climaxed with Dylan venting, "You're an idiot, babe; it's a wonder that you still know how to breathe." No Punches were pulled—this was as real as it gets.

The Dylan switch in my brain was flicked on. What about those other albums—albums that gave birth to "Like a Rolling Stone" and "Mr. Tambourine Man?" There had to be plenty of gold in those mines. I also realized that I'd reached a traffic circle in Kingston, New York, eighteen miles past New Paltz. Phil was probably wondering where I had disappeared to with his car, but I knew he'd be psyched about my revelation. I rewound the tape and listened to those four monumental songs on the way back.

Charging through the front door of our little white house I yelled, "I get it, I get it! What's the name of the album with 'Tangled Up' and 'Twist of Fate? '

Phil said, "I knew you'd get it…atta boy, Howid…You were listening to *Blood on the Tracks.*"

The sounds inside a moving car had altered my life again. The day of my *Blood on the Tracks* discovery, I retrieved my Chevy from the shop and went to see the Grateful Dead with Lenore, a pretty redhead from the sticks of Woodstock. She was one of the few women I dated that could out-drink me, but not on this day, April 6, 1987. Drinking on an empty stomach caused her to violently dry-heave in the women's room of the Brendan Byrne Arena, which is now the Continental Arena, which will one day become the Jiffy Lube Arena. Anyway, I had to haul Lenore out of the women's room while the Dead were playing "Jack Straw." Not just any "Jack Straw," but an ooh and ahh "Jack Straw." You can actually hear the crowd ooh and ahh on Doug's master.

The concert on 4-6-87 was a fine performance, and it was exactly five years earlier on 4-6-82 that I set out on my first road trip to see the Dead in Philly. But, more importantly, 4-6-87 was the commencement of my Dylan days. I hunted down every tape that was available. His albums were gateways to alternate thinking: A Jew saved by Jesus—*Slow Train Coming*; a poet and philosopher sharing the vision—*Bringing It All Back Home;* an icon airing dirty laundry—*Street Legal*; Sociology in the 70s—*Desire;* abnormal psychology—*Another Side of Bob Dylan.* I always enjoyed his voice and phrasing, but I was blown away by Dylan's musical dexterity. You couldn't pin down his sound or predict where he was headed next.

I had found the right town for Dylan studies. I was drawn to SUNY-New Paltz because it had a sensational reputation as a party school with a low academic bar. Conveniently located, New Paltz was a lovely one-hour cruise from my parents' house, ninety minutes to Yankee Stadium, and twenty minutes from Poughkeepsie and Kingston.

Having been accepted into New Paltz for the fall 1986 semester, I visited the town on a sparkling spring day. Nestled in the Hudson Valley by the Wallkill River, and facing the Shawangunk Ridge, the scenery of New Paltz was as intoxicating as the rich air. In a two-block span of Main Street, there were six bars, a Not Fade Away tie-dye shop, a record store, a pizzeria, China House, and a late night Jewish Deli. There were always peaceful hippies frolicking along Main Street. This artsy town marched to its own beat in its own style. I'd found my home, an escapist's paradise, just as the French Huguenots had when they first settled here in 1678 to circumvent religious persecution. Some of their stone houses still stand by the banks of the Wallkill River.

I sold Phil on the benefits of going to school in New Paltz. It was an unforgettable first semester: Mookie's grounder squirted through Buckner's legs—Phil's dreams, and those of Red Sox Nation were deferred again. I savored every play as the New York Giants won their first Super Bowl. And we dated an assortment of fine-looking young ladies. One day Phil cut his hair and shaved off his beard, and even more women were drawn to him.

My universe was perfectly aligned. I had found Dylan, and Garcia had bounced back from his coma and was finding his stride again. In May of 1987 it was announced that Dylan and the Dead would tour together again—except, this time, Jerry and the Boys would serve as Dylan's backing band, in addition to playing their own show. I could hardly believe it. Lady Luck was my soul mate.

In preparation for the tour, I intensified my Dylan studies, listening to his oeuvre with the zeal of a law student cramming for the Bar Exam. Fortuitously, I hadn't read much about Dylan. My mind was free to appreciate the music for what it was. *Knocked Out Loaded* and *Empire Burlesque* weren't top shelf, but I didn't care. I embraced the fantastic songs: "Seeing the Real You At Least," "Maybe Someday," and "Drifting Too Far From Shore." To me, Dylan wasn't the "Voice of a Generation." I was simply amazed by the many sides of his artistry. Dylan became my de facto professor.

The Dylan/ Dead tour started with an extra-raggy performance at Sullivan Stadium in Foxboro, Massachusetts, on July 4. Dylan hadn't toured in a year, and his nasally-whine was out of whack. The Grateful Dead were passive participants in Dylan's show after coming up flat during their own concert. Ahhhh, yawwwn, and boo hiss.

Six nights later, Dylan and the Dead reconvened in Philadelphia at JFK Stadium. Dylan blasted through his first live rendition of "The Ballad of Frankie Lee and Judas Priest." Dylan's opening set had passion, but performance styles clashed. Dylan's offbeat and up-tempo phrasing ricocheted of the Dead's easy groove. However, JFK was better than the tour opener. At the time, I thought the set was excellent, but the tapes revealed a sloppy performance with flashes of brilliance. Following Dylan, the Grateful Dead whipped through a monster set that began with "Iko Iko," "Jack Straw," "Sugaree," and "Cassidy."

After the JFK show, Jeff, Doug's lawyer friend from Hofstra, was driving us in search of a place to eat in Mt. Laurel, New Jersey. For no legitimate reason, the Mt. Laurel police pulled over Jeff's car and searched away. I think we were hassled because Doug and Jeff were wearing bandanas. Two roaches were found in the ash tray. The cops discussed whether or not we should be arrested as Doug and Jeff pleaded with the cops, telling them they were good kids, law students. Oh that must have warmed their hearts! After hearing them bitch for five minutes, the cops slapped the handcuffs on them real tight. The irony was that we hadn't smoked all day.

Inside the holding cell were two guys I knew from Rockland who had also been busted for making the mistake of driving through Mt. Laurel after the show. I engaged in some pleasant chat with Craig and Teddy, but my crew was released quickly for our offense—the tiniest marijuana bust ever. Craig and Teddy had a more complex predicament. They were busted for cocaine and acid, and they'd remain in the pokey pen until they raised substantial bail.

On the morning of Sunday July 12, 1987, two nights after JFK, I took a mighty cut at a slow-pitched softball with my aluminum bat— Ping! The ball rocketed over the left fielder's head and rolled fifty feet. I could have scampered around the bases twice, but I proved my point after touching them all once. I never hit a ball that far, and I would never hit one like that again. Later that afternoon, Don Mattingly hit a homerun in his fifth straight game before the All-Star break. I heard the call on WABC in the parking lot of Giants Stadium as I prepared for my last Dylan/ Dead show. I was hoping lightning would strike thrice.

"Total Eclipse of the Heart" was the Number One Billboard single on Sunday July, 12 1987, and Stephen's King's *Misery* topped the New York Times Bestsellers List. Like the helpless protagonist of *Misery*, Dylan was out of whack, crippled by fame. His latest album, *Knocked Out Loaded*, took a worse beating from rock critics than Joe Frazier did from George Foreman in Jamaica. Down goes Dylan! Down goes Dylan! Bob took a stab at staying current in the New Wave/ Heavy Metal era of MTV, but our beloved bard's relevancy was plummeting.

On the other hand, the Grateful Dead had just released *In the Dark*, their biggest commercial success, which would spawn their only hit song, "Touch of Grey." Jerry Garcia was the grandfatherly guru of rock-and-roll. Attending a Grateful Dead show was becoming a rite of passage for a younger generation. Newbie Deadheads were called "Touch Heads." If you dropped acid and tossed on a tie-dye, you could spin your way into the hippest counterculture scene in America. Actually loving the music was optional. Dancing and acting like you enjoyed the music was mandatory.

Surrounded by swamps, highways and sweaty hippies, the Dead ripped through two quality sets as Giants Stadium smoldered. I went to the concert with Perry and a few members of his band, The Lost Boys. I lost The Lost Boys, drifting away to watch Dylan by myself. After intermission, Dylan took the stage with the Dead by his side. The rank stench of East Rutherford was subdued by the alluring aroma of skunk bud, courtesy of an outstanding Humboldt County harvest. With his acoustic guitar slinging low, Dylan appeared scruffy cool, wearing a black beret and unbuttoned long-sleeved gold shirt—a swashbuckling rabbi. He had a fingerless black glove on his axe-picking hand and some unshaven facial hair that could pass for a beard.

During the second offering, "Stuck Inside of Mobile with the Memphis Blues Again," Garcia seized the moment, jumping all over three solos. Dylan responded, howling this way and that way—aggressive artistry. As the sun pulled away from Giants Stadium, history beckoned in the marshlands of East Rutherford.

I noticed an immense presence on the towering projection screens. It was Garcia; he came to my eyes like Buddha from the skies—hunched over a steel pedal guitar, belly protruding, mind focused, and hands busy. Jerry was playing live steel pedal guitar for the first time in sixteen years, and Dylan was rolling the dice with the rarely performed "Tomorrow Is a Long Time." The gorgeous tone of the steel pedal was the ideal counterpoint to the rugged contour of Dylan's voice.

Rolling down "Highway 61 Revisited," Dylan chuckled when he sang, "He found a promoter who nearly fell off the floor, yeah-eah, I never did engage in this kind of thing before, ah, yeah-eah." Indeed, Dylan was in unchartered territory. Always the Alpha Male in charge of the direction of his music, this time, Dylan let the Dead lead the dance. In an interview with Jonathan Lethem for the December 2006 issue of Rolling Stone, Dylan said, "The Dead did a lot of my songs, and we'd just take the whole arrangement because they did it better than me. Jerry Garcia could hear the song in all my bad recordings—the song that was buried there."

"It's All Over Now, Baby Blue" and "Ballad of a Thin Man" started tentatively and ended triumphantly. Each song teetered towards disaster, but whether it was a resounding swirl from Brent's Hammond B3, or Weir's physical energy, or pure desire from Jerry's Tiger, Dylan found the soul of his creations. The tight-rope walking was exhilarating. This was officially my sixth Dylan concert, but I was finally getting to see the real Dylan at last.

In darkness, the musicians tuned their instruments to the sparse flickering of cigarette lighters. Garcia's image suddenly appeared on the screens, brightening the night as his axe announced the coming of "The Wicked Messenger," a firecracker from *John Wesley Harding*. It was Dylan's live debut of this tune that he had forsaken since he recorded it in 1968.

As Garcia picked the blues-infused melody, Dylan stepped up to the microphone and bellowed, "There was a wicked messenger, from Eli he did come." His visceral preacher-like vocals matched the biblical flavor of the song. I was quaking in my high-topped sneakers. Dylan was reconnecting with the valiant troubadour he once was. I could feel the chills of emotional electricity rippling through me.

After Dylan exclaimed, "The soles of my feet, I swear, they're burning!" Jerry buckled Giants Stadium with a colossal jam. His lobster claw picking hand was a blur as the crazy fingers of his left hand frantically sliced and diced their way up and down the fret board. Dylan was mesmerized by the outburst, staggering around the stage, swaying like a Slinky. Jerry picked with passion 'til Dylan finished his sermon. Garcia and Weir beamed. Dylan looked possessed. Mission accomplished. The lights went out. Giants Stadium retreated to darkness.

The Grateful Dead challenged Dylan to play other songs that he'd neglected after he recorded them. "Joey," an epic gangster tale from *Desire,* was a centerpiece of this concert, and the tour. Dylan delivered the five long verses with swagger, sneering, holding his guitar like a rifle. In a 1991 interview with Paul Zollo, Dylan had some revealing comments about "Joey":

> To me, that's a great song. Yeah. And it never loses its appeal... That's a tremendous song. And you'd only know it singing it night after night. You know who got me singing that song? Garcia. Yeah. He got me singing that song again. He said that's one of the best songs ever written. Coming from him, it was hard to know which way to take that. [Laughs] He got me singing that song with them again... But, to me, Joey has a Homeric quality to it that you don't hear every day.

"All Along the Watchtower," thrilled as Jerry paid tribute to Hendrix with lashing solos. I thought "Watchtower" would end the set, but Dylan muttered, "Thank you, Grateful Dead." His only spoken words of the tour. Bob's next spoken/sung words were, "Come gather 'round, people, wherever you roam." Surprised by Dylan's choice, the band scrambled to join in on "The Times They Are A-Changin.'" Jerry filled in the space between Dylan's timeless lines with lively licks. Drifting from my friends turned out to be a prudent decision—lunatic tears of joy fell down my face.

"You're either a player, or you're not a player. It didn't occur to me until we did those shows with the Grateful Dead. If you just go out every three years or so, like I was doing for a while, that's when you lose touch. If you're going to be a performer, you—you've gotta give it your all," said Dylan, in a 1991 interview with Robert Hillburn.

The Giants Stadium concert was an affirmation of my faith in the creative powers of Dylan and Garcia. Nobody could have grasped the historical repercussions that this concert would have on Dylan's career, but I knew something was happening. I'd witnessed Dylan busy being born again, his career resuscitated by the Dead, in the swamps of East Rutherford.

Giants Stadium, East Rutherford, New Jersey

July 12, 1987

1. Slow Train Coming
2. Stuck Inside of Mobile with the Memphis Blues Again
3. Tomorrow Is a Long Time
4. Highway 61 Revisited
5. It's All Over Now, Baby Blue
6. Ballad of a Thin Man
7. John Brown
8. The Wicked Messenger
9. Queen Jane Approximately
10. Chimes of Freedom
11. Joey
12. All Along the Watchtower
13. The Times They Are A-Changin'
    (encore)
14. Touch of Grey
15. Knockin' on Heaven's Door.

The Grateful Dead returned to Madison Square Garden for the first time in four years, selling out a five-night run in September. I was there four times. That week, "Touch of Grey" ascended to Number Nine on the single charts. The accompanying MTV video, featuring skeleton puppets of the band, tickled teenage imaginations across America. First performed in 1982, "Touch of Grey" was a well received song in concert, but I don't believe anybody thought of it as a potential hit. If the song would have been released before the debut of MTV, or Jerry's coma, Touch of Grey, the hair coloring product, would have been more popular. "I will get bye-eye-eye; I will survive," sang Jerry, and his mates followed with "we will get bye-eye-eye; we will survive." "Touch of Grey" became an anthem of brotherhood in an age of greed—a call to grab a tie-dye and let your freak-flag fly.

Before heading down to the show on Friday, September 18, 1987, I scored a bag of weed from my affable supplier, Lola. This shit was so good that she used to front it to me and then forget to collect because the THC was fogging her short-term memory. I'd offer to pay on the spot, but she'd insist: "Ah, Howie. Pay me next time you see me. Don't worry about it, darling." I didn't worry about it. I proceeded to pick up my girl, strawberry-haired Lenore. We left New Paltz and headed for MSG. 9-18-87—what a lovely set of digits; the numerical date is a divine equation.

madison square garden	SMOKING IS PROHIBITED IN SEATING AREA	
MADISON SQUARE GARDEN	R 19	12
7TH AVE BET 31-33 STS.	PERF 3	10
JOHN SCHER PRESENTS	GATE 4	R
GRATEFUL DEAD	TOWER C	
7:30PM FRI SEP 18 1987	08/18	19
29581282BE0858 0600E28	$18.50	12
ICABLE TERMS AND CONDITIONS.	PRICE	NO REFUNDS OR EXCHANGES

My date and I had seats in the G-spot: nineteen rows to Garcia's right, positioned perfectly to watch Jerry's fingers roam. Following the "Hell in a Bucket" opener, Phil Lesh said, "Hey, Rocky. How come we can't levitate Garcia?" The buzz was in The Garden—something unforgettable was looming. The band rolled into a smooth groove during the first set, and the eager crowd overreacted to every gesture from the band. This run of shows was New York's first chance to express love for Jerry since his coma. The center of our universe shined upon us again; it was our duty to help him bring it on home.

"Shakedown Street" and "Women Are Smarter" riled the crowd to start the second set. Weir's falsetto screams were as entertaining as they were disturbing. Weir's weirdness set up Captain Beard as he glided into "Terrapin Station." A certain emotional threshold was surpassed, and nothing could stop the momentum. The crowd was lifting Jerry into the Twilight Zone, a place where even the Cubbies could win it all.

During drums, I reached into my bag and twisted another joint which, conversely, twisted our minds. Lenore was glowing. Out of nowhere appeared Scott Zlottlow and his girl Donna. Philly, Buffalo, and New York, was it time for another miraculous memory with Z?

A perfunctory "Goin' Down the Road" blitzed into "All Along the Watchtower!" I was breathing fire and exhaling desire as Garcia unloaded a wild jam. The Garden collectively creamed, and Weir screamed: "No reason to get excited." As I repeatedly hopped off the hallowed floor with kangaroo-like efficiency, I pined for "Morning Dew." The time was right, "Morning Dew" had never been played in Madison Square Garden.

"Watchtower" had never hooked up with "Morning Dew" before. Every muscle and nerve in my body tensed during the brief transition. Garcia crunched the golden Dew chord. MSG exploded—the loudest collective reaction you could imagine. Everybody was shaking in their shoes. The commotion of emotion swallowed Garcia, as well. Although he appeared calm, Jerry's singing portrayed pure poignancy. The crowd celebrated each line, as if each line had replaced the previous one as the greatest moment in the annals of Western Civilization.

I guess it doesn't matter, anyway. Jerry served the sacred phrase four times. The final plea sent the Garden into bedlam, eclipsing the previous emotional barrier. Jerry was compelled to go for the jugular. Emotions were too high. A cyclone of furious sound scorched MSG. Garcia's savage guitar crumpled me to the floor. I jumped up and grabbed Z, crushing him during the mad jam. Although I'd been intimate with Lenore, I don't know if she would have appreciated a beastly bear hug from a madman. I dropped to my knees and slapped the cement floor as Jerry growled the final: "I guess it doesn't matter anyway…ay, ay, aaaaa!"

7-12-87 kick-started the rest of Dylan's career and changed the pathways of my life. On 9-18-87, I let a piece of Garcia go; he gave MSG all he had left, the same way he gave Dylan his all at Giants Stadium.

Only a month after the MSG run, Jerry was keeping the wheels of commerce spinning in New York City. In the lavish Lunt Fontaine Theatre, Jerry reunited with his old buddy, Dave Nelson, and a troupe of acoustic entertainers for a run of unique concerts that featured an acoustic first set followed by Jerry Garcia Band in the second and third sets. Hearing Jerry croon "Blue Yodel # 9" and "Swing Low, Sweet Chariot," was as authentic as roots music gets.

My New Paltz friend, Scott Dwyer, and I walked past the Lunt Fontaine marquee when we heard a psychotic blast of hot air: "Hey, schoolboy! Get to the back of the line, schoooolboy!"

We looked up—it was Bill Graham, the legendary promoter, standing there like General Patton. *Gee. Sorry, Bill.* Scott and I were just walking by when Graham unloaded, and he jabbed his finger right at Scott as he unleashed his tirade with a menacing glare. One more time he growled, "Schoolboy, get to the back of the line!" *Hey, everybody. Look at me, god damn it; I'm Bill Graham.*

At least I had a great new nickname for Scott D. Every time I knocked on his apartment door, I'd say,

"It's me, schoooolboy! Open the door…Schoooolboy! Pack me a bong-hit, Schoooolboy!"

"Hey! Screw you, Buffalo Bill. You bastard," said Schoolboy.

I could always stop by Scott's for a wake and bake session. Scott loved Jerry, the Mets and the Redskins. He always had great smoke and a lovely young lady by his side. Bill Graham nailed it on the head, though; Scott did look like a handsome prep-school kid. I never stayed in Schoolboy's apartment too long. He had seven pets—all snakes. I never knew where or when one of those fanged creatures would make an appearance and slither across the shaggy carpet.

If the abrasive and innovative rock promoter would have called me schoolboy, the label would have fit like a glove. My academic life was in ruins. I was the eternal schoolboy. I might have heeded Graham's advice and spent more time in class, but I chose to run with the devil. Hedonism was pulling me away from any sense of responsibility. I enjoyed the ride. I'd face the fiddler later.

MOST LIKELY YOU GO YOUR WAY (And I'll Go Mine)

Freedom in Old Orchard Beach...Neil Young
&The Bluenotes on Pier 54...Jerry Seinfeld and
George Costanza pitching the Traveling Wilburys...
Dylan in the Grateful Dead?...Herb performs a Who
medley...A restless farewell to Doug Schmell...

A creature of habit, I gathered my friends Perry, Craig Coyne, and Craig's girl, Christie, for a ten-hour drive to Oxford, Maine, for a pair of Grateful Dead shows on July 4th weekend, 1988. Coyne was the charismatic singer and rhythm guitarist in Perry's band, The Lost Boys. My Chevy Caprice went kaput after six years of unmerciful wear and tear. I was now driving a ripe red Chevy Beretta—less manly, but a sweet ride, nonetheless. As we zipped through the flatlands of Yankee Country, Coyne and I gleefully sang to offbeat Dylan albums: *Street Legal*, *Shot of Love*, *Empire Burlesque*.

This was my third Grateful Dead pilgrimage to Maine. On my previous trips to Augusta and Portland, I developed a predilection for Maine, lobster magnet and land of lumber. People up there didn't seem to be defined by success or failure; they just were. I could picture myself spending ten years of my life here in Maine, letting time slip away without a care. But, on this July 2nd, I was stuck on the Oxford Plains

Speedway with an invasion force of 100,000 Deadheads. XTC was as popular as LSD, and everybody was hocking something.

The band played just about everything I wanted to hear: "Iko Iko," "Jack Straw," and another "All Along the Watchtower > Morning Dew," although nothing could compare to the MSG debut of that combo. During the Dew jam, No Name Bob spotted me and came running over. He said, "Catfish, holy shit! Catfish, I love you, man. This is unbelievable! I love you, man. How's Dougie Schmell?"

I feigned interest, but Bob was interrupting my flow with Jerry. He was hugging me and yapping away, while I was trying to evaluate "The Dew." I'd traveled to Maine to hear Jerry, not to get molested by an old acquaintance hopped-up on XTC. Perry and I were far from the stage, and the decibel level was tame. I wished I was back home in New Paltz, throwing slabs of meat on an open flame and sucking down a few cold ones. Instead, I was going nowhere fast on a racetrack in Oxford. The prospect of seeing the Dead again wasn't all that thrilling.

Perry and I had brunch at a local luncheonette the following afternoon. Perry munched down eggs, and then watched me maul a two-pound lobster, crunching the shell with various utensils until I'd liberated every bit of succulent lobster meat and transferred it into my belly. Despite being Norwegian, Perry hated seafood. As crustacean shell and juice went flying, my accountant casually leafed through a local tabloid. Yes, Perry had recently passed his CPA test. Without looking up from his newspaper, Perry announced,

"Hey, Howie. It says here that your boy Dylan is playing tonight at a ballpark in Old Orchard Beach."

"No way! We gotta go. I saw Dylan a few weeks ago. You'll love the band. Let's find out where Old Orchard Beach is!" I exclaimed.

Old Orchard Beach was only twenty minutes southeast of Oxford— easy pickings. Perry was eager for the Dylan adventure. Perry had reached the same threshold in his Dead following as I had. This wasn't like 1983, when we had the world at our command—so close to Jerry we could toss him a screen pass. We headed back to Camp Dead to invite

Coyne and his girlfriend along, but they opted to stay in the land of hippie oblivion. Driving towards our seaside rendezvous with Dylan, I sang, "Glory, Glory, Hallelujah" and "Camptown Races." We had staged a grateful rebellion.

Knocking back some tall boys outside of Old Orchard Beach Ballpark, Perry grinned at me and quipped, "You look like Dylan's campaign manager." My accountant was on the money. I was wearing a light blue Member's Only jacket with a Dylan button, circa 1965, and I had a Dylan concert t-shirt underneath. All I needed was a megaphone and a lunch board: Elect Bob Dylan, county sheriff.

We bought a couple of jumbo brews and easily made our way to the stage, which was planted in front of the centerfield fence. There was a nip to the summer breeze, which was heavy with the salty scent of the sea. We were strangers in Maine, mixing in with the locals, far from the familiarity of the Grateful Dead circus.

Dylan wore a stylish black leather outfit with silver buttons, and I swear he did look great—more self-assured and combative than he did when he played with the Dead. I was so close to Dylan, I could have reached across the stage and polished his boots. If only I had a shine-box. Our beloved bard was surrounded by a bare-bones electric band featuring G.E. Smith, the pony-tailed lead guitarist of Saturday Night Live fame. Bassist Kenny Aaronson and drummer Chris Parker pounded a romping tempo during "Subterranean Homesick Blues." What an exhilarating opener! I was pointing towards the heavens thanking the unknown forces that drew us here.

Dylan dashed through six electrified classics, and then he and G.E grabbed wood and loped through a trio of acoustic tunes. Then the electric quartet played three more, crowning the set with "Like a Rolling Stone." Dylan yelled his masterpiece at the sparse crowd. It was an emotional bomb, thrilling from the first drumbeat through the final chord.

Nobody loved a fresh "Jack Straw" or "Music Never Stopped" more than I, but my days of chasing after Dead tours were over. However, I could see myself going down Dylan's path, if he kept touring and he continued to mix up his set lists. It seemed as if a cosmic force was shoving me towards Dylan, and the great state of Maine was the crossroads. If Perry hadn't picked up that local tabloid at lunch, Dylan would have passed through Maine without a blimp on my radar.

In the summer of '88, my father developed a suspicious limp. Tests quickly concluded that he had incurable bone marrow cancer. Over the next three years, I'd witness the slow painful death of my father against my will. Just when my father was learning how to relax and enjoy what he'd worked so hard to achieve, he was handed a death sentence. Our relationship had been mending, but now cancer would close the door forever.

I sank deeper into New Paltz booze, women, and song. I reclaimed all the albums I'd loved on compact disc—albums that I'd forsaken to focus on the Grateful Dead. The Beatles, Rolling Stones, Doors, Pink Floyd, and Neil Young were back from exile, receiving heavy play on my stereo. My collection multiplied—suddenly I had racks of CDs, wall to wall. I explored the cannons of Van Morrison, Santana, Steely Dan, Otis Redding, The Band, Stephen Stills, Gordon Lightfoot, and Stevie Wonder. How come nobody told me that Stevie Wonder's *Innervisions* is one of the five greatest albums of all time? It's right up there with *Highway 61 Revisited*, *Blood on the Tracks*, *Bringing It All Back Home* and *The White Album*. I also discovered the joys of Miles Davis, Stevie Ray Vaughn, Robert Johnson, Robert Cray, John Coltrane, and Branford Marsalis. I could go on, but you get the idea. I was tangled up in tunes.

This Note's for You, by Neil Young & The Bluenotes was this critic's album of the year for 1988. Hearing Neil's guitar scream back and forth in rhyme with brass horns was exhilarating. I saw Neil & The Bluenotes hammer the blues at Pier 54 with my new lady, a foxy Italian brunette from New Paltz. The stage was set up so the audience faced the West Side of Manhattan—a wondrous vision. Young and his razor-sharp ensemble blasted away for hours, performing a few crowd pleasers, but mostly his new songs. Bravissimo.

The summer of '88 was steamy. Moonlit New Paltz nights were spent skinny dipping in the town pool with my olive-skinned brunette beauty with the Olive Oyl voice. I should have married that girl, but she graduated, and I was clownish. Our last show together was a Dylan concert at Radio City in September. The following night I was back at Radio City taping the show with my lawyer, Doug Schmell. We met outside of the hallowed music hall. Doug wore a Brooks Brothers suit; I wore sweat pants and an oversized Tel Aviv sweatshirt to sneak in his taping equipment. The Schmell Masters from Radio City on 10-19-88 sound immaculate. Dylan's first encore, "Wagoner's Lad," was a marvelous conversion of a tune from Harry Smith's *Anthology of Folk Music*. Dylan's rugged phrasing fit, especially when he croaked, "My horses ain't hungry, and they don't need your hay. Sit down beside me for as long as you stay. I'll go to Montana if moon show the light, but my pony can't travel this dark road tonight."

Right before the Radio City Music Hall shows in September, *The Traveling Wilburys, Volume 1* was released. This album was recorded in May of 1988 by an impromptu supergroup consisting of Dylan, George Harrison, Roy Orbison, Tom Petty, and Jeff Lynne. .

The story goes something like this: Harrison needed a B-side for a single he'd recorded. George and his producer Jeff Lynne (ELO fame) called Bob to see if they could record in his Malibu studio. Bob invited them over. George needed to pick up a guitar at Petty's place, and suddenly Petty joined the jamboree. Orbison was working with Lynne at the time, so they called Roy and invited him over for the little luau. They wrote and recorded "Handle With Care" for the B-side of George's single. The Traveling Wilburys were born. The group kept the karma rolling and decided to record an entire album over the next ten days.

The ensuing album is a loosey-goosey mix of simple songwriting, catchy rhythms, and slapstick. In fact, when I hear this CD, it reminds me of the Seinfeld episode: "The show about nothing." I can see it now:

Jerry Seinfeld and George Costanza pitching the idea for the *Traveling Wilburys, Vol. 1* to record executives:

RUSSELL: So, did you gentlemen come up with any ideas or themes for this Traveling Wilburys album?

JERRY: Well, we've thought about this in a few different ways.

GEORGE: (Interrupting) May I?

JERRY: Go right ahead.

GEORGE: You know how Dylan is the voice of his generation? Well, we thought it would be funny if the boys wrote a song like Prince, and let Dylan sing it.

SUSAN: But Dylan doesn't sound anything like Prince.

GEORGE: I know, I know. That's what's so funny about it. In his whiny voice, Dylan will sing lines like, "If you need your oil changed, I'll do it for you free," or "Oh, baby, you're such a tasty treat."

JERRY: Yes. It's wonderful stuff. George, aren't they working on a Springsteen parody? What's that song called?

GEORGE: Ah, Ah … Tweeter and The Monkey Man.

RUSSELL: Tweeter and the Monkey Man? That doesn't sound like something Springsteen would write.

GEORGE: It's more reflective of his pre-Asbury Park material.

JERRY: Yes. And the lyrics reference several Springsteen songs.

GEORGE: There you go. That's the beauty of it—Thunder Road, Jersey Girl, Mansion on the Hill. Dylan never sounded better.

RUSSELL: Dylan sings again?

SUSAN: Yuck! I don't know if I like that. What does Dylan sound like these days?

JERRY: Vibrant, alive, hungry.

GEORGE: Hungrier than a horse. The group had a barbeque after rehearsal. They were grilling meat, and Dylan was woofing it down. He was sampling pie: huckleberry, raspberry, blueberry, boysenberry.

JERRY: Apple, pear, peach.

RUSSEL: What I don't understand is, if Dylan's doing all this singing, what's the rest of band up to?

JERRY: Roy, George, and Petty are singing songs, too—adding harmonies, strumming guitar, reading music, writing songs, workshopping.

RUSSELL: They're reading and writing in the studio. The songs aren't done yet?

GEORGE: Russell, these men are legends. I will not have their artistic vision compromised.

RUSSELL: Well, I got a good feeling about you two, and these guys are legends. Let's record an album.

From "Handle With Care" through "End of the Line," the *Traveling Wilburys Volume 1* is an egoless celebration, a frolicking ode to the joy of songs, ten tunes binding five men as family: Lucky Wilbury (Dylan), Lefty Wilbury (Orbison), Nelson Wilbury (Harrison), Charlie T. Wilbury Jr. (Petty), Otis Wilbury (Lynne). The vocal adaptability of Harrison, Petty, and Lynne is balanced by the trembling, improbable pitch of Roy's voice, and Dylan's spunky cadence. These songs are spontaneous spoofs that marinate in catchy minimalist arrangements. It was the most carefree project of Dylan's career, and it outsold any of his other '80s albums.

Taking lead vocals on "Tweeter and the Monkey Man," "Dirty World," and "Congratulations," Dylan was the sparkplug of the group. I classify *The Traveling Wilburys Volume I* as a great Dylan album, essential because it yields yet another side of Bob. A gripping half-hour listen, the CD sounds fresh every time I spin it.

Dylan was torn between being a member of a group and reinventing his career as a solo artist. After sharing the stage with Tom Petty & the Heartbreakers and the Grateful Dead, and recording with the Wilburys, Dylan wanted the real thing; he wanted to become one of the boys.

Dylan showed up unexpectedly at a Grateful Dead concert on Feburary 12, 1989, in Los Angeles and played guitar on the first six songs of the second set. The Dead were having a subpar night, which became a complete disaster when Dylan joined in. Dylan didn't see it like that. The following morning, Dylan phoned the Grateful Dead office in San Rafael, California, and asked if he could become a member of the Grateful Dead, joining them on their current tour. Jerry and the Boys voted on the matter. There were five votes for Dylan, and one nay. That was enough to kill the idea. Instead of touring with the Dead, fate led Dylan to New Orleans and a recording date with producer Daniel Lanois—sessions that would produce his best album since *Blood on the Tracks*.

My 1989 summer touring season commenced with Doug Schmell and The Who at Giants Stadium on July 3rd. The Who were celebrating their revolutionary rock opera *Tommy* by recreating it live twenty years later. Doug and I arrived at the ticket gate as the music began.

Daltry sang, "It's a boy, Mrs. Walker; it's a boy."

Doug sang, "A son! He's got testicles. A son! He's got balls. I checked."

The Meadowlands security staff burst into laughter.

This Who/ Schmell moment flashed me back to the first time I tripped on mescaline. I had popped the purple pills with my friend, Tommy, before we went to the Schmell residence to pick up Doug for our magic bus ride to New York to see The Who in 1980. Unfortunately, Doug's father, Herb, didn't want his chip off the old block taking it to the streets of Manhattan on a school night. Herb was a charismatic five-foot-seven-inch brick house of Jewish power.

Doug pleaded with Herb, "Dad, I really want to see The Who tonight. They're going to play 'Pinball Wizard' and 'We Don't Get Fooled Again'."

"Doug, I love you. Don't you see? I can't let you go. You got school tomorrow, Dougie," said Herb.

"Come on, Dad. I don't want to miss 'Pinball Wizzard' and 'We Don't Get Fooled Again'," said Doug.

"Alright, Dougie. Is that what you want to hear?" asked Herb. "Here you go. (Clapping his hands to the beat) Pinball wizzardddd ...We don't get fooled again, Hey!"

When Herb said no, that was that.

I was wondering when the mescaline might strike as Tommy and I waited in the back of a Rockland Coach headed from the Nanuet Mall to the Port Authority. My mind was calm, and my thoughts were sane until we entered the Lincoln Tunnel. All of a sudden, the bricks were peeling off the tunnel wall, and the bright lights baked my brain.

"Whoa! I think this is it. I'm tripping," I said.

Tommy silently smiled—whacked off his gourd—too whacked to express himself. We didn't yap much once we got to Madison Square Garden, either. Our pockets were stuffed with cash, but we didn't say a thing, even though we had to scalp to get in. The process of talking to a stranger was too complicated, and the raw energy in the streets was imposing. Everybody was urgently tending to their business. For two hours, Tommy and I lapped circles around the Garden, trying to deal with the effects of the mescaline without getting arrested or abducted. We made it back to the Port Authority alive. The only Who we saw that night was performed by Herb Schmell.

Nine years later, Doug and I finally saw The Who perform *Tommy*. The following day we trekked eight hours up to Buffalo for the Grateful Dead on July 4th. This gave us a sixteen-hour round trip to compare, contrast, and critique different versions of "Jack Straw" "Let it Grow," "Eyes of the World," "The Other One," ...etc. The thrill of the road trip exceeded the output of the show. After Buffalo, it was Dead time again at Giants Stadium on 7-10 and 7-11. There was a distinctive "Morning Dew" jam on the 11th, but the riveting moments were few and far between. This was the last time I saw more than one Grateful Dead gig on any tour.

My July '89 tour continued when Dylan reached the East Coast. I drove out to Old Orchard Beach by myself to see Dylan on 7-15. I met my New Paltz buddy, King, at a Dylan show in Bristol, Connecticut, the next night. On 7-20, me and Phil went to see Dylan on The Boardwalk at Bally's in Atlantic City, and I closed out the month with Dylan in Holmdel, NJ (7-21), Jones Beach (7-23), and Saratoga Springs (7-26).

Dylan's performances ranged from chaotic to sloppy to inspired, and back again. His harp solos took off like wild beasts. The excitement of any song arriving at any time was always present, whether it was a dormant original, or a never-before-played cover. Dylan juggled his set lists like a drunken master chef. He had never been this adventurous with his selections before. The Dead's influence on Dylan was evident.

The show at the Garden State Performing Arts Center in Holmdel was the best of that pack. That night I had the pleasure of turning my date, Jenny, on to her first Dylan concert. Jenny was a country beauty: fair skin, thick ruby lips, blue eyes and blonde hair that flowed down close to her robust bottom. We shared a handful of nights together, and somehow I lost her in the shuffle of my college/ touring/ drinking days. Wistfully, I recall Jenny, and all those fine young women that I dated from New Paltz. Jenny was amazing, but I was on a never ending musical quest.

Doug brought his girl, Judy, to the GSPAC concert. We went our own ways with our women, but I convinced Doug to sneak in his taping equipment in to capture Dylan's performance. Doug enjoyed Dylan, but his real passion burned only for Jerry.

Dylan's rowdy performance began with "Trouble," a 1982 obscurity. Then Bob barked an edgy version of Van Morrrison's "One Irish Rover," a new tune for these ears. G.E. Smith finished it off with a powerful solo spurred on by Dylan's emphatic crooning. The first harp blasts of the night came at the start of "I Don't Believe You." Dylan rocked it madly just as he had during his 1966 tour of Europe. The real trouble started when Dylan broke into "Just Like A Woman." Doug was approached by a female usher who saw some weird activity going on by his seat. This is where my narrative stops. Here's the conversation between Doug and the usher, as transcribed from the master boot on 7-21-89.

Usher: Can I see what you have in there? What do you have in that bag? Why is there a red light on?

Doug: I got a flashlight.

Usher: If it's a tape recorder, shut it off right now... I have to take the tape. I'm going to get a security guard. I have to get a security guard, then. Give me the tape, or I'll get a security guard.

Doug: I don't understand. What's wrong?

Usher: Is that a tape recorder?

Doug: No, it's a camera with a flashlight blinking.

Usher: If it's a camera, why is the light on? Listen, if it's a camera, let me see it, or I'll have to call a security guard over.

Doug: The light's not even on. Don't worry; I'll shut it off.

Usher: I know, but you're not listening to me. You still have to check it with a security guard.

Doug: I'll shut it off. Don't worry.

Usher: Yeah, but even if you shut it off ...

Doug: OK. I'll shut it off.

Usher: I'll call a security guard if you don't come with me now and check it in. You're not listening to me (In the midst of this bickering, Dylan was twenty-feet away, blowing a lyrical harp solo).

Doug: I don't understand what the big deal is.

Usher: There are no cameras or anything allowed in the theatre. I have to check that with a security guard.

Doug: It's not a camera.

Usher: What is it?

Doug: It's a flashlight. I told you already.

Usher: Can I see it then, sir? Whatever it is, I have to check it with security.

Doug: Miss, believe me. It's nothing; it's not worth the hassle. It's just me and my girlfriend. I swear to God, it's nothing. Please trust me.

Usher: I don't care what it is. You have to check it with a security guard.

Doug: I'll come back tomorrow.

Usher: No, you can't come around tomorrow.

Doug: I don't see what the big deal is.

Usher: It's not allowed. If it's a camera or anything, anywhere, or recording device, it must be checked in with a security guard.

At this point, the usher disappeared as if Doug wished her off to a cornfield. The kid had some real chutzpah. I may have folded under that pressure. Doug spoke to the usher in hushed tones, doing his best to protect the audio integrity of the tape. He was a master taper all the way, still interested in turning out a quality tape under serious duress. And, wow! This tape's precious.

G.E. Smith's solo roared during "I Shall Be Released," setting the stage for a manic "Like a Rolling Stone." The garbled lines gushed out of Dylan. During the extended instrumentals, Dylan stomped around the stage and occasionally stopped to pose like a guitar hero. "Mr. Tambourine Man" was especially pleasing as the final encore. Bob's cadence had comic texture: "I'll come following, ah…..you!" *Maybe someday Mr. Dylan, but for the foreseeable future, I'll be following you.*

My time following Jerry and the Dead was dwindling down. Doug, the man who loved Jerry Garcia's music with purer enthusiasm than anyone I've ever met, was still taping, but not as frequently. He knew better than anybody that it wasn't the same, but he still taped in vain.

Our last journey together ended on an amusing and fitting low note coming back from a JGB show at Merriweather Post Pavilion on 9-2-89. My Chevy Beretta was running below empty before I finally pulled off Exit 4 on the New Jersey Turnpike in Camden for fuel. We were fifty feet from the Mobile Gas Station when the tires stopped spinning. After all our road shenanigans, we had finally run out of gas. Doug pushed the car as I steered us into Mobile. We were friends for eternity, but our road odyssey was over.

RING THEM BELLS

*Oh Mercy! curriculum for a Dylanhead...The Woodstock
Triangle...Smile, you're on the front page of the
Poughkeepsie Journal...Friday the 13th: Dylan walks
into the crowd and splits through the side door
of the Beacon ...The White House Parties...*

*O*h Mercy. Now there's a brilliant title for an album: two words, seven letters. Oh Mercy! After reading the four-star review of *Oh Mercy* in *Rolling Stone*, and previewing the cover featuring graffiti art from a brick building in Manhattan, I was salivating. For the first time in my twenty-five-year-old existence, I would have ten new Bob Dylan songs that I could cherish and nurture from the day of their release, Tuesday, September 19, 1989. *Oh Mercy* Indeed.

Habitually, I awoke around noon in those days, but for the release of *Oh Mercy*, I arose from my futon early and guzzled a twenty-ounce cup of muddy java from Mc Peady's. I was pacing around the front of the town record shop by 8:45 AM. A gangly Caucasian with dreadlocks and ripped jeans fumbled through his pockets for keys as he sauntered towards the door. I'd purchased many CDs at this store, but this would be our first substantial conversation.

"Hey, bro. You got the new Dylan album in there?" I asked.

"The what?" said the record store attendant as if I asked him when the next train from Ronkonkoma would be pulling into the station.

"*Oh Mercy*. The new Dylan album coming out this morning," I said.

"I don't know, dude. I only work here on Tuesdays and Saturdays. Let me open up the shop, and I'll let you know," he said.

Okay. Maybe I was coming on a little strong here, but my heart was racing. If *Oh Mercy* wasn't here, I'd have to drive at a 100 MPH clip to get to the Poughkeepsie Gallery and the next record store in the area. I was stepping on the attendant's heels when he snapped the lights on.

Oh Mercy. There it was. Several CDs were lined up like pretty maids in a row behind the counter.

Dylan heaved the opening line like it was a State of the Union Address: "We live in a political world; love don't have any place. We're living in times when men commit crimes, and crime don't have a face." "Political World" rocked ahead with gnawing intensity. This was Dylan as he sounded live: raw boned and unmasked.`

"People don't live or die; people just float," Dylan sings in "Man in the Long Black Coat." The narrator in this album believes in a way of life that's been abandoned. The music was concise—from another realm—old-timey, but not dated. It was moody with a swampy texture. As someone who had tried to absorb Dylan's thirty-year career in two years, I was ecstatic with *Oh Mercy.*

In "Ring Them Bells" Dylan twinkles the piano and exhales like a preacher offering redemption through soulful sound. Dylan deadpans a witty line that's as visual as it is haunting: "Time is running backwards, and so is the bride."

Oh Mercy was like a paternal presence in my life. I lacked the companionship of a big brother or father figure for advice on matters of the heart. I bonded with this new batch of songs. In "Most of the Time," I heard a kindred spirit boast: "I don't compromise/ and I don't pretend/ I don't even care if I ever see her again/ most of the time." You can move on, you can be proud, but there's always something haunting about a past love. For millions of fans, Dylan seems to speak their minds, most of the time.

I thought "What Was It You Wanted?" was about a relationship with a woman, but it was about fanatics who always want something from Dylan—the price of fame. I didn't scrutinize lyrics closely back then. I just kind of let the songs wander into my mind through repeated listening. Dylan's best lyrics transcend time and meaning—they're as elusive as "The Man in the Long Black Coat."

I probably would have skipped every class, anyway, but *Oh Mercy* was my curriculum as the leaves of New Paltz turned brown and piled onto cold ground. After drinking the night away in bars on Main Street, I used to invite college girls back to my disheveled bachelor's pad and force them to listen to *Oh Mercy*. If they enjoyed that, consensual sex could be a rewarding conclusion to the night. If they didn't pass the litmus test, I chased them out the door and yelled, "Infidel! Infidel!" Ho, ho, ho. *The Traveling Wilbury's Vol. I* was a hit with the ladies. The darker *Oh Mercy* didn't fare as well.

Some of my fantasies came alive in the immediate aftermath of *Oh Mercy*. Dylan announced a tour with several shows in the Woodstock Triangle. Woodstock is in the center of this imaginary triangle, and New York City would be at the tip. Dylan has his mojo working whenever he performs in the triangle. In this zone, Dylan kicks ass and takes names. Or is that kicks ass and takes no names? If you're kicking ass, jotting down names seems frivolous.

On a chilly Monday morning, I waited on line for tickets for Dylan's concert on October 20th in Poughkeepsie. I planted myself in front of the door of the Mid-Hudson Civic Center at 3 AM with a blanket. I took a nap and awoke with a line of twenty behind me. These folks weren't sure if I was a bum or the first person on line. To my astonishment, when the ticket window opened, I was actually rewarded with the six best seats in the house. In addition to that, the Poughkeepsie Journal ran a story on Dylan's upcoming return to the Hudson Valley, which featured a photo of me in a London Hard Rock sweatshirt and a New York Knicks hat. I'd gone four days without shaving, and I looked bedraggled, but I had six tickets fanned out in front of me. Below that, the caption read:

OH MERCY!

Howard Weiner, 26, of New Paltz, New York, displays his front row tickets for Bob Dylan's concert at the Mid-Hudson Civic Center on October 20.

By now, Dylan had been touring solid for two years, and some fans and journalists began referring to this as the "Never Ending Tour." That notion sounded good to me.

On Friday, the 13th day of October 1989, Dylan shuffled on to the stage of the Beacon Theatre wearing a gold lamé suit with pointy white boots. Sitting in the first row of the balcony with my friend Blaise, we were amazed by Dylan's fashion statement, and we had a fabulous view of his bouffant hairdo.

Dylan's musical presentation seethed. Rare songs from his recent catalog like "Precious Memories" and "Man of Peace" danced along with "Everything Is Broken" and "What Good Am I?" from *Oh Mercy.* I had seen the three powerful Beacon shows to kick the tour off, but this final night crackled with boundless suspense. Dylan was pushing his band, and the audience, to the brink. If someone didn't know what Dylan looked like, they may have thought the guy in the golden suit was part of the opening act.

During the acoustic segment, Dylan raced through the first song he wrote when he first arrived in Greenwich Village, "Song to Woody." The bard's vault was open. Any song past or present was possible, and chances were Dylan was going to play it in a way we'd never heard before.

"It Takes a Lot to Laugh, It Takes A Train to Cry," "In the Garden," and "Like a Rolling Stone" closed the set out with a heavy metal punch. The chaotic pace of these songs was exhilarating, even if the output was sloppy. Dylan flashed through "Like a Rolling Stone." It was a hurried performance until he neared the finish line, then Dylan lingered in the moment of his greatest anthem and tacked a leisurely three-minute harp solo on before leaving the stage.

"The Man in the Long Black Coat" debuted as the first encore of the evening. Blaise and I were delirious. Being in the front row of the balcony felt unsafe. Pure ecstasy might catapult me over the railing into the orchestra pit below.

Things got stranger by many degrees in the midst of "Leopard-Skin Pill-Box Hat." Dylan laid his axe down, sang a verse center stage, then grabbed the mic and went for a stroll while blowing harmonica. Running out of real estate, Dylan dropped to his knees to complete his harp jam on the right side of the stage. He then dropped his harp, walked into the crowd, and shook hands with a few fans in the front row before walking out the side exit. Surreal! Was Bob going for a walk in the park? Was he coming back?

The house lights were on, and the band kept playing. Nobody, I mean nobody, knew what to expect. The jam ended, and the stunned crowd applauded for more, but Dylan had left the building—not a word heard goodbye, not even a shabbat shalom. Folklore says he got on a bicycle and pedaled to his Manhattan apartment.

The Beacon Theatre, New York City

October 13, 1989

1. Seeing the Real You at Last
2. What Good Am I?
3. Man of Peace
4. Precious Memories
5. Simple Twist of Fate
6. Stuck Inside of Mobile with the Memphis Blues Again
7. Don't Think Twice It's Alright
8. Song to Woody
9. The Lonesome Death of Hattie Carroll
10. Everything Is Broken
11. I'll Remember You
12. It Takes a Lot to Laugh, It Takes a Train to Cry
13. In the Garden
14. Like a Rolling Stone
    (encore)
15. Man in the Long Black Coat
16. Leopard-Skin Pill-Box Hat

I awarded my extra front row tickets for Dylan's Mid-Hudson Civic Center concert to Phil, Perry, Doug Barthel, and the Sackett brothers, King and Blaise. Raised in Woodstock, the Sackett siblings were schooled at SUNY-New Paltz and home educated on American roots music, with a concentration on Dylan. King was the chief connoisseur; he exuded an unbridled passion for Dylan's music. Doug Barthel was also a Woodstock denizen until he moved into the apartment across from me in New Paltz. One morning, I awoke to the sound of *Street*

Legal blasting in the halls, which meant I had either successfully brainwashed the Chinese couple next door, or a diehard Dylan fan had just moved in.

The Mid-Hudson Civic Center is a faceless dump, an ideal place for roller derby or professional wrestling; however, those details get lost when you're standing in the front row with five psyched friends as Dylan kicks off the festivities off with "The Times They Are A-Changin'."

I had a stare-off with Dylan as he sang, "What Good Am I...while you softly weep, and I hear in my head what you say in your sleep, and I freeze in the moment, like the rest that don't try." Dylan avoided direct eye contact with me the rest of the night, but for those thirty seconds we were frozen in the moment. In 1998, during Dylan's Grammy Award winning speech for *Time Out Of Mind,* Dylan spoke of a night in Duluth when he went to a Buddy Holly concert and Buddy looked right at him, and somehow Buddy's spirit was in the recording studio when *Time Out Of Mind* was recorded. Eyeballing Dylan was a peculiar experience, almost uncomfortable, like staring at the sun.

Showing me love for the front row seats, my friends bombarded me with beer. I was doubled-fisted with fresh beers lined up below my seat all night. By the time Dylan was playing piano, I was seeing double. Playing piano? Yes, it was the first time he had tickled the ivories at a show in many years. I do recall a superb "Most of the Time" encore.

Dylan's Wilbury brothers enjoyed the sweet smell of success from their most recent solo projects: George Harrison, *Cloud Nine*; Tom Petty, *Full Moon Fever*; and Roy Orbison, *Mystery Girl*. Tragically, Roy suffered a fatal heart attack and passed away at the top his game, at age fifty-two. Producer Jeff Lynne captured Roy's soul and spirit in the studio. Daniel Lanois achieved the same result with Dylan. *Oh Mercy* was a monster from a strange land, a tell-tale sign Dylan was clicking.

The Grateful Dead released *Built to Last* in 1989. Based on the success of *In the Dark*, I hoped this new effort would start a trend of strong studio efforts from a band that's more comfortable without a script. Following five or six listens, I was disappointed. I usually give a new CD a grace period of six listens before I draw conclusions. I rounded-up my friends Tom, Bo, Phil, and Doug B. for a critical listening soiree. We combined valium with bong hits and Molsons, and I gave *Built to Last* another hopeful spin. Our tribal committee rejected the CD after hearing one too many Brent tunes. I ejected the CD and tossed it like a Frisbee deep into the woods of New Paltz. Let the raccoons try to figure that one out. *Built to Toss* would have been a more fitting title.

I moved into "The White House," at 20 Pencil Hill Road, behind the student housing at Southside and University Gardens. It was there that I became the Bill Graham of New Paltz. I hosted parties featuring The Lost Boys on the back porch. Hillbilly Jim, a six-foot-nine, 300-pound mountain man, collected the five-dollar admission so I could keep the fresh kegs flowing. I just wanted to organize a good time with great tunes, but I started turning a handsome profit for providing this community service. The town police harassed me a bit and handed out a few citations, but most of them were more interested in joining the party when they were off duty.

The White House was an awful structure that should have been condemned. One mighty huff and puff from the big bad wolf would have blown this drifter's paradise to pieces. The gray porch overlooked a slanted yard that gave way to the woods—a natural amphitheatre. Somehow, I was still blind to my impending, and inevitable, downfall.

The White House, New Paltz, New York

IT'S ALL OVER NOW,
BABY BLUE

Jack Nicholson and Uncle Bobby at the Grammys...
Tangled up in barbed wire...death of a student,
birth of a salesman...My father's last smile...He's
Gone in Vermont...My orange birthday suit...

Dylan had to be thinking that there must be some kind of way out of here as he stood on stage before his peers in front of a worldwide television audience. Dylan had just terrified the crowd with a ramshackle rendition of "Masters of War." Dylan's face was bloated, his sinuses were clogged, his lyrics were indecipherable, and his band without G.E. Smith sounded trashy. Bob's wardrobe was pretty hip, though. He wore a white hat with black trimming, black shirt, bow tie and purple jacket. His guitar strap featured a red lightning bolt, and there was a harmonica rack by his neck, although he didn't blow a note.

I felt helpless watching Dylan. The performance was an embarrassment, and I let out a sigh of relief when it was over. That proved to be premature.

Jack Nicholson, who had earlier introduced Dylan as "Uncle Bobby," was waiting to present his favorite honorary relative a Lifetime Achievement Grammy. Appearing befuddled, Dylan stumbled towards the front of the stage and offered Jack a handshake. Not noticing Dylan's gesture, Jack left him hanging and just patted him on the shoulder. The amused crowd was giving Dylan a heartfelt standing ovation. Dylan looked at Jack and started to applaud for him. Happy Jack was clapping for Dylan; after all it was his night. The cameras zoomed in on the iconic duo as Jack went back to the podium and praised Dylan. Bob swayed back and forth like a pendulum and fidgeted with his hat. Jack handed the Grammy to Dylan, who immediately spun around and looked for an exit, but two foxy presenters in multi-thousand-dollar gowns blocked his escape route. Dylan was either sick, and/or intoxicated, and now he had to improvise an acceptance speech that he never planned on making. He said:

"Thank you. Well, alright, yeah. Well…my daddy didn't leave me too much. You know he was a very simple man, and he didn't leave me a lot but what he did tell me was this…(Dylan nods as he looks at the Grammy. The restless audience giggles) He said so many things (laughter). He said, 'Son, you know it's possible to become so defiled in the world that your mother and father will abandon you. And if that happens, God will always believe in your own ability to mend your own ways.' Thank you."

The spontaneous rally rescued Dylan from a Titanic moment. His resiliency was amazing. These were strange times. As Dylan bombed at the Grammys, millions of Americans were transfixed on the bombs being dropped on Baghdad. CNN'S Wolf Blitzer introduced us to new war jargon: flying sorties.

I was routinely getting bombed in the bars of Main Street, New Paltz-style, lots of unnecessary shots with the bartenders at 4:30 AM. I had flunked out of college—academically disqualified and disgraced. Phil, King, Blaise and Doug Barthel had all recently graduated from New Paltz. Ten years after my college career commenced, I was still thirty-six credits short of a four-year degree. The metabolism of my twenty-seven-year-old body was slowing down. I could bench 325 pounds, but I ballooned to 215 pounds, forty pounds heavier than I should have been. While all this was happening, my father was hanging on to life by a thread at Mt. Sinai Hospital. His body was little more than a brittle skeleton.

I hoped whatever demons beleaguered Dylan at the Grammys would be long gone by July 4, 1991. In my new black Honda Prelude, I drove up the Thruway and across the New York border to the Tanglewood Music Shed in Lennox, Massachusetts, for fireworks, The Boston Pops Orchestra, and Dylan. My traveling companions were hippie cats named Tommy and Surrey. Surrey was a skinny Swedish babe with stringy blonde hair, and Tommy was the male version of Surrey. We met King, Blaise, and some of their Woodstock pals outside of Tanglewood for a pre-show barbeque. We gathered around my Prelude and paid homage to the recently released *Bob Dylan Bootleg Series: Volumes 1-3*. Featuring unreleased outtakes and alternate versions, this solidified Dylan as emperor of the songwriting universe. Compositions like "Mama You Been on My Mind," "She's Your Lover Now," "Series of Dreams," and "Blind Willie McTell" were officially available for the first time.

I made an unusual entrance into the Tanglewood Music Shed that night. The line to get in was quite long. Tommy and Surrey didn't have tickets, so they scampered up and over the barbed wire fence like squirrels charging up tree bark. Tommy said, "Hey, Catfish. Come on over dude; don't wait on that line," as if this option were as simple as strolling through the gate. I had a ticket, but I lacked patience. My climb upwards was cake until I reached the top and stuck my right leg over the barbed wire. My blue mesh Yankee shorts got caught on the barbed wire. Duh! That skin-slicing wire is supposed to be a deterrent. A few minutes earlier I had been enjoying a glorious July 4th, but now my nut sack was in grave danger.

With one foot straddled over each side of the barbed wire fence, my hands were holding on to an iron rail in the middle. In one panicked move, fueled by adrenaline and love of my genitalia, I swung my left leg over the barbed wire, freed my mesh shorts, leaped off the top of the fence like a stunt actor, and landed onto the concert grounds ten feet below. My heart was stomping. Tommy said, "Hey, Catfish, dude, are you all right? I was worried about you there at the top." Jumping Jesus! I was all right once my heart pumped its way back into my chest. I looked at the back of my calf and noticed a six-inch slash. Luckily, it was just a surface scrape that wouldn't require stitches, just a tetanus shot from my doctor the following day.

After getting tangled in barbed wire at Tanglewood, I expected a fine evening of music. I last saw Dylan four times at The Beacon Theatre in October of 1990. New guitarists were auditioning to take G.E. Smith's place in the band during those shows. G.E. was packing it in after three years on the road. The Beacon run was G.E.'s farewell to The Never Ending Tour.

I couldn't even identify the opening song at Tanglewood; between the rushed arrangement and the whiny, nasally hailstorm of words emanating from Dylan, I was stumped. A few years later, I discovered it was "New Morning" after checking out some set lists in the Dylan Fanzine, *Isis*. G.E. Smith's competency and leadership were sorely missed. The entire concert was atrocious, a continuum of that awful Grammy outing. What happened? It appeared Dylan was on a summer-long bender of booze and bad performances. Uncharacteristically, Dylan did a lot of yapping between songs, gibberish that was tough to understand, but funny once it was transcribed, and I had a chance to read it.

I saw Dylan barf out another silly show at the Garden State Performing Arts Center a week later. Between "Wiggle Wiggle" and "I'll Be Your Baby Tonight," Dylan said,

"That's my ecology song for tonight. It's all about fishing. Well, here is one of my older songs, not to be confused with Whitney Houston's new song. It's got the same title. It's not the same thing, though."

Between "I'll Be Your Baby Tonight" and "When I Paint My Masterpiece," Dylan quipped,

"That's my attempt to do one of Whitney Houston's songs. Actually, it sounds more like hers than mine. Anyway, this is some kind of foreign language one."

Oh, the horror! Et tu, Dylan? My last three Grateful Dead shows were uninspired, and now Dylan had fallen into some insane funk. My Glory Days were fading fast. My desire to see either Dylan or the Dead had been officially wiped out until I heard audio evidence of improvement.

Comes a time when a man must stand and face the fire, whether he's ready or not. I was not ready. If I'd planned for the future, I might have positioned myself to take over El Bandido from my father, but I hatched that dream too late. I had taken a few journalism classes and considered being a sports reporter; however, most journalists at least have a degree on their résumé. Doug Barthel told me he had just started working for an insurance agency. All I had to do was pass an insurance test and go through two weeks of training, and I'd have an adult job. It didn't strike me as an exciting occupation, but it was something. I figured I'd give it a whirl.

I sold my first Medicare supplement in Cherry Valley, New York. There's a certain thrill to walking into a stranger's house and getting them to sign the dotted line and hand over a check. The president of our company was a handsome womanizing boozer, a quick-talking huckster who could charm and sell. Doug and I would rent hotel rooms in upstate New York strongholds like Oneonta and Oswego, and sell insurance to senior citizens in the surrounding cowtowns. We were hardcore traveling salesmen—out on the dirt roads fighting for our meals and gas money. Breaking out the roadmaps and listening to tunes along the way was familiar turf for me. I was a natural-born Yankee Peddler, wheeling, dealing, pitching, and pleading, until I got a call from my mom. The situation at Mt. Sinai Hospital was dire.

Dad was skin and bones breathing beneath a mask and hospital gown—multiple tubes were connected to him. My siblings, Michael and Risa, my mom, and Uncle Walter and Aunt Susan were all in the room when I arrived. Dad was incoherent until he noticed me. When he saw me, he ripped off his oxygen mask and smiled. It might have been the same smile he had when he first laid eyes on me in Maryland. We were the two people in the room with the longest history together. I kissed him and told him I loved him. A nurse placed the mask back over his nose.

Two days later I shoveled earth on top of my father's casket in a New Jersey graveyard—a bizarre ritual at a Jewish funeral. It was a steamy August afternoon. Soaked in sweat, I turned to face the somber crowd. I saw their empathy for me—the oldest son losing his father. At least 150 mourners showed up—friends, business associates, and family. Most of these people had a spouse or a blood relative by their side. I felt like I was twice removed from humanity—forever a stranger, and I'd just lost the one person who'd looked after me since the day I was born.

My Dad was buried next to his first wife—the mother I couldn't remember, Doris. All these years after her death I'd still never met any-one from her family. All the mysteries of my early life were buried at this cemetery. I wondered if Doris was the one who was responsible for my father's record collection. Maybe that's why I'd clung to those albums, *West Side Story* and *Fiddler on the Roof,* when I was a boy. She was the one who was probably listening to those Harry Bellefonte and Joan Baez records. I didn't care for Joan's sound when I was a child, but I can't forget her face from that cover. Maybe my mother looked like that. I'll never know. I never saw a picture of her.

At age thirty-nine, Jimmy Connors was thrilling Queens with an unlikely run at the U.S. Open Championship. While Connors was diving after tennis balls in jungle-like heat, I was lounging in the air-conditioned comfort of my Mom's downstairs sofa, cheering. Our fam-ily was sitting Shiva, which means everybody who had ever known my father stopped by to pay respect and drop off a box of pastries. Those close to the family brought over trays featuring mounds of kosher meat: roast beef, corned beef, pastrami, and turkey. There were bags of bagels, trays of lox, containers of egg salad and cole slaw—ten times more food than any civilized gathering of Jews can eat. This went on for seven days. Connors was finally bounced in the semi-finals by young Jim Courier. Outside of grazing for food, I spent seven days on the couch.

My three cats were ecstatic upon my return to New Paltz. Elisa Gomez, a dear friend of mine in The White House, fed my cat collection and cleaned out the litter box. I'd acquired this cat pack over the past eighteen months. Otto was the large, goofy male with a tail like a snake. The female felines were Face, the furball calico and Shagville, my fat lap cat with the fateful name. When Shaquille O'Neal was a freshman at LSU, I thought Shaquille would be a clever name for my first pet. However, I was outdone by my veterinarian. Following my tabby's fist checkup, my vet handed me a pill bottle with medication for Shagville. Shaquille was clever, but Shagville was pure genius. Yeah baby, Shagville, it is.

I was back on the road again, pitching insurance policies in the obscure villages and hamlets of Upstate New York. I rolled into places I never heard of before and never wanted to see again: Valatie, East Jewett, Ghent, Hannibal, Scriba, Hartwick, Austerlitz, Pittstown, Pawling, Tivoli, Minisink, Lake Sheldrake, Sundown. Rambling from town to town, I was overwhelmed by the vast randomness of these odd places—places that would never experience a Dead or Dylan concert—places under the radar and out of range—places where traveling salesmen can get lost in an awful time warp.

In the village of Parish, near the outskirts of Oswego, things got ugly during one sales call. I was explaining Medicare benefits to a couple at the dining room table, when the husband began to tremble in rage. He jumped to his feet and declared, "Nobody is going to come into my house and tell me about my Medicare."

"No! Oh my God! William, calm down. Don't, William, don't," cried his wife.

Sitting there in a blue dress shirt and paisley black tie, I sensed mayhem, and I hadn't even started my sales pitch.

"Oh, William, please sit down. Oh please, please," said the wife.

William's teeth clattered. "Nobody's gonna tell me 'bout my business." William slammed his fist on the table and started walking down the hall towards his bedroom.

His wife didn't have to warn me, but she cried, "You better leave."

I was high-flying out the door with my valise of brochures. I wasn't sure if William had a rifle or an axe stashed in his bedroom, but I wasn't sticking around to find out. William was pretty hot-headed for a senior citizen. He probably could have used the hospital indemnity policy that I was about to pitch. I heard wild screaming and pleading from William's wife as I ducked into my Honda Prelude and tore ass out of Parish. A year earlier I was pursuing Dylan and Garcia, now I was being chased out of trailer parks by enraged seniors.

Accumulating mileage on my Honda Prelude, I studied the arsenals of four legends: Van Morrison, Otis Redding, Stevie Ray Vaughn, and Miles Davis. One of the brilliant innovators in jazz, Miles died a month after my father. Otis and Stevie Ray were cut down in their primes at different times.

Dylan staged a return to his roots in 1992 with *As Good As I Been to You.* This was my *Self Portrait.* Many Dylan fans were angered by *Self Portrait* in 1970. Their hero released a rambling ragtag collection of songs. I felt the same way about *As Good As I Been to You.* After the awful concerts of 1991, I wanted to get excited about Dylan's future. I knew *As Good As I Been to You* was all covers, but I thought this might set off a creative spark in Dylan. What I heard were some cool folk tunes that had once inspired Dylan, but he seemed emotionally detached from them in his performances. The vocals were overly nasal and lazy. I thought Dylan might be washed up. I could relate. I wasn't exactly on a roll.

One job tumbled into the next. I pitched product after bloody product. Insurance policies became replacement windows, which begot security systems and then above-ground swimming pools. I was broke and hunting to stay alive. I moved from apartment to basement cave to stone houses throughout Ulster County, dragging my cats along for the ride. Luckily, I clung to my musical dreams. The promise of song held off despair.

I was thirty-one when I moved into a tiny two-bedroom apartment in Kingston with a lunatic who sold comic books at a local shop. Not that there's anything wrong with selling comic books; in fact, Doug Schmell quit law to start a successful comic book business. It was in this strange living arrangement that I met the landlord's daughter, Joanne. She was a shapely red-haired girl who had just graduated high school. She worked in a local bagel shop, and by some bizarre twist of fate, loved Bob Dylan. Dear landlord, please don't shoot me for lusting after your lovely daughter.

Speaking of fate, Dylan was opening for the Grateful Dead again in mammoth venues in the summer of 1995. Regardless of how far Jerry's virtuosity and health continued to decline, the Dead could still fill the Grand Canyon with fans. With Joanne and our New Paltz friend, Kim, I ventured off for a show in Highgate, Vermont. I had last seen Dylan on pay-per-view during his 1994 Woodstock Festival appearance. Dylan had regained his performing edge and put on a rocking show at this Woodstock which was held in Saugerties. I was optimistic as I headed to Vermont with two beautiful ladies by my side.

Vermont was bleeding green—flat, fertile and woodsy. We stayed at a bed and breakfast and feasted on blueberry pancakes topped with homemade syrup the morning of the show. Joanne and Kim had tickets for the show. I was prepared to scalp, but to my consternation there were no extras, so I patiently waited for the freaks to tear the fences down. Fence destruction had become a ritual on recent Grateful Dead tours. Hell, if they were going to tear the place apart, I might as well walk in. And, sure enough, by Dylan's third song, these scumbags ripped down a substantial section of fence because they believed it was their birthright to see the concert for free. The peaceful reputation of Deadheads was being tarnished.

I only saw half of Dylan's concert. Bob had IT going on again. "Like a Rolling Stone" gave me goose bumps. Dylan was in a groove—really exploring his songs, finding new meaning in them. Bob was on the cusp of something, he had the look. He never needs to write another song, but the idea of a new album with new originals was compelling to me.

When the Grateful Dead concert began, I spotted Joanne and Kim in the field of Deadheads, far from the stage. They were a sensuous vision to my eyes—pot brownie smiles, flowers in their hair, bosoms swaying to the beat. We huddled, hugged, and merrily danced to familiar jingles like "Jack-A-Roe." I shut down the inner critic of my mind. This was Vermont, baby, the Green Mountain state. I was a carefree explorer shuffling on virgin territory.

My harem wanted to move closer to the stage for the second set, and that's where the good times stalled. Jerry looked like a skeleton puppet from the "Touch of Grey" video. Jerry was fifty-three going on eighty. I was deeply saddened by his appearance and sound. I knew this was the last time I'd see him. Jerry was reading lyrics off a monitor and still missing verses. A return to physical well-being seemed impossible. During drums, after enduring a lifeless "He's Gone," I talked the girls into leaving. I couldn't watch Jerry suffer anymore, and I wanted to avoid the traffic nightmare on the one-lane road leading out of "Hell Gate."

I learned of Jerry's death in my Kingston apartment at noon, on August 9, 1995. I went to Doug Barthel's house in Woodstock and had a few beers, but the real grief didn't strike me until his obituary footage led off the Eyewitness News at Eleven. It was unbelievable. Jerry had become an American icon. His legend and popularity mushroomed during the band's least prolific period.

The day after Jerry's peaceful passing, I was moved by a tape of an obscene "Jack Straw" jam from Philly 8-30-80, which also happened to be Doug Schmell's first show. I had to pull off to the side of the New York State Thruway to shed a few tears for Jerry. But Jerry Garcia left behind an endless arsenal of recorded concerts that far exceeded anything done by any other musician. Jerry's spirit would thrive. His music presence could never fade away.

However, nobody could capture Jerry's essence in words quite like Dylan. Here was Dylan's press release regarding Jerry's death:

There's no way to measure his greatness or magnitude as a person or as a player. I don't think any eulogizing will do him justice. He was that great, much more than a superb musician, with an uncanny ear and dexterity. He's the very spirit personified of whatever is Muddy River country at its core and screams up into the spheres. He really had no equal. To me he wasn't only a musician and friend, he was more like a big brother who taught and showed me more than he'll ever know. There's a lot of spaces and advances between The Carter Family, Buddy Holly and, say, Ornette Coleman—a lot of universes, but he filled them all without being a member of any school. His playing was moody, awesome, sophisticated, hypnotic and subtle. There's no way to convey the loss. It just digs down really deep.

Now it was time for the death of a traveling salesman.

Route 9W between Highland and Kingston is a curious stretch of flat road populated with monasteries, wineries, and cemeteries. I was stuck in the middle of that nowhere land renting a stone apartment in West Park, N.Y. Hustling up and down the Taconic Parkway, I sold security systems to homeowners who had nothing to fear in Dutchess and Putnam Counties. Since my college daze, my career hadn't taken off, and I wasn't drinking or socializing much. I decided to make up for some lost time on my 33rd birthday, 11-4-96.

I rattled into New Paltz in an old Honda Accord that I'd recently purchased for $700 and parked in a lot behind the shops and honky-tonks that lined Main Street. It was Monday night, and an evening of debauchery loomed. I arranged to spend the night at a friend's place, a few blocks away. I loosened up with a few cocktails at Snug Harbor and Bacchus before ending up at Cabaloosa, a charming place with live bands and a patio. The foxy red-headed bartender, Noel, was a fantastic singer in a funky band. She had fabulous cleavage, a pretty face with a nose ring, and a heart of gold.

King, Dave, Glen the Viking, and a few other friends were on hand to make sure I got loaded and stoned. I knocked back a birthday shot of Jameson with every pint, and we torched one-hitters while the band was on break. My head was reeling from the onslaught. I hadn't smoked in a few years, and my drinking tolerance wasn't what it used to be. Noel had taken my car keys away from me, but by 4:30AM, I had my keys back. I'd convinced Noel that I was crashing at my friend Rich's pad, and I was, except my bewildered brain decided that it would be quicker to hop into my car and drive there.

Pulling out of the almost vacant lot, I nearly smashed into a cop car. I turned right and continued down the road, as if nothing had happened. If I hadn't been completely whacked, I would have stopped right there and begged for mercy. The cop casually followed my maroon Honda Accord with the partially rebuilt engine. I was busted, but I also noticed an increasing distance between myself and the cop. I pressed the petal a little harder, and the cop car in my rearview mirror became smaller. This is where the hard booze and potent THC created delusions of escape. I tried a Burt Reynolds maneuver and floored the Accord. I left the cop in the dust—for three seconds. He was on my bumper instantly.

What was I thinking? I was behaving like a street thug on an episode of *COPS*. How could I outrun a patrol car in my jalopy with the bald tires and blown-out engine? I pulled over to the side of the road and tried to regain my composure. At this point, I made nice with the officer, and he somehow took pity on me. During the sobriety test, the cop asked me why I was stumbling. I told I him I strained my calf muscle jumping rope that morning. I turned down his request to take the breathalyzer, which meant an automatic suspension of my license in New York State, but blowing into that tube wasn't going to help me in court.

The town judge sent me to jail, even though the merciful cop recommended that he should just let me go home without posting bail. As the sun began to rise, my birthday bash was over. I was greeted with a strip search and an orange uniform at the county jail in Kingston.

I passed out on a twin bed amongst the general lock-up population for a couple of hours and was offered breakfast when I awoke. I was too hungover to eat, and I don't dig milk in my coffee. Hot black coffee is a potential weapon. They served me mashed potatoes and chicken for lunch—sickly-looking, bloody chicken! I nearly puked.

One of the inmates said, "Yo, Holmes. Are you gonna eat that?"

I said, "I'm not hungry. I'll pass."

Four inmates dove at my tray, and the first one to gain possession of the tray got all the spoils—alpha male jail rules. My throbbing headache prevented me from meeting the other guys to find out what they were doing time for. The zit-faced guard never called the inmates by their names. He repeatedly called them fuck-faces. Being incarcerated with dealers, thieves, and hoodlums wasn't the frightening part of the prison experience. The loss of freedom, dignity, and spirit was terrifying. I was scared straight. I'm a very picky eater, and I didn't enjoy being a member of the fuck-faces. And, worst of all, there was no music. I was released at 8 PM and given my clothes back, minus the forty plus dollars in my jeans. The authorities actually clipped my cash. I didn't even have a quarter to make a phone call. I walked to the nearest Stewart's Shop and bummed a quarter. King swung by to pick me up. My cats roared in unison upon my return. They were famished. It had been a tough twenty-four hours for the four of us.

The arrest was a blessing; I would never drive drunk again. I could have killed somebody, including myself. My refusal to take the breathalyzer paid off in court. I was convicted of a Driving While Impaired offense—much better that Driving While Intoxicated, which is a felony. With a license suspension and car insurance rates that would skyrocket, my traveling sales career was over.

The curtain fell on ten years, in and around, New Paltz. I frittered away the last five years—busy dying. I hung around New Paltz a day too long. I had to find home—a vibrant place where I could start anew—a place where I might redeem some lost time. I gathered my cats and CDs and headed back to New York City.

Main Street, New Paltz, New York

NEW MORNING

The day the music stopped...Temporarily like Judas...
This Land Is Your Land...Performing for pirates at a piano
bar in Tampa Bay...Dylan finally joins Little Richard...
Champagne in the Garden, Wo Hop for dessert...

In the shuffling madness of Manhattan, I found my groove in the shade of the skyscrapers. When I first arrived in New York City, Dylan released *Time Out of Mind* (1997), a colossal comeback effort that earned him a Grammy for Album of the Year. Earlier in the year, Dylan was hospitalized with a mysterious heart ailment, but he recovered swiftly and resumed the Never Ending Tour. It was a feel good story. Everybody was pulling for Dylan and *Time Out of Mind* was sensational. The arcane twangs of that album accompanied me as I launched my comeback in Manhattan.

I landed a salaried position as a copier rep, and for part-time work, I discovered the joys of hosting karaoke: extra cash, free booze, lovely ladies. Each year brought more prosperity than the year before. The Yankees closed out the millennium with a championship and began the 21st century with another title. I rented a duplex in the desirable Yorkville neighborhood on the Upper East Side. It was a fabulous apartment for a swinging bachelor with three cats.

Love & Theft, Dylan's first album in four years, was being released on September 11, 2001. Those numbers were entrenched in my mind: 9-11-01. This was the day I had most anticipated since *Oh Mercy* was released on 9-17-89. The coming of a great Dylan album is monumental to me. The songs live on in my life like they're my own children. Some people anxiously anticipate birthdays, weddings, and religious ceremonies; I anxiously anticipate Dylan albums. I counted down the final ten days prior to the arrival of *Love & Theft*. The critics unanimously praised *Love & Theft* in their reviews, just like they had lovingly embraced *Time Out of Mind*.

Technology further fueled my expectations for 9-11. Way behind the Internet curve, I purchased my first big ass PC and monitor in 2001. Welcome to the future, Catfish. The rumor was true. By tapping a few buttons, Grateful Dead concerts could be downloaded on these devices and burnt on to CDs. For thirty-eight years, I'd thirsted for an endless supply of music; now I was tapping into the dream. I started corresponding with other music lovers on the Internet, as well.

I wore a brazen purple Jerry Garcia tie to work on 9-11. That tie had a distinct texture, silkier than my other ties. The colors and patterns of Garcia's artwork were audacious. It was a loud tie that rejected conformity in any degree. I might have to adhere to a dress code to make a living, but I could still thumb my nose at Corporate America and look dashing at the same time.

The weather was absolutely gorgeous. Another morning could never compare. The transition from summer to fall was seamless—Joe DiMaggio handing off centerfield to the Mick. Honestly, I was hopping and skipping to the subway that morning. I usually straggled into work late, but that day I was seven minutes early. I punched in at 8:23 AM, a time card frozen in my mind.

I was employed by Garden State Copier. I don't know why a company that sold and serviced office equipment in Manhattan took a Jersey name, and I never investigated further. It was a laid-back office, and I had a long leash. When I was supposed to be out cold calling businesses,

I could usually be found napping in my apartment. I became friendly with my manager, Dave Humphreys. Dave looked like a copper-cropped Abraham Lincoln. Mr. Humphreys was a well-rounded Twentieth Century man: baseball enthusiast, Civil War buff, avid nonfiction reader, Dylan admirer. Our first appointment of the day was going to be a *Love & Theft* acquisition at Nobody Beats The Wiz in Herald Square. After that, Dave would head back to the office, and I would dash off to my apartment and crank *Love & Theft*. Of this, I was certain.

Dave and I were chatting about Roger Clemens's current nineteen-game winning streak behind the closed door of his office when his secretary Theresa busted in and yelled,

"You guys ain't gawna fuckin' believe this. A god damn plane just flew into the fuckin' World Trade Center."

We rushed into the compact copier showroom with the other technicians, secretaries, and salesmen. This was an incomprehensible tragedy, whatever was happening. Hundreds of people had to be dead, and how were they going to put out that fire and patch that gaping hole?

Dave said, "Hey, Catfish. Let's go to The Wiz and get the Dylan album. We could see the World Trade Center from Sixth Avenue." His tone was somber and scientific. Maybe if we could see this with our own eyes, we could make some sense of it.

With our soles planted on the corner of Sixth Avenue and 29th Street, we stared at the venomous gray smoke which billowed from the tower's head. An odd thought entered my mind—I had walked this block on my way to work every day and had never noticed this breathtaking view of the Towers. Now, I couldn't look anymore; this was grotesque, the ugliest thing I'd ever seen, but I hadn't seen anything yet. Out of nowhere, a fireball explosion engulfed half of the other tower. I never saw the other plane fly into it. I'd lived in New York City for four years and never before seen a violent crime. Here, in a split second, I was witnessing mass murder.

Dave broke the silence by saying, "Let's go to The Wiz and get the Dylan album. We can find out what's happening on TV."

It wasn't a bad idea. Maybe my heart would stop beating so fast, and this whole thing would seem less real if we went back to viewing it on TV. We actually bought *Love & Theft* and then watched President Bush read to school children before he declared the nation was under a terrorist attack. Then we heard reports that a plane was flown into the Pentagon. I thought our military had a defense system in place that might protect against an attack like this. With all that Star Wars defense talk, I never imagined someone could attack New York and Washington D.C. from the skies by simply flying a plane into a building.

After watching the last tower crumble, I walked home with *Love & Theft* in my right hand. I had no desire to listen to the CD, however, my mind kept replaying a few lines from a 1962 Dylan song: "Some time ago a crazy dream came to me; I dreamt I was walking in World War Three…I lit a cigarette off a parking meter and walked on down the road. It was a normal day."

September 12th was another day of brilliant sunshine and low humidity, but the deadly stench from Ground Zero blanketed all of Manhattan. It's a smell you could never purge from your memory. Flesh burning in an eternal electrical fire. I went for a walk and finally listened to *Love & Theft*. After all that anticipation, I never heard the CD on 9-11.

Every step of the way we walk the line/ your days are numbered/ so are mine. I was instantly gripped by the opening lines of the second song, "Mississippi." I adopted that as a mantra in the bleak, anxiety-ridden climate after 9-11. It had an FDR ring to it—"The only thing we have to fear is fear itself."

The media and government warned us that another terrorist attack was inevitable. Al Qaeda had infiltrated America with numerous sleeper cells. The time had come to start worrying about dirty bombs and biological terrorism. Anthrax packages began arriving all over the city. *Every step of the way we walk the line/ your days are numbered/ so are mine.* The mantra delivered peace of mind—sprinkled sanity in nervous times.

"High Water," the nucleus of *Love & Theft*, is a blues stomp anchored by the terrific banjo playing of Larrry Campbell. In "High Water," folks are traveling around in wagons and hopped-up Mustang Fords. The grizzled narrator of "High Water" witnesses the devastating Mississippi Floods of 1927, a disaster that America endured, and the nation was strengthened through shared tragedy. The singer of these songs is a wise drifter from another era looking for salvation. In the aftermath of 9-11, *Love & Theft* presented itself as an American manifesto on how to keep on keepin' on.

"Bye and Bye" was the sly, lilting tune that delivered a heavy wallop with each listen. It had an old-timey Bing Crosby feel with a finger-snapping groove that delivered instant coolness. The crooner of the song breathes a lover's sigh and paints the town, but his self-reflections are haunting: "Well, I'm scufflin' and I'm shufflin' and I'm walkin' on briars; I'm not even acquainted with my own desires...Well the future for me is already a thing of the past."

I was ambushed by these lines as I walked through Grand Central Station two days after 9-11. The sonic rhyme of scufflin' and shufflin' was pleasing, but the connotation was disturbing. I had been scufflin' and shufflin' about Manhattan for four years, simply content with a nine-to-five job, but I wasn't going anywhere or pursuing anything meaningful. I looked at the photos of missing loved ones from Ground Zero—people who would never get another shot at their dreams. I was out of touch with my own desires, but it wasn't too late to change that.

I felt like a goon as I looked at the somber patrons. I was a Judas. I loathed what I was about to do, but this was my part-time job. I had to host my Friday night karaoke show at Iggy's Famous Bar on Second Avenue between 75th and 76th Streets, three days after 9-11. I wished Iggy had canceled karaoke, possibly forever. I slammed a few shots of Jack Daniels and pondered my presentation. I usually greeted the crowd in my party guy voice before kicking the revelry off by singing "Midnight Hour," "Stuck in the Middle with You," Pride and Joy," or fill in the Dylan song. The city was mourning, and singing karaoke seemed inappropriate, but asking for a moment of silence or playing the National Anthem wasn't my style, either. How could I get out of this mess? I slugged another shot of Jack and let inspiration move me brightly.

A portrait of the Golden Gate Bridge popped on to the karaoke screen as violins screeched in time to acoustic guitar. I grabbed the mic and channeled my best Woody, Okie style: "This land is your land, this land is my land, from California to the New York Island, from the redwood forest to the Gulf Stream waters, this land was made for you and me." People were pleased. They clapped along, to my incredulity. I was relieved until I noticed a construction worker striding from the far end of the bar towards the stage. This giant laborer had the dusty grime of Ground Zero all over his t-shirt, skin, and jeans. He'd been in the hell pit all day, and now he was coming my way.

The big fella pulled an American flag out of his back pocket and bear hugged me off the stage during the brief instrumental interlude. He whispered, "Thank you" in my ear. His eyes were moist as he placed me back on the stage. Yee-ha! Now the joint was jumping; folks were swinging their partners 'round and 'round. I finished off Woody Guthrie's most famous tune on fire. Out of collective sadness, the night went ballistic. Customers filled out their song requests in droves. There was an indomitable spirit ignited in the room by music, even though much of the singing was foul. I put out a bucket and asked my fellow New Yorkers to donate money for our local firefighters. I dropped off $1200 at the firehouse on 85th Street the following day. I waited in a line of other New Yorkers who were writing personal checks to the fire department. Everyone was doing what they could.

During the course of that karaoke night, I decided to leave my day job. I could better serve the world spreading music, even if it was karaoke. The healing powers of music were immense. Jams and jingles had bolstered my spirits as far back as I could remember. In addition to providing an escape for stressed-out people, if I could pull off a living in karaoke, I could stay at home during the day and download Grateful

Dead concerts. Just about every public breath Jerry has taken since 1965 has been recorded, and Deadheads were sharing and converting their tapes into high quality SHN files for everyone with an Internet connection to enjoy. I could collect and analyze any and every Dead show while propagating and sharing Jerry's music with others.

This is where Jim Kerr Jr. comes into the story—son of the famous FM radio host, Jim Kerr. Junior Jim was playing acoustic guitar by himself late one night at the Australia Bar on the corner of 90th and First Avenue. A long-haired, wild-eyed wiry cat with tattoos, Jim ended his set in front of the sparse gathering of boozehounds with "Going Down the Road, Feelin' Bad." It was 4 AM Sunday morning, but I had to rap with this guy. He had a magical vibe about him. We sang "Cold Rain and Snow" and "We Bid You Goodnight," for the bartender and a few stragglers.

Jim lived down the block from me on York Avenue. He turned me on to rogue Grateful Dead websites—downloading parties by invitation. There was one brilliant site where only five people could download at the same time. The site featured a smorgasbord of shows. If you were lucky enough to get on to the site, you could download one show at a time, but you would be booted off if you didn't pick a new show to download within three minutes of the last one being completed. I used to set my alarm to wake me up in the middle of the night so I could grab another show before being logged off. When I was on my game, I'd download twenty-five shows in a forty-eight hour period.

There were concerts I never heard before; others were old friends that were lost or in critical condition (old battered tapes). I would have snorted speed and stayed up night after night for those downloads. Luckily, I got up every time my alarm clock went off. Deadication.

Jim turned me on to the Dew board—a site that emerged from the Morning Dew Radio show on WBAI. Since 1988, WBAI had broadcast live Dead shows weekly. This message board altered my life. These nuts loved every Jerry jam, and they were willing to argue and debate every note. My Internet name was 6-16-82 Catfish. I chatted with Doberwolf, Cosmic Chuck, Cosmic Johnny, Crazy Chester, The Boxer,

Kingofallmailmen, Basil, Bud Chief, Dire Wolf, Ramble on Rob, Basil, Grateful Dead Woman, Dark Star Girl, Son of Jerry, Brian, and the moderator who was the host of the radio show, Mandrake.

Our Internet digressions were enough to make somebody want to chew their own foot off. We debated the merit of everything Grateful Dead-related. The rhetoric became heated at times as we pitted different versions against each other: 8-6-74 "Eyes of the World" versus the 9-3-77 Englishtown version. 8-6-74 won by TKO.

Our Internet community spawned many friendships and social gatherings. There were new fans who had never seen the band, and veterans like Harold and Basil who saw the band back at the Fillmore East in 1969. The Dew board also gave birth to my writing. Without consciously noticing it, I was sharpening my verbiage, writing op-ed pieces, rebuking other opinions, crafting two-minute memoirs about past shows, and penning reviews of whatever concerts I was attending. I wasn't a proponent for random Internet chat, but this rekindled my passion for the Grateful Dead, and all the road tales gave me restless fever; I'd been sequestered in Manhattan too long.

I pined for my glory days of touring with the Dead. As I accumulated Grateful Dead concerts, the dates appeared like mathematical equations, and the venues sounded more exotic than ever: 10-19-72 Fox Theatre, 11-11-73 Winterland, 9-1-79 Hollander Stadium, 5-9-77 Buffalo War Memorial, 8-7-82 Alpine Valley, 6-18-74 Louisville, 3-21-81 Rainbow Theatre, 10-16-81 The Melkweg.

Yankee Baseball was a divine diversion for New York City into early November. Tino Martinez and Scott Brosius smashed improbable game-tying homeruns in the ninth inning of two World Series games, putting the Yankees on the threshold of their fourth straight championship. It was rumored that even a few Yankee haters were rooting for New York. The deciding Game 7 was on my birthday, November 4th. All the ducks were lined up for a massive celebration, but a bloop hit off the great Mariano Rivera in the ninth inning killed the dream. Once upon a time, that loss would have been heartbreaking to me. After 9-11, I'd changed. Outcomes of baseball games were nothing to fret about. Derek Jeter and company would wake up the next day and still be millionaires.

Clinging to my Upper East Side neighborhood, I played it close to the vest, running karaoke shows by night and digging tunes during the day. I was slowly rolling out of the thick fog created by the 9-11 nightmare, proceeding with caution. The chorus of "Things Have Changed," Dylan's Oscar winning song from the film *Wonder Boys*, captured my mood: "People are crazy, and times are strange; I'm locked in tight; I'm out of range; I used to care, but things have changed."

Perry, Stan and my ex-manager, Dave, joined me for Dylan's concert at Madison Square Garden on November 19, 2001. This was the first event I attended at a major venue since the new measuring stick of time, 9-11. Dylan was in the midst of a tour, and this stop was as emotional as it gets. As "Rainy Day Women," began, Dylan said, "Most of the songs we're playing here tonight were written here, and those that weren't were recorded here. So no one has to ask me how I feel about this town."

Yes, this is where young Bob Dylan revolutionized songwriting with "A Hard Rain's A-Gonna Fall," and he's continually been drawn back for inspiration. *Time Out of Mind* was written here, and *Love & Theft* was recorded in a New York studio. Dylan emerged from hibernation at Madison Square Garden in 1971 with a scintillating performance for the people of Bangladesh. The idea for the Rolling Thunder Revue was hatched on the streets of New York, and that's where he met the loves of his life—Suze and Sara.

Dylan wore a pink suit for his big night at MSG. Outside of his Pink Panther outfit, and that wide-stance corkscrew twist during the "Just Like a Woman" harp jam, the ambiance of Dylan's showmanship was dignified. He seized the moment without strutting. The show was reserved, although I experienced an odd epiphany during "Summer Days" when Dylan sang, "She says, 'You can't repeat the past.' I say, 'You can't? Of course you can.'" Repeating the past didn't work out too well for Jay Gatsby, but that was fiction. I'd been tantalized with the promise of that line since I first listened to *Love & Theft*. When I heard Dylan sing this live, it struck me as a call to action. My vision wasn't clear, but I knew it involved Dylan's Never Ending Tour and a road map. It was time to ride again without defining the mission or worrying about the outcome. At thirty-eight, I changed my occupation like it was a pair of khaki shorts. Now wasn't the time for rational behavior.

I woke up in a Ramada Inn feelin' bad. Briefly, I wasn't sure where I was, or who I was. My only certainty was the shooting pain in my brain. Then I remembered the concert at a hockey rink in Tampa Bay. *Was that me singing "Like a Rolling Stone" at a piano bar before a bunch of pirates?* Ah yes, I had stumbled into the Gasparilla Festival and a lot of intoxicated fun after Dylan's performance. My hangover raged. I planned on spending the day at Busch Gardens or visiting a cousin who lived nearby, but my nutrient-depleted body demanded plan C: caffeine, fried food, Gatorade, and immobility. I lay on my funky hotel mattress all day and ordered in lobster tails and a baked potato for my Super Bowl feast. Tom Brady and the bloody Patriots knocked-off the airborne Rams 17-14. I didn't flex a limb all day—complete vegetation, the sweet reward of traveling solo.

Two nights earlier, on January 31, I watched Dylan launch his 2002 tour with a workmanlike performance in Orlando. I snuck in a compact camera and made a shaky bootleg of what was drummer George Recile's first outing in Dylan's band. The show was unremarkable, and my bootleg was much worse, but it was exhilarating to be a traveling witness to musical history again. To get to Tampa, I had to endure a Greyhound across Central, Florida. Without a driver's license, I might have to sacrifice a slice of my civility here and there.

In Tampa Bay, I lodged near Buccaneer Stadium and Legends' Field, spring training home for Yankee Baseball. Besides these stadiums, this strip of highway was packed with strip joints and XXX shops—a very adult area. Rolling through Florida in February was a rush, yet heading back to New York City was a welcomed comfort. I dig the certainty of having either a Starbucks or Duane Reade on every corner.

Dylan was drawn back to Madison Square Garden for a pair of shows in November 2002. Following the progress of this tour, I learned Dylan was performing at least half of his songs on a Yamaha keyboard. Below Bob's photo in the 1959 Hibbing High School Yearbook was his goal: "To join Little Richard." At age sixty-one, Dylan was following through on his ambition in spirit.

On the floor of Madison Square Garden, a silver-haired gentleman in a red vest yelled out, "Champagne, champagne!" Why not? I splurged on a round for myself and the Paletta brothers. There was a sense of revelry in the MSG air. Even the date was numerically optimistic and harmonious: 11-11-02. At last, the slow sad drag of 9-11 had lifted from my daily existence. I didn't know anyone who had perished on September 11th, but my naïve sense of invincibility had been shattered when my beloved city was attacked. I was vaguely familiar with Don Henley's, "End of Innocence," but when Dylan barked his interpretation of Henley's classic as the fourth song of the night, he'd once again picked the right words to express where we stood at this moment in history, even though those words were created in another time by another artist.

"Yeah Heavy and a Bottle of Bread," the second number of the night, was a token of unlimited devotion. A spunky jingle from Dylan's 1967 *Basement Tapes* with The Band, this offering was obscure enough to pleasantly shock any Dylanhead. We were the chosen ones, New York City, and Bob was walking the line for us out there in his suave black suit with red trimming and silver buttons. The live debut of "Yeah Heavy and a Bottle of Bread" was a gift to the hardcore fans.

Riding in on an exotic calypso beat, the swirling sensation of the song was swiftly passing by when Dylan exclaimed: "Yeah Heavy and a Bottle of Breaaaaadddddd!" His Bobness turned his back to the crowd and shuffled to the equipment rack to grab a harmonica, and then hustled back to his Yamaha keyboard and unloaded a few shrill blasts. The band faded as if an engineer was controlling the volume. Dylan moved two steps to the left and four to the right as he lightly caressed sound from his harp. At this point, it seemed like Dylan was floating. Tony

Garnier smiled behind his stand-up bass. He had been on the road with Dylan for thirteen years now, and he was still amazed. The music faded to absolute silence before the faithful roared. Dylan stopped time in The City That Never Sleeps.

"I was born to rock the boat; some will sink, but we will float. Grab your coat; let's get out of here. You're my witness; I'm your Mutineer," sang Dylan in a poignant tribute to the song's author Warren Zevon, who was ailing from Mesothelioma, a rare, fatal, lung disease. "Mutineer" was an ideal cover song for Dylan, who was positively born to rock the boat. Bob also paid homage to the Rolling Stones and Neil Young by covering "Brown Sugar" and "Old Man." Dylan's nod to his contemporary peers was an enjoyable and different twist for an artist who preferred shining the light on lesser-known influences.

"Bye and Bye" became the sixth song that I saw Dylan perform for the first time on this night. Charlie Sexton and Larry Campbell traded guitar licks against Dylan's keyboard riffs as if they were conversing in a smoky jazz lounge—musical intimacy for the masses. With Dylan joining the ruckus on electric guitar, the set closed with "Summer Days," now a tour de force. The exuberant jam was long, exploding with dance hall intensity all the way. A year earlier it was a feel good limb rattler; now it was Dylan's "Free Bird."

Madison Square Garden, New York City

November 11, 2002

1. Tweedle Dum & Tweedle Dee
2. Yeah Heavy and a Bottle of Bread!
3. Tombstone Blues
4. End of Innocence
5. Things Have Changed
6. Brown Sugar
7. Masters of War

8. It's Alright Ma (I'm Only Bleeding)
9. Just Like a Woman
10. Drifter's Escape
11. Shelter From the Storm
12. Old Man
13. Honest With Me
14. The Lonesome Death of Hattie Carroll
15. High Water
16. Mutineer
17. Bye and Bye
18. Summer Days
     (encore)
19. Knockin' on Heaven's Door
20. All Along the Watchtower

After a night of rest, I was back in the Garden with Perry and Stan for the companion MSG show. Knowing that many diehards would see both shows, Dylan came out inspired again, opening with "Seeing the Real You at Last," and following with Van Morrison's "Carrying a Torch." Dylan really has a feel for more obscure Van tunes. There was a spirited "You Ain't Going Nowhere," and a "Summer Days" that somehow rocked harder than the previous one.

After his standard encores, Bob came back one more time to pay tribute to his recently deceased pal, George Harrison. The band nailed a tight arrangement of "Something," true to the original as Dylan crooned it in his own sweet, nasally way.

The night demanded that we keep on rolling. We huffed a bone and zipped over to Lucille's, the companion bar to B.B. King's Blues Club downstairs in Times Square. We jammed with the blues cats 'til the joint closed at three. Then we hopped in Stan's Lexus, boogied down to Chinatown, and pulled up curbside by bursting trash bags dripping with grease. Across the street was Wo Hop, the undisputed late night bastion of inexpensive, yet succulent, Chinese cuisine. Paradise on Mott Street.

The sodium parade began with golden egg rolls, followed by fried dumplings stuffed with tender pork. Soon, plates of chicken in black bean sauce, steak har kew, and chicken almond ding were competing for our affections. It was a wild scene down there. Hammered patrons woofed down Chinese grub in a cramped basement with wobbly tables and autographed celebrity photos cluttering the walls. The food was tremendous. We had no choice but to keep chowing until our insides begged for mercy. Dylan at MSG > Lucille's > Wo Hop's—only in New York.

TONIGHT I'LL BE STAYING
HERE WITH YOU

*Cajun fantasies in the French Quarters...Dylan
versus a Georgia peach at Jazzfest...Hey look at
me, Bob; it's Nils...NYC Blackout/ Block Party
2003...Top of the karaoke heap at JFK...*

Ramblin' fever was burnin' in my brain, again. When I found out Dylan was the headline performer for opening weekend at the 2003 New Orleans Jazzfest, I decided to head on down to Sugartown for a week. I'd passed through many exotic locations during my Grateful Dead days, but my interaction with those places was wham! bam! thank you maam! This time around I wanted to slow things down and soak in the local culture. The Big Easy was an ideal launching pad for a new traveling philosophy.

I established camp at the Econo Lodge in Metairie, Louisiana, a hog-eyed suburb eight miles north of New Orleans. I would have preferred staying closer to the action, but saving a grand on hotel accommodations was a no-brainer. I left my bags behind and hailed a cab down to the French Quarter and dove into the action, sampling chilled oysters and clams from their shells and chasing them with hurricanes that had me reeling on Bourbon Street. I sang "Folsom Prison Blues" at the Cat's Meow and staggered on down the road, double-fisted, beer spilling on cobblestone. A lazy buzz charged the humid night. The Big Easy was beginning to bake, and debauchery was the inevitable outcome.

As darkness caressed the French Quarters I was in a stone bar from colonial times on the corner of Rue Bourbon and Rue St. Philippe, sipping frozen purple concoctions containing grain alcohol. The slanted ceiling was inches from the top of my hairless head, and the piano player smiled like Louie Armstrong in the flickering candlelight. I remember the pearly whites singing: "There I go; there I go; there I go; pretty baby you are the soul that starts my control." Somehow I flagged down a taxi and managed to instruct the driver to take me back to the Econo Lodge. I awoke the next morning free of any contusions, scars, or punctured organs.

An unpretentious racetrack hosted the New Orleans Jazz and Heritage Festival. Jazzfest featured an eclectic gathering of musicians jamming authentic American music. Simultaneously, there were anywhere from seven to eleven bands playing on different stages on the outer circumference of the track. On the infield, vendors sold beer, jambalaya, crawfish, catfish, fresh baked pies, po' boys, paintings, bracelets, anklets, earrings, tie dyes, funky hats, posters, jazz t-shirts, ponchos, and all sorts of voodoo trinkets.

I don't bet on horses or go to the track often. I never grasped the enormity of it all before. Heavy horses need space to gallop, and racetracks are wonderful grounds for musical festivals. Lovely scantily-clad Dixie talent circled the racetrack as blues, jazz, reggae, rock, roots, zydeco, and gospel music filled the air. It was a divine infiltration of my senses.

The crowd was melting when Bobby hit the stage late in the afternoon on Friday, April 25, 2003. His white, ten-gallon cowboy hat and black suit looked uncomfortable on this sizzling day, but if you're a legend, you dress to impress. I'd never traveled this far south in pursuit of anything. I glowed like a Master of the Universe.

Bob got his southern mojo working with a pair from *Nashville Skyline*, "To Be Alone with You" and "Tonight I'll be Staying Here with You." Dylan could go anywhere and assimilate his songs into the local landscape. An unusually early "Highway 61 Revisited" roared in the third spot. Two tunes later, "It's All Over Now Baby Blue" was thrust upon us. This wheel was on fire.

A spooky "Mr. Tambourine Man" followed on the heels of "Dignity." Rearranged classics frolicked with fresh meat. I fetched a can of beer. *Here's to you, Mr. Dylan.* Against a background of pure blue skies and a retreating sun, Dylan's image beamed down from the video screens on the side of the stage. Through seven songs, Dylan dominated like a pitcher en route to a perfect game. It was scary; we were only halfway through the show. I had that same old feeling of destiny. I was in the right place at the right time—a witness to history.

As I shuffled solo to "Bye and Bye," a tanned brunette beauty in jeans shorts and a cut-off Florida Gators t-shirt bounced into my space. She grabbed my hand, and we began to tango to the ping-pong waltz. It was espresso love at first sight. My swamped brain went dizzy, torn between Dylan and mammalian attraction.

Oh, you're from Atlanta, and you're a hair stylist. That's nice. I'm a lunatic from Manhattan, who owns a karaoke business and travels solo. Really, you're meeting some friends here at Jazzfest? Wow, I'm actually here...New Orleans! I don't believe it. Dylan's playing "Saving Grace," another Festivus miracle! My first "Saving Grace." Dear, sweet, merciful Jesus, give me the strength to keep entertaining my Georgia peach. Oh no! A Hard Rain's A-Gonna Fall. Where have you been, my blue-eyed peach? Dylan, I love you; Julie, I love you too. I feel her breath whispering in one ear; Uncle Bobby's growling in the other one: "Black is the color, and none is the number. I'll tell it and think it and speak it and breathe it." She's grabbing my hand again, and we're moving towards Dylan. She's like Moses, parting the sea of sweaty baldness before us. Female Power. We made it to the front row. Dylan's galloping back for the encore with that huge cowboy hat planted on his head. Giddy up. Do it, Bob! The drummer strikes; it's the beat everybody's been waiting for. "How does it Feel? How does it feeeelll?"

New Orleans Jazz & Heritage Festival

April 25, 2003

1. To Be Alone With You
2. Tonight I'll Be Staying Here With You
3. Highway 61 Revisited
4. Things Have Changed
5. It's All Over Now, Baby Blue
6. Dignity
7. Mr. Tambourine Man
8. Drifter's Escape
9. Bye and Bye
10. Stuck Inside of Mobile with the Memphis Blues Again
11. Saving Grace
12. Honest With Me
13. A Hard Rain's A-Gonna Fall
14. Summer Days
    (encore)
15. Like a Rolling Stone
16. All Along the Watchtower

I stole a few kisses from Julie while waiting for the Bourbon Street Shuttle. My heart was a-reeling. Julie mentioned she was twenty-three. I was thirty-nine-and-a-half, but I don't recall volunteering that info. The French Quarter was bopping for Jazzfest—carousing in the streets without the *Girls Gone Wild* crunch of Mardi Gras. We met up with Julie's pack of Texas girlfriends at The Cat's Meow. I was looking forward to a karaoke-less vacation, but this gave me an opportunity to show off. I cut loose a tolerable "Midnight Hour," and the crowd roared like I was Wilson Pickett reincarnated.

Julie and I slipped away from her friends. They were adorable cretins who wanted to consume booze all night. I walked Julie back to the

Holiday Inn. I told her about my hardship, that I was staying in a dump in Metairie. In her saw-throat southern drawl, she said, "No you're not; you're staying with me." Sassy.

We grinded in the sheets, showered, and then grinded in the shower. I had fallen asleep by Julie's side. I couldn't envision life outside of this bed, and I was content in that state of mind until her bombed friends came sailing through the door. Some of them were staying in this room; some were shacking up next door. But everybody was heaving in this room—a Texas Pukefest. I hung around long enough to make sure nobody was going to need medical attention for alcohol poisoning, and then I decided that maybe this Yankee ought to retreat back to the Econo Lodge. Julie spent her final day in New Orleans with her friends at Jazzfest. I had a date with Dylan and his band at the New Orleans Municipal Auditorium.

My Grateful Dead excursions didn't yield much sexual experience. Sure, there were lots of braless beauties with loose morals spinning around, but when you're living out of a Chevy with four other guys, creating privacy and the proper ambiance for seduction is challenging. There's a perception of promiscuous sex attached to the Grateful Dead scene—free love, baby. Well, it didn't materialize that way for me. Our road trips were musical pilgrimages that resulted in bootleg orgies—lots of male bonding. I liked my new role as the stranger in town following Dylan. This gig was paying off in spades.

Cajun cuisine lived up to its advance billing, although I don't care much for fried foods, mayo, swine or beignets, and New Orleans is too hot for gumbo. I also prefer black beans to red beans. After a week of raw seafood, fried chicken, and po' boys, my body craved fresh broccoli and carrots. The lazy flow of New Orleans was appealing to me. It's the kind of place that would ruin me if I stayed too long. I would return for Jazzfest in 2004.

My next stop on Dylan's Never Ending Tour was for three shows at the Hammerstein Ballroom on the Westside of Manhattan. A spicy "Silvio" kicked off opening night. Dylan summoned the remnants of his shattered voice and blasted away. Dylan wasn't going to receive any accolades for his singing during this residency. His modern-day performance voice is an acquired taste. Only eighty-three people were fluent in Dylan growling, and I happened to be one of them. A few numbers in, Nils Lofgren appeared on the stage, unannounced. With Freddy Koella and Larry Campbell providing supporting axe work, Lofgren's noteworthy licks were secondary to his stage antics. The tiny veteran from Neil Young's band charged towards Dylan, playing for him in an overly animated fashion: Look, Bob! It's me, Nils. Dylan seemed pleased, and the ballroom buzzed. "Love Sick" and "Highway 61 Revisited" were the highlights. The following evening, Dylan empowered the set list with "Every Grain of Sand" and "Desolation Row."

"Stan the Man" was primed to join me for the final Hammerstein showcase on August 14, 2003. I grabbed my ticket, Metro Card, and a modest wad of cash. I was about to shut off the air conditioner when it shut off by itself. Everything stopped. A woman was stuck in the elevator of my building. George the super was on top of that situation. I stepped outside to see how widespread the electrical outage was. An Indian cab driver had WINS News blasting from his car. The announcer said something like, "The power is out in New York City. There appears to be a massive failure to the power grid in the Northeast from Washington D.C. all the way up to Canada. There is no electricity in New York City, Philadelphia, and Boston. The reason is unknown at this time." Looking at me, the cabby shook his head and said, "I think this de work of the de terrorists." That thought initially crossed everyone's mind.

Fears subsided quickly. This wasn't Al Qaeda; it was just another failure of America's decaying infrastructure—that we could deal with. In fact, that news triggered a massive celebration in Manhattan. I walked over to Brother Jimmy's, one of the places where I hosted karaoke, and handed out cups of water to the workingmen and women of Manhattan who had to walk home. Rivulets of sweat soaked through their suits and blouses. It was going to be a steamy night without air conditioners, televisions, or the Internet. New Yorkers had two choices: stay in and suffer, or go out and meet your neighbors, those same people that you dodge daily on the way to the train.

I finally got to hang out with some neighbors in my building. Paul and Dianne invited us in to their courtyard for a barbeque, encouraging us to drink their beer while it was still chilled. They were a kind couple who split their time living in Boston and New York. Paul was a jazz bassist, and he had a big ole German Shepherd named Jack. I mistakenly called Paul Jack for awhile. Jack was the one dumping on sidewalks; Paul was in charge of the scooping operation.

I finally got to meet Sarah, the smoking Swedish stewardess on the fourth floor, but I never followed through on that lead. I was the bad boy of the building, the outlaw who crashed through the front doors with giant JBL speakers at 5 AM and beat up the lavish marble floors with my hand-truck, yet my neighbors seemed to like me, at least on this night.

The tenants' gathering dissipated around midnight. Too hot to sleep, I charged into the streets and joined the greatest block party ever, already in progress. It was the antithesis of the 1977 blackout, which exposed the rotten core of the Big Apple. Instead of looting and shooting, New York was a Grateful Dead show in darkness. In between First and Second Avenues, a sizeable crowd cheered on a ragtag group of entertainers—percussionists, guitarists, dancers. I joined the jamboree and sang "La Bamba" right into "Good Lovin'." After my performance, the cops on the corner stepped in to break it up; some people were trying to rest peacefully at 3 AM.

Twenty-seven hours after the blackout began, electricity was restored to the Upper East Side. And Dylan didn't bail on New Yorkers who wanted to see the last Hammerstein show. Near the end of a grueling summer tour, the concert on the 14th was rescheduled for the 20th. Legends don't rebate, they rage on. Me, Stan, and his Harley-riding brother-in-law, Joey, enjoyed the amazing finale at the Hammerstein. Appearing in the second hole, "Señor" made the night: *Señor, señor; I can see that painted wagon; Smell the tail of the dragon; Can't stand the suspense anymore; Can you tell me who to contact here, Señor?*

I was born eighteen days before JFK's assassination. Thirty-one days after the national tragedy, Idlewild Airport was renamed JFK Airport. Thirty-eight days after that, on February 7, 1964, the Beatles arrived in America on a Pan Am flight, landing at JFK.

On the fortieth anniversary of the Beatle's arrival in America, Jet Blue threw a Beatles bash at the immortal arrival gate, and they hired yours truly. They wanted me to engage the transient crowd with Beatles karaoke. This gig could get ugly without warning, so I brought along a sidekick, my talented and trusted employee, Matt Hamm. Besides, I needed someone to run the show while I was getting inebriated with nervous passengers at the bar.

With a mop-top wig covering my cranium, and groovy peace beads around my neck, I sang "With a Little Help from My Friends" to kick off the festivities. Me and Mr. Hamm followed with a dazzling duet of "Come Together." Our mission was to attract other singers to pick out a Beatles song to perform before their peers. Needless to say, nobody hails a cab to JFK and fantasizes about singing before the stressed masses boarding flights to Zurich, Rome, Berlin, and Brussels. And, even if some loony was harboring these strange karaoke dreams, what are the chances that he or she would imagine singing from a Beatles Playbook?

A Fiona Apple clone stunned the airport with an operatic version of "Let It Be" before boarding a flight to Tel Aviv. Maybe it really was Fiona. A few other brave souls belted out Apple Record recordings in vain, but mostly it was me and Matt singing for red-eyed travelers, stewardesses, pilots, and security personnel.

After a few cocktails, I had that warm, fuzzy feeling and crooned any ole Beatle song. I delivered "Happiness Is a Warm Gun," "I Feel Fine," "She Came in Through the Bathroom Window," "Baby You're A Rich Man," "Please Please Me," "Help," "I'm Only Sleeping," and, I'm sure nobody will ever forget my live debut of "Nowhere Man." I can't remember half of the songs I butchered, but I received warm smatterings of applause. Matty was the stronger singer of our dynamic duo, but he wasn't as familiar as I was with the Fab Four catalog. We finished the gig with "All You Need Is Love," confidently trading Lennon's lines as if we'd done it a thousand times before.

After wandering around for four decades, I was back where my musical odyssey began—New York City. From the lonesome confines of Grandma Tilly's apartment on Walton Avenue in the South Bronx, I'd reached the top of the karaoke heap at JFK.

CATFISH

It's a wonderful life pretending you're in the Doug Flutie Band...Steaming on a Greyhound bound for Delaware... Baby Blue Paradise in Kahunaville...Cooperstown Freeze Out...Shuffling beneath the baseball diamond skies...Honey, why are the tires on the Lexus still smoking?...Discovering your life in literature...

For someone who had racked-up more road mileage than Jack Kerouac, I was acclimating myself to the role of submissive public passenger. My next rendezvous with Dylan was at the Mohegan Sun in Uncasville, Connecticut, on June 5, 2004. Bob arrived on his tour bus. I arrived on a casino bus, door to door service from the Upper East Side. Walking through the sliding doors of the colossal gambling complex on Indian Territory, I deeply inhaled the suntan lotion scent and saw my New Paltz homeboy waiting for my arrival.

"Whatta you say there, Howid," said Phil Hyman, in a voice that accurately nailed my father's accent.

"I feel like a hundred bucks after that three-hour ride," I said, shaking Phil's hand prior to a brief hug.

"This is incredible. I haven't seen you in, like, ten years," Phil said.

"Truly amazing," I said." I packed some KY jelly in my rucksack for later."

"Ha! I didn't think you still cared. I got a headboard tied to the roof of the cawr," said Phil.

"You pahcked your cawr in the lot," I said.

"Hey, everybody. Get this a guy a cup of caww-fee; he's a Yankee fan," said Phil.

I said, "Well, ya got the Patrick Uwin…You got the da Kete Lee…You got yaw Eddie Pick-knee…You yaw Eggs Over Easy at Mc Donald's—the X-man, Xavier Mc Daniel."

We were ten years older, but thankfully, our conversation hadn't matured.

Phil's wife had friends in high places at the Mohegan Sun. We were hooked up with third row seats and a VIP suite. A Mohegan Sun employee showed us to our room and said, "You guys are in Doug Flutie's Band, right?"

I didn't know Doug Flutie had a band, but apparently the former NFL quarterback had a group that was playing somewhere on this Indian land. Flutie was Houdini on the gridiron. I would have enjoyed seeing him scramble from a tiger in a steel cage, but seeing him jam was another thing, although Flutie is a musical surname.

Phil decided we should loosen up with some martinis before Dylan's show. After a couple of rounds, the bartender dropped the tab in front of me. Without glancing at the bill, I jokingly said, "Sir, we're in the Doug Flutie Band."

The bartender said, "The drinks are on the house."

It's a wonderful life pretending you're in the Doug Flutie Band.

The concert was positively solid. Stu Kimball, who had played on *Empire Burlesque*, replaced Freddy Koella on guitar in Bob's band. Stu was about the size of Bad Bad Leroy Brown. With Larry Campbell, George Recile, and the mainstay, Tony Garnier on bass, Dylan's band could brawl with anybody. They looked like they could stave off a raid by Israeli commandos.

The following morning I said adios to Phil. We'd meet again next time Dylan was in New England country. I had a ticket for Dylan's show that night at The Borgata in Atlantic City, but I had to eat the ticket. I couldn't bus to New York and then Atlantic City in time for the show.

I missed out on a desirable set list at The Borgata. This pissed me off. After hosting a karaoke gig at Opal in the Murray Hill section of Manhattan on Monday night, I viewed the Boblinks page on the Internet. Dylan was playing in Wilmington, Delaware, the next night at a place called Kahunaville. With a few strokes of the keys and the insertion of some credit card digits, I had bus tickets, hotel reservations, and great expectations for Tuesday June 8, 2004.

Manhattan sizzled as only she can on a summer day. The asphalt below my feet was ready to buckle from the dual battering of the sun and exhaust fumes as I made my way to the Subway, where things only got uglier. I was a soaking, stinking, hungover mess by the time I reached the Port Authority and stepped on to a Greyhound bound for Wilmington. I went to the back of the bus and felt hot air crawling on to my skin. The bus began to pack, but nobody mentioned anything about the lack of AC. It was noon, and I pondered taking a 2:30 bus. I asked the bus driver if there was anything wrong with the AC. Ralph Kramden calmly replied, "Ah, don't worry about a thing. Once this bus gets rolling, the cool air will kick in; don't worry about a thing." *Well, hardy har har har.*

The old Greyhound was doing sixty once we emerged from the Lincoln Tunnel. Still, there was no cool air in the bus, and the windows didn't open. By the time we passed the Meadowlands Complex on our right, I could have put some oil on my head and fried an egg. The sun was immense, shining beyond her glory. It happened to be a historic day. For the first time in 112 years, Venus orbited between the sun and earth. This occurrence is known as the Venus Transit, and many believe the event was supposed to trigger a major breakthrough in human consciousness. At this point, I was an infidel.

Why must I be such a freak? Normal people are satisfied with spending their evenings in loveseats eating Doritos and watching American Idol. Oh, to just be in my apartment watching Yankee Baseball with the AC cranked. Look at these poor people on the bus, elderly, obese, just sitting there sweating and breathing heavily. Every second is hotter and hotter, more unbearable. Oh, the pain, the pain! I gotta ask Ralph Kramden to pull over. I'll hitchhike to Wilmington. Come on now, mate. Just suck it up. Dylan and Delaware are oh so close. Only an hour away. An hour? Sweet Jesus, help! I feel like a rotisserie chicken. I must have cool fresh air. Oh, the pain, the pain!

Greyhound delivered us to Delaware, but they haven't heard the last from me on this matter. That's my vow to you, dear reader, although I've yet to do anything to date. I was overwhelmed by relief; just stepping off the bus was euphoric. I checked into the Wilmington Days Inn with a six-pack and dozed off to the steady, rumbling hum of the AC, full blast.

I sucked the Molson out of a couple of tall boys and jumped into a taxi headed towards the Kahunaville Summerstage. I only knew of Wilmington, DE, as the destination of credit card payments—usually late ones. It doesn't matter how well off I am financially at any given time. I avoid timely payments of bills. It all started with Columbia House. Enjoy great tunes now, pay later.

The taxi driver dropped me off in a gravel lot overlooking Wilmington's scenic waterfront. To my left was a Minor League ball-park, to my right was the Kahunaville—a faceless compound that could have housed a Home Depot, or a medium-sized religious cult. Inside, Kahunaville was a Hawaiian-themed restaurant, bar, and video arcade rolled into one.

Sliding patio doors led to a long wooden deck and Summerstage. Scantily-clad Kahuna girls wearing hula skirts and bikini tops were selling plastic bottles of Budweiser and test tube shots filled with a cheap tequila/ Hawaiian Punch-like mix. As a kid, there were few beverages I craved like Hawaiian Punch. I loved the sound of the can opener as it punched a triangle hole on top of the can. A rushing stream of Hawaiian Punch would soon quench my thirst. But on this night, my heart was with the "king" of beers.

I walked to the front of the stage without any hassle. Was Dylan really going to step out and play here? The atmosphere was reminiscent of the start of a college keg party. Dylan strolled out with a white cowboy hat and a slick black suit with red trimming. His band played possessed from the onset; you could see the wildness in their facial expressions. "To Be Alone with You" was the opener. Larry Campbell was cross-eyed. Either the band was stoned, or they were enjoying the effects of the Venus Transit. David Bromberg, the entertainer extraordinaire from Wilmington, stood off to the side and drooled. The big fella with his trademark beatnik beard and black-rimmed glasses would have loved to grab Campbell's idle banjo and join the ceremony.

With my right palm placed upon the stage, I was face to face with the maestro as he waltzed into "It's All Over Now, Baby Blue." After my hellish journey, I laughed when Dylan sang, "This highway is for gamblers. Better use your sense." This was amazing; I was trying to absorb it all: Dylan's choppy singing—tossing each line out like it was a song within itself, Campbell's hypnotic steel guitar—sweet as country pie. As the sun faded west, Dylan sang, "The sky too is folding over you-ooh-ooooh...It's All Over Now Baby Blue." A slight breeze blew in from the Christina River as Dylan exhaled a playful harp solo. My grueling two-hour bus ride was a small sacrifice for Baby Blue Paradise.

For the Grateful Dead, "It's All Over Now, Baby Blue" was performed as a fixed encore, a poignant goodnight lullaby. Dylan liked slipping it into his shows early, usually in the second spot. When Dylan sings, "Strike another match; go start anew, It's All Over Now, Baby Blue," those words convey the anticipatory promise of racing into a new experience. "Baby Blue" strikes that same chord of suspense that "Senor" does when I see it live. The momentum of this show was unstoppable. "Lonesome Day Blues" was incendiary. Dylan growled emphatically as the band hammered the blues. That was followed by a rare "If Not for You," a tender jingle from Dylan's domestic Woodstock days when he was married to Sara. By the way, Sara was born in Wilmington.

If I stayed up close any longer I might have burst into flames. It was finally getting packed up front. I backed away from the stage and shuffled to the music under the cover of night. The satisfied crowd filed out after the show. Most adults go to work on Wednesday morning. I had nowhere to go. It was open mic night at the Kahuna Bar, except there were no musicians. That didn't stop me from grabbing a Sennheiser and singing all four verses of "Like a Rolling Stone" a cappella. A few more nightcaps hit the spot before I copped some sleep at the Days Inn and begrudgingly boarded a Greyhound for my return trip to my beloved island, Manhattan.

On January 12, 1990, Dylan played a four-set, fifty-song concert at Toad's Place, a small club in New Haven. Dylan used this intimate space to perform a batch of songs that he'd never done before, like Bruce Springsteen's "Dancing in the Dark" and the Traveling Wilburys's "Congratulations." It was a legendary night, an extended public prac-tice to kick off a tour. When it was announced Dylan would play in Poughkeepsie at The Chance in advance of his first ever Minor League Ballpark Tour in August of '04, I began to salivate. Could this be another Toad's? What was up Dylan's sleeve? Maybe he'd break out a baseball-related oddity like "Catfish." *Lazy stadium night/ Catfish on the mound/ "Strike three," the umpire said/ Batter have to go back and sit down.*

The 900 tickets sold out instantly. Doug Barthel scored two, and after he managed to talk his wife Jamie out of going (she's not fond of Bob's vocals), I was gifted the ticket.

Well, Dylan never fails to surprise. The Chance set list was as ordinary as watching Derek Jeter gobble up another grounder at short. Additionally, The Chance was way overcrowded—a general admission nightmare. I couldn't see a thing, and there was no breathing space. Strike one.

Two days later on August 6, 2004, Willie Nelson opened for Dylan on the hallowed grounds of Doubleday Field in Cooperstown. It was a windy fifty-degree night. Dylan wore a long black jacket for warmth.

The chill reminded me of an April night in Yankee Stadium—just cold enough to make you wish you were someplace else. I generally dig a loud sound system, but Dylan's band had the fences shaking. I didn't find much to get excited about in the set list, either. I was left wondering whether Dylan was losing his edge, or if this was a personal malaise from bearing witness to one too many shows. I salvaged the night by watching DVD bootleg videos of Dylan with King, Blaise, and Doug B. in the warmth of our hotel room. Thanks to a horrendous traffic jam into town, I missed out on a visit to the Baseball Hall of Fame. Strike two.

When I was eleven, Cooperstown was the destination of my one and only father and son road trip. Dad was a Brooklyn Dodgers fan, and he remained a Dodgers fan until the end of Sandy Koufax's career before shifting allegiance to the Mets. I was a Cincinnati Reds fan in those days. I loved the Big Red Machine: Johnny Bench, Pete Rose (Charlie Hustle), Joe Morgan, Tony Perez (Doggie), Ken Griffey, Cesar Geronimo, Dave Concepcion. Even though my old man wasn't passionate about baseball, it was the primary bond that connected us.

My last Ballpark show of 2004 was with "Stan the Man" at Dutchess Stadium in Fishkill, home of the Hudson Valley Renegades. I passed that ballpark often during my stint as in-home security systems consultant. I never looked at that ballpark and imagined that inspirational music would be created in front of the centerfield fence. The Hot Club of Cowtown and Willie Nelson were the opening acts.

On August 10th, it felt like summer again in Fishkill, New York, a welcomed change from the Cooperstown freeze out. The parking lots were filled beyond capacity. Stan parked his Lexus on a side street in an upscale housing development. We arrived late and heard Willie singing "Poncho and Lefty" as we walked towards the stadium—"Living on the road, my friend, was going to keep you free and clean." Tickets were sold out and tough to find. I scrounged one ticket for ten bucks, and Stan charmed his way past the lady at the gate as Dylan took the stage and sang, "Everybody must get stoned."

"Here you go Howie, baby. Try some of this," said Stan as he handed me a burning bone.

Harsh on the lungs, the smoke immediately opened my head to Bob's thundering voice:

"Tweedle Dee Dum said to Tweedle Dee Dee, your presence is obnoxious to me." Stan and I traded leads on air-guitar by the soundboard. "My pretty baby, she's beginning to boil, she's dripping with garlic and olive oil," grumbled Dylan. For some reason, "Tweedle Dum & Tweedle Dee" is the Rodney Dangerfield of *Love & Theft*. I've always found this number charming, and it smokes live.

Dylan was in the zone. You could hear it in his growl, see it in the way he pounced and pawed at his keyboard. "It's All Over Now Baby Blue" followed. All the mechanisms for a great evening were activated. The songs were alive, they magically communicated with this crowd on this night, and the songs spoke to each other, one song supporting the next. "Lay Lady Lay" and "Bye and Bye" turned the outfield grass into a ballroom beneath the sparkling sky. During "Stuck Inside of Mobile," Dylan answered his own question: "Oh, mama, is this really the end? I don't know." When Bob plays a solo round of Jeopardy, it's a tell-tale sign that he's on a roll.

Pulling imaginary pistols from his imaginary holster, Dylan peppered the crowd with gunfire during the jam in "Honest With Me." I'd never seen Dylan this relaxed before. It was moving—yet another side of Bob Dylan. It was a spirited turnaround from the frigid performances in Poughkeepsie and Cooperstown.

Leaving Fishkill, there was a monster backup of vehicles heading towards Route 84, so Stan turned left in search of the nearest honky-tonk joint on 9D, which happened to be a place called the Leaping Frog. There was a big ass ceramic amphibian on the lawn. A local TV crew was inside interviewing patrons about the upcoming NFL season. Stan and I went out into the parking lot with the sports reporter and gave Hudson Valley viewers our assessment of the 2004 Giants on live TV. After reestablishing ourselves at the bar, a French-kissing lesbian couple challenged us to pool and mopped the table with us repeatedly. Losing was never so wonderful.

It must have been 2 AM when we descended upon a diner off Route 84. We loaded up on ham, eggs, pancakes, and chicken tenders before heading home.

Zooming down Route 6 East, Stan didn't see any signs signaling the road's end. Facing a traffic circle, Stan slammed on the brakes as the tires on his Lexus squealed across the pavement into the heart of the round grass island. The music never stopped. Neil Young was singing, "This note, this note, this note's for you." It was like sliding into home plate safely. There was no reason to get excited—it happened too quickly.

I slept at my mom's house in Nanuet and called Stan the following morning to catch a ride back to The City on his way to work.

I said, "Stan, that was a helluva evening."

Stan replied, "Howie, Dylan was awesome last night baby. I'll pick you up in ten minutes. One thing, though. Betty (Stan's wife) got up this morning, looked out the window, and asked me why the tires on the Lexus are still smoking."

I missed all of Dylan's fall tour; however, it turned out to be a fateful autumn. I read *On the Road* for the first time. Outside of a handful of nonfiction books, literature was a nonfactor in my brain. I was drawn in by Kerouac's prose, but more than that, his journey was mine. I'd lived a Beat lifestyle since I started touring with the Dead. Doug Schmell was the Jewish Dean Moriarity, and I was Sal Paradise minus the writing. At last, I'd discovered a major source of inspiration to Dylan and the whole Grateful Dead scene.

Dylan's memoir, *Chronicles, Vol. 1*, arrived a few weeks after I read *On the Road*. Dylan chose to write about five essential periods during his career, and one of them was entitled *Oh Mercy*. It's a compelling chapter with reflections on his time with the Grateful Dead and the *Oh Mercy* sessions in New Orleans. Dylan did it again. He revealed a lot, but he never revealed the mystery behind his greatest songs, and he didn't dish out dirty laundry. Almost everything Dylan does enhances the fascination and mystery that surrounds him. I picked up a copy of the audio CD with Sean Penn's narration. It's absolutely Dylanesque. It's impossible to listen to *Chronicles* and not fall under the illusion that you're listening to Dylan.

As thought-provoking as these books were, my destiny was altered by an everyday email. Harold, a member of the Morning Dew Internet community, sent a message which read:

Hey Catfish,

They are offering a course called Discussing Dylan over at The New School. You should be teaching it. Here's the link.

I SHALL BE RELEASED

*Yankee Baseball Blues...Dancing Fools...Planet
Waves in Beantown...Scoring after the Beacon...My
Struggle...Sunday sermon in Lancaster...Otisville USA...
Road trip to Little Rock with a Memphis Cabbie...*

The New School. Hmm, I'd never heard of it before. They didn't field a baseball team, but their course catalog offered Discussing Dylan 101 with Professor Robert Levinson. Matriculating students could earn three credits towards their degree, and non-credit students could plunk down 400 dollars to discuss Dylan in an esteemed academic environment. I didn't think twice about enrolling. I saw myself as a potential mentor helping somebody out, perhaps a sexy brunette student with a Chinese dragon tattooed above her ass, a young lady struggling with her post *Blonde on Blonde* Dylan studies. Unfortunately, most of the men and the women in the class looked like they were my kin.

Professor Levinson, aka Bob, was more Merv Griffin than Ivy League professor. Every week there was a guest, usually an author who had contributed to the potpourri of Dylan Lit. He interviewed Rob Sheffield, David Hadju, Oliver Trager, David Fricke and Joe Levy. The class also hosted some legendary music talent: Garth Hudson, Odetta, Paul Travers, and Carolyn Hester. The poet Robert Polito was one guest who had a feel for live Dylan. He saw Dylan at both Cooperstown and

Fishkill, and his assessments of the shows were on par with mine. I asked Professor Bob to pass a copy of the Dutchess show on to Polito. I'm a pusher—always spreading the tunes.

The 2005 touring season commenced in Seattle without Larry Campbell. Larry had been replaced by Denny Freeman on lead guitar, and Donnie Herron in the instrumental handyman slot. It was a blow to the Never Ending Tour. Campbell was that amazing, filling all the roles Dylan asked him to play since 1996. It was going to take at least two talented musicians to fill Larry's shoes.

My first tour stop was at Boston's Orpheum Theatre. I zipped up to Beantown on the Acela express and was greeted by a city blanketed in Red Sox paraphernalia. Baseball season had just begun, and the Boston Red Sox were the reigning World Champions. It was living hell. It was a treat to watch Red Sox fans suffer year after year, but they had finally reversed the curse by winning the World Series after an unprecedented comeback against the Yankees in the American League Championship Series. As a Yankee fan, I could stomach the loss, but I couldn't get used to the smug look of a happy Red Sox fan.

Speaking of smug-looking Red Sox fans, I met Mr. Phil Hyman at my little hotel near the Orpheum Theatre. I had ninety minutes to put on a dog and pony show for Phil before Dylan hit the stage. I opened with a few numbers from Boston Music Hall 11-21-75. Following "Romance in Durango," Dylan says, "This is a song about marriage. This is called Isis. This is for Sam Peckinpaugh, if he's still here." I love the cadence of that announcement. Then I played some Born Again Christian songs from the Warfield run in 1980, including the night when Carlos Santana took the stage with Dylan. Of course I had to play that amazing "To Ramona" when Jerry Garcia appeared with Dylan during that same run. After listening to Bob's 53-second version of "Talking Hava Nagila Blues" five times in a row, I went for the jugular.

Phil said, "It's getting close to show time, Howid. Should we start heading over?"

I said, "Not so quick; we got twenty minutes. Dig this."

I clicked on the "Eyes of the World" from Roosevelt Stadium, 8-6-74—the royal rhapsody. The groove is thick and luxurious from the onset. The timing and anticipation of the musicians is uncanny. Every nuance adds to the collective sound, and the harmonies are equally mesmerizing—a perfect launching pad for two of the best Jerry solos you'll ever hear—concise, volatile, lyrical. The final ten-minute jam is a typical master blaster a la 1974, the Grateful Dead at their improvisational peak as a band. Phil and I were dancing fools, tossing various items around the hotel room like we were twenty-five.

Serious rock history had transpired in Boston's Orpheum Theatre, but the place was Plain Jane past her prime. It lacked the stylish ambiance of most big city theatres; however, this was exactly the type of time-battered building that would inspire Dylan.

Showing off his new band, Dylan experimented with a pair of songs from *Planet Waves*, the underappreciated jewel that preceded *Blood on the Tracks*. "Tough Mama," one of my all-time favorites, was rocked with concise and tasty jams from Denny Freeman. Bob went for a harp stroll during "Hazel," a love ballad he hadn't played since *The Last Waltz* concert with The Band. Those numbers thrilled the critic within, and it was my debut encounter with both tunes live. Dylan continued to pile on to the feast with "If Dogs Run Free," "Tomorrow Is a Long Time" and "Chimes of Freedom." Dylan tested the elasticity of his band. It was confirmed; he had himself an ass kicking cohesive unit—a wall of antique sound. The fantasy overload continued when my first "Mississippi" arrived as an encore. Driven by Dylan's swampy keyboard sound, it took a few verses for me to settle into that one. When you think you've seen and heard it all, that's when Dylan starts to amaze you.

Phil and I were back at The Orpheum for night two. The evening came down to one song, my first "Blind Willie McTell." On *The Bootleg Series Vol.1- 3*, "Blind Willie McTell" was sung with spiritual reverence against an elegant acoustic landscape. In Boston, Dylan's band thundered the chords as if they were standing on top of Mt. Zion. Saturday night was dominated by "Blind Willie McTell." Sometimes a single performance by Dylan or Garcia can loom so large that it hijacks the identity of an entire show.

On this tour, it appeared that Dylan was consciously grouping songs to create theme-based shows. It was audacious. Grouchy Bill Graham's most famous proclamation was "They're (the Grateful Dead) not the best at what they do; they're the only ones who do what they do." Those words fit Dylan's career, and now more than ever, Dylan was in spirit with that Grateful Dead performing philosophy.

After witnessing a religious revival with Dylan down at The Borgata in Atlantic City on Sunday August 24, 2005, I reunited with Stan at The Beacon Theatre on Tuesday. The highlight of that night was our post-show Wo Hop gorge. Our friendship had no foundation except as witnesses to live music. Eight years older than Perry, Stan was an accountant with a wife and two kids in Valley Cottage. I knew nothing of his wedding, anniversaries, kid's graduations, and we didn't talk about our jobs or speak on the phone about anything except music. We only saw each other at Grateful Dead shows, Dylan concerts, and Perry's gigs. It was a pleasure, a friendship based on music without any baggage.

April 28th, the third show of Dylan's five-night run at The Beacon was the zenith of a terrific first tour with his new band. I hailed a cab west to Amsterdam Avenue and met Perry a few hours before the show. Perry looked great. He's one of those people who appears healthier each time you see him, and you wonder how he does it. A happily married accountant with three kids, Perry played mandolin in two or three bands. About twelve years earlier, Perry gave up electric guitar in favor of the mandolin, jam bands for quick picking bluegrass—Jerry Garcia's path in reverse.

We stopped by Brother Jimmy's and enjoyed barbeque, trashy décor, and the vision of tender waitresses in tight jeans with t-shirts knotted at the navel. Our southern-style spread consisted of meaty dry-rubbed ribs, thick chicken wings in barbeque sauce, and chicken tenders. I downed a bucket of peel and eat shrimp by myself. The Paletta brothers will devour the beef from a 1,000 cows, but they won't nibble on anything that swims in the sea. On our way to the Beacon, we stumbled into the Bear Bar next door. The beer was flat, the surroundings dirty, and the cookies behind the bar were 95% naked. I was completely content, but hearing Dylan on the jukebox reminded us it was time to claim our third row seats, which I had scored through a bobdylan.com presale.

Dylan set the mood for the night, delivering "Senor" in the two-hole. My accountant was giddy at the sight of Dylan going for a stroll during the harp solo. Even wilder was Bob's new vocal technique—up-singing. Dylan was finishing off his vocal flurries by suddenly singing in a noticeably higher pitch—an exaggerated experiment to break away from the steady force of his booming howls. It was one of those nights. Dylan unloaded a jackhammer rendition of "Down along the Cove" and the always spellbinding "Blind Willie McTell."

"Mississippi" made its presence felt as the first encore. Dylan nailed a southern groove, part Delta Blues, part Cajun voodoo. I was thrilled to see my accountant under Dylan's command. I could see the wear and tear of the Never Ending Tour on Dylan's pale mug. He was a dogged public servant, yet his spirit was forever young.

Perry and I extended our night at the Westside Brewery across the street. A nice looking dirty-haired blonde with enormous hooters started hitting on Perry. My buddy is happy at home, so he gifted those mounds to me—if only I could capitalize.

Perry said, "Howie, I'd like you to meet Jillian. She's here by herself for the Dylan show. You two should hang out. Jillian says she lives in Queens and she came to the show by herself. Howie, I think you two have a lot in common."

Erotic single women are a dying species on Dylan's tour, but Perry found me a wild one.

Perry retreated to domestic bliss, while I jumped in Jilian's car and scored cocaine on the East Side. I'd outgrown blow decades ago, but sometimes you have to roll with the flow. Jillian's dealer jumped into the front seat. I'd been demoted to the back. This was getting weird, my mind was racing.

Honestly, your honor. I just met this girl at a Dylan show. I never met that Puerto Rican gentleman in the passenger seat with the revolver and the blow before. Honestly.

Like most deals, this one went down smooth. Since we were parked by Iggy's, one of my karaoke joints on Second Avenue, I brought Jillian in for a cocktail. The bartenders, Christy, Peter, and Linea rolled out the velvet carpet for us, but Jillian just wanted to head back to my place to focus on her stash.

We rolled and tumbled and listened to Dylan all night long. At 8 AM, we were singing karaoke, the lyrics flashing on my big screen TV as the neighbors were heading to work. I tried every Buddy Holly tune that I never had the nerve to sing in front of an audience before: "True Love Ways," "It Don't Matter Anymore," "Peggy Sue." If my neighbors weren't already convinced I was Judas, they now had audio confirmation.

I was back at the glorious Beacon on Saturday night, the 30th day of April, for the tour finale. I impressed the stranger sitting next to me by identifying just about every song on the first chord. This bearded hippie turned me on to some wacky weed. I smoked seven or so bowls during the show—five more than I'd smoked all year. "I Shall Be Released" was a psychedelic, peaceful odyssey that seemed like it flowed for a half hour, but it may have only been about five minutes. My mind was running on Pluto time. I walked home across Central Park stoned to my soul, in no hurry to get anywhere, simply enjoying the moonlight and the memories.

On Monday morning May 2, 2005, I tossed my laptop into a back-pack and sashayed to Starbucks early in the morning. I decided I was going to write a book about Dylan's Never Ending Tour and vowed to return to Starbucks every morning to write. I ordered a venti iced-coffee with vanilla syrup and claimed a chessboard table in the corner. My prose journey began with my impressions of the Dylan-Dead concert from 7-12-87.

During the past two weeks, I'd seen a batch of amazing performances by Dylan, and spent precious time with cronies and strangers. Winding down from my first semester in Discussing Dylan 101, I thought about all the authors I'd listened to. They seemed to be twisting similar stories on Dylan from the '60s and '70s with brilliant insight. Their prose styles and verbiage were stupefying. It seemed that writing about Dylan had become an academic pissing contest. I wanted to know more about the guy in the cowboy hat who was thundering across the land in a tour bus for his eighteenth consecutive year. That's where my story resided. I had the passion and persistence to reach the finish line, but I didn't know the first thing about crafting a book.

I penned my first book when I was eight years old. It was titled: *Maryland Terrapin Scrapbook*. The Terps were my favorite college team because I was born in Maryland. I cut out articles on the football team from the *Rockland Journal News* and pasted them on colored pieces of construction paper. I contributed written commentary on every game, and at the end of the year, I had myself a book. Maryland went 11-0 that season, but they got trounced by Houston in the Cotton Bowl, ending my chances for a New York Times Bestseller. My urge to write received no support from teachers because my penmanship was awful. It still is. Adding to my discord with English teachers was my distaste for reading literature. I was immediately turned off by the old-fashioned language of the classics.

My second writing project was a journal of a two-week trip through Europe around Christmas in 1988. I visited an ex-girlfriend, who was an exchange student in Germany. We Eurailed from Munich to Innsbruck, and followed that with excursions to Venice and Paris before rolling on back to Munich. I penned observations over dark roast coffee every morning and came away with three unshakeable conclusions: I loved being American; I was a natural-born traveler; and I wasn't getting married anytime soon. I called this diary *My Struggle*, and I left it out on a coffee table. My New Paltz friends enjoyed reading these passages, which were styled after Jim Bouton's *Ball Four*. Somehow *My Struggle* got lost in the shuffle of time—it disappeared like a puff of wind.

Now I was officially on a quest. The impending book gave me further reason to really dive into the beast and pursue my muse like never before. I wasn't sure if I was exploring the Never Ending Tour, or if I was just trying to find my identity. Either way, more traveling research equaled more strange tales.

Speeding through Amish countryside on Amtrak, I couldn't wait to get Lancaster for Dylan's concert at Clipper Magazine Stadium on June 19, 2005. Once there, I discovered an odd blue-collared town. After picking at a brutal batch of chicken wings, I wandered into a dusty old brick house tavern and tossed back a few pints of Yuengling with the local booze hounds. It was Sunday, the day of rest in this God-fearing town, yet for many locals, this tavern was church, and Yuengling was the Holy Water.

Bouncing around the outfield grass—in the gap between first and second bases, I reveled in my first "God Knows." "Tryin' to Get to Heaven" was sublime—another sacred Sunday spiritual. Dylan finally did justice to "New Morning," atoning for those shoddy versions that started gigs in 1991. Lancaster was further blessed with "Visions of Johanna," which came off as the most pious sermon of the night. I wrote my first Dylan review, and lo and behold, it was published on boblinks. com. My next ballpark show was a few nights later in Montclair, New Jersey, Yogi Berra's hometown, and my first trip to the land of the Delta Blues was on deck.

After touching down in Memphis, a blue trolley car transported me from my hotel to Beale Street. I was here, in the heart of Memphis, the crossroads of American music. The living was nice and easy: barbeque joints, music shops, blues clubs, small outdoor stages. The business of Beale Street is rhythm & blues, rockabilly, country, soul and jazz. Beale was real; my kind of street.

Exquisitely perched atop the banks of the Mississippi River, Beale Street bleeds music. The sounds of Elvis, Johnny Cash, Otis Redding,

Carl Perkins, B.B. King and Isaac Hayes filled the air. While consuming tender barbeque meats at the Rum Boogie Café, I admired Stevie Ray Vaughn's guitar encased on the wall before me. Everywhere I turned, I sensed the presence of the past. If there is a sacred musical vortex in the universe, it resides here.

On the second day of my trip, I pulled myself away from Beale to visit the red pandas and giraffes at the Memphis Zoo. What are the deals with those necks? As a creature with no neck, I'm infatuated with the giraffes. Then my inquisitive mind pondered what I was doing at the zoo on a humid 101-degree afternoon after an all-night booze binge on Beale.

I never made it to Graceland or Sun Studios, but I took a taxi to the Stax Museum, on the bad side of town. The marquee simply read, "STAX SOULSVILE U S A. This was a replica of the building that had stood there, the birthplace of Memphis soul, Otis Redding's office. The masses go wild for "Respect" and "Hard to Handle," but many don't realize that those songs were the brainstorms of the same man who wrote "Dock of the Bay."

Otis was the buzz. His performances were as immense as his physical stature. Nothing grooves with as much soul as live Otis. If you doubt this, all you got to do is listen to any live version of "Try a Little Tenderness." CD number four from the *OTIS* box set is the finest hodgepodge of live music ever thrown together. Listening to "Fa-Fa-Fa-Fa-Fa (Sad Song) in Stax," I placed my right hand on the soundboard that had channeled Otis through its veins. It was soul stirring; you could feel Otis in the house.

Behind Otis, my top Stax artists are Isaac Hayes, Albert King, and Booker T. & the MGs. Isaac Hayes's 1969 *Hot Buttered Soul* is the pride and joy of Stax, the best album ever recorded on that label, and Albert King's *Lovejoy* is a dyn-o-mite blues record.

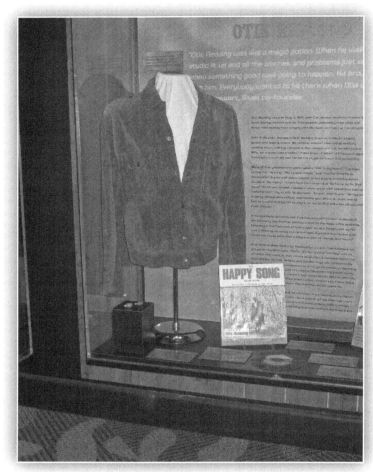

Otis

My only Memphis hiccup occurred as I tried to head on to the field of Autozone Park before Dylan's show on the first day of July. A pair of elderly ushers impeded my progress. Apparently, I didn't have field access. Outraged, I demanded to speak to the highest ranking official. I hadn't traveled to Memphis to sit in the stands, 350 feet from the stage, while others were dancing on the grass. All of the previous ballpark shows had been general admission affairs.

A few minutes later, I was talking to an important person in the Autozone hierarchy. A man in a dark blue three-piece suit handed me his shiny business card and said "Hi. I'm Jerry. How can I help you, sir?" Jerry was the number two guy in Autozone Park, the VP of Operations.

I said, "Hi. My name is Howie Weiner. I'm a freelance journalist. I write about music for *The New York Times* and *Creem Magazine*. I'm covering the southern leg of Bob Dylan's tour, and I was hoping I could get on to the field so I could capture the temperament of Dylan's performance and mingle with the fanatics."

"Well, Howie. Welcome to Memphis. Are you from New York?"

"Good call. I am a New Yorker, sir. And I just want to let you know this is a beautiful ballpark."

"Fabulous. Gentlemen, let Mr. Weiner on to the field. And if you need anything at all, my number's on the card."

I could have used a couple of cocktails, a backstage pass, and a rub-down from a pretty Dixie chicken, but this touch of southern hospitality would suffice. My exaggerated claims of writing prowess reminded me of a lesson I learned from George Costanza, "It's not a lie, if you believe it."

Yes, Dylan played "Stuck Inside of Mobile with the Memphis Blues Again" and "Highway 61 Revisited." The music crackled through the evening skies—everything sounds better in Memphis. "Things Have Changed" and "Love Sick" encore were the jewels of the night.

The following afternoon, July 2nd, I was on line waiting for a Greyhound bound for Little Rock with the Memphis flu again. This virus was a condition brought on by stifling Delta heat and excessive booze consumption. When I planned my vacation, the excursion to see Dylan in Little Rock would be a game time decision. On the last full day of my vacation, I had three options:

1. I could call the whole thing off, take a nap, and then rage on Beale all night long.

2.   I could endure a five-hour round trip Greyhound adventure with many stops in between. The bus was late, the line was long, and the people reeked, but I was getting used to these conditions. I was a tough guy; maybe I should just stay the course.

3.   My final alternative was expensive. I asked a cab driver outside of the station how much a round trip to Little Rock would cost. Dispatch told him $400. Between my Greyhound tickets and the ensuing cab rides to and from Little Rock, I would be about $200 in the hole, anyway. The idea of being chauffeured door to door was appealing. I had a Visa, and I wasn't scared off by the idea of having to pay 18.5% interest. Hmm.

I opted for door number three.

Yeah hah! Rural Arkansas, here I come—a 137-mile jaunt down Interstate 40 West to Little Rock. I wanted to visually explore Arkansas terrain, but my cabbie battered me with meaningless gab. He meant well, but this was almost as tedious as being stuck on a Greyhound. I told my new friend I had to lie down because I drank too much the night before—a convenient truth. I popped on *Planet Waves* and woke up in the capital of Arkansas.

Rolling through Little Rock, I thought about Bill Clinton, Levon Helm and those great Arkansas Razorback basketball teams. My mind had limited Arkansas associations. Now we had to find Ray Winder Field. My Pakistani chauffeur had never been to Little Rock, either. We got directions the old-fashioned way, by pulling over and asking a committee of locals. I was rejuvenated after my nap, and I began to bond with Maneesh Waleed, my garrulous cabbie. We were quite a team, a Yankee and a Pakistani chasing down kicks in Razorback Country.

I scored a ticket and checked on Maneesh before I headed into the show.

"Maneesh, what are you going to do when I'm inside?" I asked.

"Ohhh, nothing sir. I sit here and wait for you," he said in an attentive tone.

"Hey man, feel free to get a bite to eat. This is going to take a while. There's an opening act, then Willie Nelson, then Dylan," I said.

"That's OK, sir. I wait here for you."

This was brilliant. I bought baseball souvenirs for my nephews Lucas and Logan and brought them out to my little orange taxi for safekeeping. The stands of Ray Winder Field creaked when I copped a squat. This was the oldest Minor League ballpark, and it was due for demolition after the season. Ray Winder Field had a clumsy, disheveled appearance. I didn't think anyone would stand in front of a wrecking ball to save this place. When the new stadium, based on old-timey ballpark models stood in its place, nobody would be weeping for Ray Winder.

Dylan put on an aggressive show that whistled above the audience's head. This crowd preferred the predictably soothing twangs of Willie Nelson over the rambunctious wildness of Dylan's art. There was no compromise in Bob's attitude. He either connects with a crowd through his presentation, or people grumble. Hell, I was grumbling. Dylan turned in a set list similar to the Memphis show. There was no holy water sprinkled on this show; however, I was grateful I made the trip to Ray Winder Stadium, and I was even happier that I had a chauffeur waiting outside.

Whipped from my vacation, I split during the last encore. I wanted Maneesh to get a good jump on the traffic out of Little Rock.

Eager to see me, Maneesh said, "Sir, you enjoy concert?"

"Yes I did. Yes I did," I affirmed. But what I really loved was that I had avoided a grueling Greyhound ordeal. After another nap on I-40, I was in Memphis, my beloved city on the banks of the Mississippi.

Maneesh pulled into the lot of my hotel and said,

"Oh my God, sir. I remember you, do you remember me?"

I was thinking, *Maneesh, this is no time to get weird*. I laughed and said, "Ah, no. What are you talking about?"

"I pick you up at airport and drop you off here. You say to me, how much for ride to Little Rock...Remember?"

Oh, horse feathers! I did remember. This was the cabbie that picked me up when I landed at the airport. I never saw his face, but I asked the driver how much a fare to Little Rock would set me back. There was no way I could have remembered Maneesh, I never saw his face. But how many people land in Memphis and inquire about the fare to Little Rock? The answer is one. And, what are the odds that this guy, out of all the Memphis cabbies, would be sitting outside the Greyhound terminal when I made a spontaneous decision to hail a cab. That is destiny. After spending twelve hours as my chauffeur, most of that time in Arkansas, how did Maneesh not remember me until he had pulled up in front of my hotel? The human brain is composed of strange tissue.

BLIND WILLIE MCTELL

The levees break, Dylan's soundtrack is released...
Captain Fantastic and the rebellious passenger...
Twisting bones in Amsterdam...The ordinary life of Franz
Pilsner...An American rendezvous in Rotterdam...

Memphis was right up there with New Orleans as my favorite southern city. I envisioned repeated pilgrimages to these musical holy lands. About two months after my Memphis excursion, New Orleans was in grave danger.

Katrina brewed in the Gulf of Mexico—a monster hurricane bearing down on New Orleans. I'd been to Sugartown three times in the past two years, and I'd developed a strong predilection for that voodoo village. Katrina had an evil eye, Lake Pontchartrain was on the rise, and the Superdome became an evacuation center. This was a nightmare equation.

Katrina was vicious; however, it appeared the worst devastation had passed when I picked up the new Dylan soundtrack, *No Direction Home,* on Tuesday, August 30, 2005. The seventh volume of Dylan's Bootleg series was released on the morning the levees protecting New Orleans were breeched. It was the second major tragedy to strike an American metropolis in the new millennium, and Dylan releases coincided with both events.

The New Orleans tragedy was a shameful American episode. The citizens of New Orleans were betrayed by poor public planning and government response on the municipal, state, and federal levels. Those images are indelibly embedded in the nation's consciousness: shooting and looting in the streets, the hole in the Superdome roof—a peak into the chaos and suffering inside. Watching CNN, I was chilled by an image of a skinny, African American man carrying a bed over his head on Route 10. That's all he had left in this world—a defiled mattress. "What Good Am I?" played in my head as I watched this footage:

What Good Am I, If I'm like all the rest? If I just turn away when I see how you're dressed? If I turn a deaf ear to the thunder in the sky; What Good Am I?

With the extremely unpopular occupation of Iraq, America's reputation was taking a pounding on multiple fronts. After my successful summer expeditions to Memphis and Little Rock, I had an itch to go international. I booked a brief trip overseas to catch Dylan in Rotterdam. While passing through, I could spend a few days in Amsterdam. October was the rainy season in the Netherlands, so in a country where they named every city after a dam, I took heed and packed an umbrella. However the weather turned out to be immaculate; I couldn't have programmed it better with a thermostat and sun dial: 55-75 degrees with a sunburn index of 7.5—not a drop of rain in sight.

In the hour of my departure for Amsterdam, I was enjoying the remnants of a supersized Sam Adams, when the airport PA system screamed, "Mr. Howard Weiner, please report to gate 14 for the flight to Amsterdam. This is the final boarding call." I gulped the final three ounces of my beer, tipped the bartender, grabbed my over-stuffed backpack, piled it on top of my carry-on luggage, and schlepped my belongings towards the gate.

The captain of the plane was waiting to greet me at the gate with a flight attendant by his side. His chest was flexed, and his expression was stern. His body language suggested he had the right stuff. *Oh boy, I'm in trouble.*

"You must be Mr. Weiner," said the captain, calmly, as he began to breathe harder. "Where were you?"

I wanted to say, "I was loosening at the bar, you Nazi," but pissing off the man who will be flying you across the ocean isn't a prudent move. I respected this guy because he was a pilot, forget about the captain designation. There are two classes of people—those who can fly a plane, and those who can't. I just said, "Sorry, sir. There's still twenty minutes to go before takeoff."

Captain Fantastic didn't realize I was the cool king of the last minute arrival—the antithesis of my old man. My father was always uptight and under duress in airports—constantly striving to be earlier than early. My father wasn't a powerful man, but if Mike Tyson was dilly-dallying in front of him on an airport line, Dad would have stomped him. I vowed to never be like that. I never rushed anywhere, but I could never be late. This leaves a slim window of opportunity for arrival, especially when I'm super-sizing my beers at the terminal bar. Oh, show me the way to the next terminal bar. Oh, don't ask why.

As soon as we were hurling over the Atlantic Ocean, somewhere between Nova Scotia and Bermuda, I passed out to the remixed version of *Captain Fantastic and the Brown Dirt Cowboy,* my favorite Elton John album. I'm a sucker for CD reissues. Give me three bonus tracks and make a token attempt to improve the sound quality, and I'm a happy guy; you got my $14.98 again. I couldn't get this album out of my head. "Better Off Dead" and "Tower of Babel" were tattooed to my brain while I was in Europe.

I landed in Amsterdam early in the morning. Jetlagged, I'd already lost track of what day it was. I almost settled into my little bed and breakfast suite, which was cozier than advertised, but I had an action-packed agenda. I tossed my belongings aside and called my girl, Sharon. I'd met this Dutch divorcée at a party in Chelsea six weeks earlier. Sharon insisted that I visit her when I was in Amsterdam, and she sealed my fate with a smoke-drenched kiss.

I had time to burn before Sharon got off work. I grabbed a snack, had two Heinekens for lunch, and stopped in a dimly lit coffee shop on the outskirts of the Red Light District. They really did have marijuana menus. I ordered a bag of California skunk and twisted a beautiful bone. I hadn't rolled one in a long time, but it's like riding a bicycle, I suppose.

Stoned silly at a table in a park, I listened to some Grateful Dead and watched Dutch folk bicycle through the streets of Amsterdam on a splendid autumn day. A wave of déjà vu overcame me. Maybe I had Dutch blood. I could see myself answering to the name Franz Pilsner—an ordinary Dutch citizen who commutes by bike, owns a chocolate shop overlooking an ancient canal, and is hitched to a fine woman like Sharon. It then occurred to me that I was practically going out on a blind date with this woman. I remembered that tender, smoky kiss, and recalled a striking brunette woman, but I couldn't fill in too many other details. I was pleased when I recognized Sharon coming my way. She was even sexier in Amsterdam than she was in Chelsea. I patted myself on the back. You've done well, Franz.

It was like any other first date I ever had, with a few exceptions: 1) the people in the background were speaking a foreign language; 2) I was on another continent; 3) She invited me back to her place.

Sharon drove me to my bed and breakfast early the next morning. She had plans for the weekend, and so did I. My unopened bags looked like they enjoyed a restful stay in my $250-a-night room. I stacked my luggage and dashed off for a train to Rotterdam. I was determined to get my money's worth out of the hotel over there.

The Netherlands countryside was flat as a pancake, and the towns were neat and orderly. The Dutch people were reserved and amiable; everybody tended to their own business—Germany on Prozac. The Dutch served their coffee with chocolates and wafers, a delicious custom. If I were exiled from America, I think I could make it in the Netherlands.

I was happy to meet an English-speaking sweetheart inside Ahoy before the show. I fired up a joint and asked her what she was doing in Rotterdam.

She said, "I'm just following Dylan around Europe."

"No way," I said." Where are you following him to?"

"I'm gonna see a few shows in Germany, then Brussels and Paris, and then I'm heading back to Jersey."

She had a pretty face and a sly smile. She looked like Sabrina, a bubbly brunette who hosted karaoke for me. But who was this girl? Was she by herself? Were there actually female versions of me running around Europe? Impossible. The lights went out, and an usher cleared the aisle. She disappeared with my joint as Dylan moseyed on to the stage. So long, Sabrina.

Forty years after Dylan shocked the folkies at Newport by going electric with "Maggie's Farm," Dylan blitzed Rotterdam with a ragged "Maggie's Farm" opener. Howling, kicking, and twisting behind the keyboard, Dylan was still challenging his audience. "Here I am, the eternal troubadour, performing on my own terms. Take this Holland, may it serve you well."

Dylan coaxed us into a world of domestic tranquility with a trio of ballads penned in Woodstock. "Lay Lady Lay" was exceptional. Donnie Herron channeled the Nashville sound—the twangs of his pedal steel flowed with Dylan's keyboards, setting a seductive ambiance. Dylan growled his mating call, "I long to see you in the morning light. I long to reach out for ya, in the dead of night." The tug-of-war between the singer and the song was amazing. Dylan reinvented his love ballad with a steady booming howl and an age-defying swagger.

I picked this Rotterdam concert out of Dylan's European tour dates on a whim, and I drank from the Holy Grail when Dylan busted out "Blind Willie McTell" in the sixth spot: "Seen the arrow on the doorpost sayin' this land is condemned; All the way from New Orleans to Jerusalem." After watching Katrina turn New Orleans into a condemned land, this sacred hymn had more clout than ever before.

Nobody can sing the blues like Blind Willie McTell, but nobody can sing the tales of America like this guy from the North Country. "Love Sick," Tangled Up in Blue," Chimes of Freedom," "Highway 61 Revisited," the thrill of America rolled across Ahoy. Rotterdam's love for Dylan's performance grew with each Yankee anthem—from the Great North Woods down to New Orleans and all along the Mississippi River aboard the Jackson Queen. What an ambassador!

Ahoy, Rotterdam, The Netherlands

October 28, 2005

1. Maggie's Farm
2. Tonight I'll Be Staying Here With You
3. Watching the River Flow
4. Lay Lady Lay
5. Stuck Inside of Mobile with the Memphis Blues Again
6. Blind Willie McTell
7. I'll Be Your Baby Tonight
8. Ballad of a Thin Man
9. I Don't Believe You
10. Love Sick
11. Tangled Up in Blue
12. Down Along the Cove
13. Chimes of Freedom
14. Highway 61 Revisited
    (encore)
15. Like a Rolling Stone
16. All Along the Watchtower

Ending the night at a Chinese karaoke lounge near my hotel, I sang in front of a gathering of European and Asian strangers. Back at the hotel, I couldn't sleep. My brain and body were crossed, deliriously out of whack. I watched the sun rise like a soft yolk over a Rotterdam canal and typed a review for boblinks.com. This was my mission, although I was never given the assignment. I returned to Amsterdam and checked into the very same bed and breakfast I had forsaken the day before. I didn't have the desire to see Van Gogh's art or visit the Anne Frank House before leaving Amsterdam. I was content. My faith in America was restored.

My appetite for touring was insatiable. I impatiently waited for Dylan's 2006 tour dates to be posted online. Where would fate lead me next?

POSITIVELY 4th STREET

Matzo balls and champagne in the desert...
Dear Mr. Sobriety, thanks for the buzz kill...Dylan
taps into Pavarotti...Sailing the Mississippi...
Country roads to Boonsboro...Hard Rain in
Manchester...Johnny Appleseed strikes again...

Gazing out the oval window, I saw the canyons and deserts of Nevada for the first time. I was hoping to see those bats that Dr. Hunter S. Thompson and his Samoan lawyer had encountered on their iconic journey to Las Vegas. As the flight descended, there were no bats to be seen—there was just a massive neon owl staring at me, courtesy of the Hooter's Hotel, restaurant, and casino.

On April 6, 2006, twenty-four years after my long, strange trip had begun with a Grateful Dead show in Philly, I'd finally made it to Sin City. I checked into The Mirage and observed the action. Everyday people tossed away hard-earned pay at card tables with names like Let It Ride and Casino War. We all know what happens when you let it ride, and I'm not going to war with any casinos. Making my way through the rat maze, I couldn't help but eyeball the sexy cocktail waitresses. The burly security guards wearing blazers three sizes too small were sizing me up because I had headphones on. I was listening to Sly & the Family Stone in an attempt to drown out the clanging jingle-jangle of the slot machines. But anyone wearing headphones is a person of interest to casino security.

After a bumpy plane ride, I gorged on a mile-high turkey on rye and scrumptious matzo balls the size of grapefruits at the Carnegie Delicatessen in The Mirage. I had flown halfway around the globe for an All-American experience in Amsterdam, and now I was in the desert, sucking on sour pickles and devouring matzo balls like a New York Jew.

I headed down the Strip to preview the Aladdin Performing Arts Center, the place where Dylan would be working the following night. I discovered the Desert Passageway, a shopping arcade of odd stores, restaurants, and theatres linked to the Aladdin Hotel & Casino. The shop next to the Performing Arts Center was packed with desirable music memorabilia/ Big ticket merchandise. I saw an exquisitely framed and autographed copy of *Blood on the Tracks* and thought, "I will have you." I inquired about the price tag.

"My friend, we had that piece sent here just for the Dylan show tomorrow night," said the store's proprietor. "This valuable comes with a certificate of authenticity, and we will ship it anywhere you want. This rare piece of memorabilia is selling for 1,000 dollars."

I carefully thought it over for ten seconds. I was planning on possibly blowing a grand in the casinos, anyway. That was my cap. I countered with a tough question.

"How long will it take to get to Manhattan?"

"That can be shipped express tomorrow (Friday) and be delivered in three business days."

Perfect timing; I was getting back to Manhattan Monday night. I charged it on the same plastic I used for the Little Rock taxi excursion, except this was a bigger matzo ball. I'm not a memorabilia collector, but a signed *Blood on the Tracks* would look fabulous hanging behind my big ass TV, and it was a safer bet than blackjack or roulette. So the transaction was written, and so it was signed.

When I made the purchase, it didn't occur to me that it was exactly nineteen years to the day of my *Blood on the Tracks* epiphany in New Paltz. Who keeps track of dates? Ho, ho, ho.

At the Aladdin the following night, Merle Haggard opened and snarled his cowboy classics about hard living and tough times. He looked battle-tested, just as his surname suggests. Like Dylan, he didn't waste time on small talk. His songs were enormous: "Sing Me Back Home," "Mama Tried." And he always sang his mind, even if he was protesting against marijuana smoking hippies who were burning their draft cards down on Main Street.

When the lights came on, a familiar looking woman was seated to my right. Hey! It was that Jersey girl I met at the Rotterdam show. Wow! Other traveling Dylanheads do exist. I'm not alone. This mysterious diva was now following Dylan out West, driving around with a small posse that included her boyfriend. Suddenly, I felt like an underachiever; there were people hustling around, catching entire tours. I was merely a slacker who jet-set around the globe.

On April 7, 2006, Dylan's charismatic presence illuminated the stage. His sassy turquoise-colored shirt shined against his black suit and black top hat. He looked like a panther. Crouched behind a shiny silver organ, Dylan burst into "Things Have Changed." Blown away again! How many times and ways can he continue to thrill me? The master composer altered the sonic landscape of the band, thanks to the new organ that replaced his Yamaha keyboard. The organ produced suspenseful sounds, sounds of a cathedral nature. Sometimes the organ plinking made me feel like I was skating in an indoor hockey rink; other times, I heard a carnival and pictured the clowns, snow cones, cotton candy, and Ferris wheel.

"The Times They Are A-Changin'" followed "Things Have Changed." It was a contrast of songs that reflected moments in time and foreshadowed the future. In his '60s anthem, Dylan sings of battle lines being drawn, and if you're not hip, you'll sink like a stone. "Things Have Changed" also captured a moment in time. We were in the new millennium, where people are crazy and times are strange. Yet, both songs had a timeless quality. The line in the sand was hazy. Everybody and everything was subject to change. *What's good is bad; what's bad is good; You'll find out when you reach the top, you're on the bottom.*

Las Vegas was Dylan's fifth show of 2006. On the first four nights, Bob played similar set lists, but on this night, he played an entirely different assortment of songs. I prepared for Sloppy Joe, and Dylan delivered a ripe mango. For those who followed the tour in person, or via the Internet, Bob's set lists were a never ending soap opera. The highlights of this night were "Love Sick," and "Cat's in the Well" as a set closer. The last raspy grunt of the set was "Goodnight, my love; may the Lord have mercy on us all." Amen.

Emboldened by great art and the charged atmosphere of Friday night in Vegas, I went out to paint the town and found a lively blonde at the roulette wheel. Her light blue eyes were sensual, and her braided ponytail and black tattoo set her apart from the ritzy crowd at The Mirage. The rectangular black patch on her upper arm was a failed tattoo attempt. Crystal, an implant from Kansas, worked an assortment of odd jobs at the Imperial Palace across the street. After bawdy talk and several vodka drinks, I discovered her pierced tongue. This was my debut make out session with a pierced tongue. In a mousy whisper, she boasted of other body piercings—one on her navel; one left for my imagination.

We floated to Room 724, where I fumbled with the room key/card and an uncooperative slot. I was about to go to the front desk, but then it occurred to me that I was slightly shitfaced. I was in Room 708. Crystal hopped on to the queen bed overlooking the Strip. I put on *Infidels* and asked her to get comfortable. After pouring a few glasses of wine from the mini fridge and brushing my teeth, I came out to the soothing snore of a blonde goddess, too peaceful to wake. I lowered the lights and watched her sleep, but I had a burning desire that had to be quelled. I called the deli below and ordered a quart of matzo ball soup. When I awoke, the rising sun was reflecting off the hotel across the street, and my fully clothed mystery girl rolled towards me, pecked me on the cheek and thanked me for a wonderful time.

Crystal headed off to work to chase her Vegas dream. I headed down to the champagne buffet brunch at Cravings. Stations with smorgasbords of delectable foods lined the perimeter, and accommodating Mexican waitresses served coffee, juice, water, and champagne with a smile. "Would you like some more champagne, señor?" How could I refuse?

During the course of my three-hour stay, I feasted on waffles, grapefruit, hash browns, fresh turkey slices, dim sum, crab legs, California roll, olives, broccoli, lox, moo goo gai pan, asparagus, shrimp, more broccoli and chicken breast. If only they had black beans, all my cravings would have been met—a little something for management to mull over. All the while, I was typing a review for boblinks.com, freezing the moment, sharing it with others on the Internet. Breaking down a great performance is rewarding.

Following a Cravings-induced siesta, I went to a Billy Joel concert at the MGM Grand Hotel. I bought the ticket online; now I had to take the ride. I was impressed with the scores of Christie Brinkley wannabes in the front rows—the blonde-haired cookies were swooning. Otherwise, it was a pre-packaged greatest hits snoozefest. I'd enjoyed all these songs at some point in my life, but there were no kicks to be had tonight. Billy Joel actually sang:

"A bottle of red, a bottle of white, I won't be drinking either one tonight." Dear Mr. Sobriety, thanks for the buzz kill. Joel should have taken his own advice and left a tender moment alone.

Standing to the side of the stage, I noticed that Billy had the same male-pattern baldness I did, and he was reading his lyrics and between-song banter off a monitor. My mind kept picturing Dylan, the raging panther. Billy Joel was an amazing musician serving the audience, while Dylan was painting on a canvas on stage in the city of Bugsy, Sinatra, Sammy, Dean and Elvis. I think those cats would have preferred Dylan's old-school presentation.

Two weeks after Vegas, I was thrilled to be back in Memphis, on the historic corner of Beale and Main for a pair of shows at the Orpheum Theatre on April 24 and 25, 2006. I could get lost on Beale Street for a decade or two. Just off Beale, there's a place called the Flying Sorcerer, where the waitresses are super-fine and the Paulaners are only two dollars a pint during Happy Hour. Oh, mama! I warmed up there before both shows.

This Orpheum Theatre is a luxurious red cushion with gold gilding. These were amazing times in majestic places. Destiny was knocking on my door, and I answered. Dylan was going to rip this joint, and I'd bear witness.

"Maggie's Farm" kicked the party off. The tight instrumental whistled like a steaming tea pot before it poured into my first "She Belongs to Me." It was a grotesque masterpiece—Dylan's vocals rumbled the ground on the final rhyme of each line—a powerful grunt reminiscent of Lurch from the *Addams Family*. Last year he created up-singing; now he was shifting his voice into an exaggerated lower register—down-singing. Zimmy's vocal shenanigans were as creative as they were humorous, although nothing could prepare me for the vocal inflections to come. When I rolled out of bed, I didn't realize I was going to see Pavarotti.

"Positively 4th Street" was the seventh song in the thick of an unforgettable evening. The instrumental prelude took its own sweet time developing. A voice grumbled, "You gotta a lot of nerve to say you are my friend," as if the man behind the organ was Rip Van Winkle awakening in the wiry frame of Bob Dylan. The crowd was giddy, and Bob was on a roll, but the song was sinking. Dylan reverted to more vocal chicanery—exaggerated up-singing and a constant shuffling of cadence. Just when I thought I could start singing along, Dylan would throw a knuckleball. Each line was more pleasing and hilarious than the previous. "Positively Fourth Street" teetered between sarcasm and ecstasy. The band playfully mimicked Dylan's outbursts during the jam. As great as the lyrics are, the presentation became bigger than the words. Instead of questioning the nerve of others, Dylan seemed to be poking fun at himself—the young man who had had the audacity to write this song in the first place.

"A Hard Rain's A-Gonna Fall" brought this exhilarating set to a boil. Dylan's scowling tone gave the tune a biblical feel, as if Bob was channeling prophecy. A teenage kid who looked like Kurt Cobain rocked out next to me during the encores.

Generation Y had seen the light. The youngster was talking like a hurricane, "Hey, man. I never heard Dylan before. This guy is way cool, man. I didn't know he rocked like that. I gotta go backstage and meet him. Yo, like I never heard him before. That man was great. He's awesome man—awesome! Whatta you think? Ah man! Do you think I can get backstage? I want to meet him."

I slapped him a high-five and said "Good luck." Beale, here I come.

It was getting harder and harder for me to put these concerts in perspective, but opening night in Memphis was up there with Giants Stadium '87, Beacon Theatre '89, MSG 2002, New Orleans 2003, and Rotterdam 2005. After all these years, something in the moonlight still hounds Bob Dylan.

A brain-busting hangover greeted me the following afternoon as I sailed the Mississippi River with a group of straight-laced tourists on the Riverboat Queen. Between the blown out speakers and the Captain's announcements, I wanted to puke and jump overboard.

"Chaachhh...testing, testing, one two...Ladies and gentleman... Welcome aboard the Riverboat Queen...Chaachhh...Many famous celebrities live in Memphis...Chaachhh Over there, the fourth house on the left is Cybill Shepherd's house...Chaachhh."

True sailing is dead.

Thankfully, I drowned out this clown on my Walkman with Captain Trips: "Mississippi River, deep and wide; Got a lovin' woman on the other side; No she's gone, gone, gone, I don't worry; because Im sitting on top of the world."

As we returned, Memphis was an awe-inspiring vision sitting on the banks of the Mississippi, frozen in time. It may have lost its luster the day Martin Luther King was assassinated, but it still looked like the Promised Land from a distance.

The second show at the Orpheum featured an even better song selection, although Dylan would have to reinvent Western music again to better his opening night performance. "Down Along the Cove," "Absolutely Sweet Marie," and "High Water," had me thinking about my afternoon sailing expedition with their river references. The inclusion of "Masters of War," "The Lonesome Death of Hattie Carroll," and "Blind Willie McTell" made the proceedings almost too good. Sometimes, when you get everything you want, it can leave you feeling flat. During both shows, the crowd in the orchestra danced and pitched a wang dang doodle all night long.

Dylan's new compositions shined besides his classics, and help was on the way. Before the start of this spring tour, Bob dropped by the Bardavon in Poughkeepsie to record a studio album with his traveling Cowboy Band, an old-timey collection that would be called *Modern Times*. Dylan was omnipresent in 2006, leaving an inspirational trail that was astounding for someone aged sixty-four. "Will you still need me when I'm sixty-four?" Yesssss.

Howard Stern and Bob Dylan attracted millions of baby boomers to satellite radio, Sirius and XM, respectively. Of course, I could cough up ten bucks a month for satellite radio when the programming featured *Theme Time Radio* with your host Bob Dylan—every week, same Bob time, same Bob channel. Dylan was the professor dishing out life lessons through short jingles, most of them from pre-Vietnam America, although any artist could arise during any episode. Critics loved the show. Dylan was witty and arcane—a DJ with a predilection for reciting poems.

I jumped into the radio fray, joining Limbaugh, Stern, and Dylan on the New York airwaves. It all crystallized like chain lightning. Through the WBAI Dew Board, I met Lance Neal, the host of the Morning Dew Radio show. He'd been hosting Dead-dominated radio on 99.5 FM since 1988. On a couple of occasions, I went down to the WBAI studio on Wall Street and played bits and pieces from my Grateful Dead archive. My live commentary was all right, but Lance was delighted with the bottle of pear brandy I brought to the studio. Anyway, I mentioned that I'd love to host a Dylan show, and Lance took me seriously. He put in the good word and told me call the program director.

I put together a proposal for a show called *Visions of Dylan*. From my Upper East Side music archive, I arranged a show featuring an eclectic mix of Dylan's studio works, his live recordings, and other artists' interpretations of Dylan's compositions. And here's the kicker—each episode would have a theme!

"This sounds fantastic, Howie," said Janet (WBAI director). "Could you put together a demo on CD? I like the idea of the show, and I like the sound of your voice."

Could I put together a demo? I told her I could, but I didn't know the first thing about recording demos. My resume in radio was a blank page—not even a spot on the college airwaves. But I was one step away from fulfilling a dream, reality be damned. I didn't have time to pay dues. The gig was mine for the taking. I left my meeting with Janet and went to Guitar World and purchased some rudimentary equipment for a home recording studio. The Guitar World guy suggested I purchase a software program called Cue Base. This was a complex little program, but I had an ally—Jim Kerr Jr.

A master of sound, Jim learned well from the old man. He rigged my equipment so I could cut a professional-sounding demo. Janet liked the CD I gave her. She suggested a few minor changes and asked me to make two one-hour segments that she hoped to play.

Visions of Dylan aired on the first Monday in August, only a few months after Dylan's debut as a radio host. The theme of my first episode was protest songs. I felt the WBAI listenership might be impressed with that. WBAI was a predominantly African American station with a radically liberal agenda. It wasn't the type of station where you would expect to hear Dylan or the Dead, but that's the beauty of public radio. To complete the loop of twisted fate, Dylan performed on WBAI for the Cynthia Gooding show back in 1962, and he later appeared on WBAI during the Bob Fass Show in 1966.

Here's one difference between *Theme Time Radio* and *Visions of Dylan*: Bob's shows were recorded on the road in a mobile studio; my shows were recorded in my studio apartment with my cats meowing in the background.

Over the course of a year, I produced nine two-hour episodes, each one taking about thirty hours of my spare time. Listening to my show on the radio in my apartment as it was broadcast live over New York airwaves was surreal. Somewhere, a truck driver on 95 South was fiddling with the FM dial, and he or she was digging Dylan. My best episodes were "Bringing It All Back Home," Dylan in the mid-'60s, "Nothing but the Blues," and "Dylan in Hollywood." My own radio show was something I'd never pursued or even imagined, but destiny appeared on my doorstep, again.

The legendary rock DJ and morning man, Jim Kerr, called me during my second show and said, "Hey, Catfish. I like you're show a lot. You sound great, and you're doing a great job." That was a gratifying phone call.

Two weeks after the debut of *Visions of Dylan*, I was out on the Dylan trail again. Frederick, Maryland, was the initial stop. I took a train from Penn Station to a hillbilly town in Maryland, the name of which slips me. A guy named Butch picked me up at the station. We only knew each other from corresponding on The Dew Board. He was 10ACJed, and I was 6-16-82 Catfish. Butch looked like the Philadelphia Flyer pugilist, Dave Schultz, and I looked like The Commish, actor Mike Chiklis. I had pictured Jed as a flower-carrying, long-haired pacifist. *Well, well, well; you can never tell.*

Frederick was the beginning of my third year as a witness to "The Bob Dylan Show" in Minor League ballparks. On this year's bill were the legendary guitarist Junior Brown and Stevie's brother, Jimmy Vaughn. In Frederick, Dylan stormed the stage in black garb, exuding a military presence. His band was dressed in gray. I wasn't sure if we were witnessing a concert or a Civil War re-enactment.

Dylan's performance lacked gusto, but the twenty-four hours with Butch and his lovely wife Amy were memorable. While Butch and I were inebriated, his tiny wife drove a black pickup truck through windy back roads in complete darkness like a champ. The roads from Frederick to Boonsboro were graveyards, hills and mountains that had been drenched with Civil War blood. Butch and Amy were wonderful hosts, extending me kindness based on the camaraderie of an Internet community which was spawned by the spirit of the Grateful Dead.

Sweet Jesus, I don't want to die today. Those words replayed in my mind as Butch drove me to the station the next morning. His mad-dog driving would have had Neal Cassady blushing. I considered ejecting myself from the passenger seat as we swerved through the backwoods of Maryland. My Civil War brothers, here I come! But Clutch Butch delivered me to the train station alive. My next stop was a Minor League park in Manchester, New Hampshire, where I would have a reunion with Mr. Phil Hyman.

I listened to a bootleg copy of *Modern Times* on the Amtrak to Manchester a week before its official release. The future was like the past; it was another Dylan masterpiece. In Manchester, I was staying at a hotel that was part of the Minor League ballpark. My room was just beyond the centerfield fence, a 500-foot poke from home plate. Phil arrived with his hometown friend, Rich Zuppan. Rich had a twin brother Dave, who, for some unfathomable reason was absent—that kid loves Dylan. We hunkered-down in my room and lounged around the lobby bar before venturing out into the lazy drizzle. I bought a poncho and dug in with my Bostonian friends. If it were a baseball game, they never would have come out of the dugout. It had been overcast and rainy all afternoon, and the forecast called for torrential rain.

A thousand die-hard Dylanheads had a sing-along with Bob during the second tune, "You Ain't Going Nowhere." If you didn't dig Dylan, you were on your way home or headed for the exit. The rest of us were in for an enchanted evening. Dylan slid into a playful "Just Like a Woman." The precipitation intensified as he yelled, "Nobody feels any pain tonight as I stand inside the rain." On August, 27, 2006, the Lord said, "Let it rain on that tiny ballpark in New Hampshire." And so it rained—a relentless downpour, similar to the ending of *Grapes of Wrath*.

Dylan loves the slop. He could have written the night off as a lost cause and shortened the show, saving his best tunes for another gig with a bigger crowd. However, Dylan felt a kinship with these New Englanders. Dylan performed as if he wanted to put on a poncho and serenade us from the pitcher's mound. It was a soggy fantasy camp.

Another plane took off from Manchester airport and sailed through the clouds, fifty feet above the stage. Dylan howled, "Where have you been, my blue-eyed son? Where have you been, my darling young one?" Phil, Rich and I moved closer to the stage. There may have been 1,000 fans left to hear "A Hard Rain's A-Gonna Fall." Standing in the pelting rain, we were invigorated. Sometimes a cigar is just a cigar, and sometimes "Hard Rain" is just hard rain.

"Highway 61 Revisited" left burn marks. "Tangled Up in Blue" was better than any version I'd heard since 1998. Almost every night we get "Like a Rolling Stone," but Bob was more deliberate with it on this night. Denny Freeman kicked out a great solo. The band was in no hurry to leave. They may never play in front of such loyalists again.

If you were Bob Dylan, how would you say goodnight? Dylan started off with his usual routine, taking bows with his ten-gallon hat in hand and his Cowboy Band stoically lined-up behind him. Suddenly, Dylan reached into his hat and grabbed a fistful of a mystery dust and soft-tossed it at the crowd, as if he was performing a baptism. I was snapping a picture on my camera as Dylan sprinkled the crowd with the powdery substance. Johnny Appleseed strikes again!

Dylan was ubiquitous. With the release of Modern Times backed by the announcement of a major tour, Dylan would keep me busy through the end of 2006. And with the overload of Dylan knowledge rattling around in my brain, I finally landed a paying gig.

THUNDER ON THE MOUNTAIN

*Dylan expert for hire...The Titanic on Broadway...The
upside of global warming...A cumbersome souvenir...
The Cowboy Band rumbles Portland...Breaking and
entering and napping...Boston turkey sausage...*

I found myself in the thick of a new Dylan project coming to the theatre district. Twyla Tharp, who had success bringing Billy Joel's music to Broadway with *Movin' Out*, had now created a musical based on Dylan's songs. Ready or not, *The Times They Are A-Changin'* was a-comin' to Brooks Atkinson Theatre. Through another twist of Internet fate, I was hired as a Dylan expert to entertain guests at the opening night party in the Roseland Ballroom.

My friends from the Morning Dew Board alerted me to this opportunity, which appeared on Craigslist. One of my brothers posted: "Catfish. Somebody's looking to hire a Dylan expert; the gig pays $300." That night I emailed my credentials to the anonymous employer. The following morning, I emailed a more sober reply.

John Henry from Maker's Mark informed me that I was in the running for the Dylan expert, and he asked me to meet him for an interview. Being that John Henry was a hard-working executive from a liquor company, I was a shoe-in. I'm confident and collected during job interviews. I may not be the ideal employee, but I can play the role for fifteen minutes.

The opening night party for *The Times They Are A-Changin'* had a carnival theme. I was the barker who challenged people to stump me on Dylan trivia. For the occasion I dressed in a black outfit with a matching cowboy hat. In preparation for my performance, I actually spent a few days cramming more Dylan trivia into my overloaded brain. I was stumped once or twice, but mostly people asked, "Where's Bob tonight?" Bob was on the road heading for another joint.

One gentleman, who resembled Eric Clapton, asked me, "Which guitar player played the most shows for Dylan in the 1990s?

I answered, "That would be you, old sport. J.J. Jackson."

J.J. was also the guitarist and musical director of *The Times They Are A-Changin'*. I rapped with J.J. for a while. He was excited about this gig. John Henry gave me a pair of tickets to see one of the rehearsals, and this was my review which was published in *Isis*, a Dylan fanzine:

PLEASE MRS. THARP

When the Titanic set sail from Southampton, the luxurious ship was stocked with the finest food and drink, a hopping band, and some of the most intriguing people of the day. Unfortunately, all anyone remembers is that damn iceberg. There were a lot of things to admire about Twyla Tharp's Broadway musical *The Times They Are A-Changin'*, but thanks to a hideous plot, this production will sink like a stone.

Here's how the playbill describes this story that exists in a dreamscape of a struggling circus:

"Captain Ahrab is a tyrannical leader crippled by greed. Coyote sees the faults of his father and wants his life and everyone else's to change. Cleo has found shelter at the circus and is trying to survive. She sees Ahrab's greed and doesn't like it, but does not know otherwise. The clowns want to live their lives. Like children, they know that they need direction but are getting tired of Ahrab's rules.

A tale of fathers and sons, of men and women, of leaders and followers, of immobility and change, The Times They Are A-Changin' uses prophecy, parable, metaphor, accusation and confession- like the Dylan songs which comprise it- to confront us with images and ideas of who we are and who it is possible to be."

I know what you're thinking that description wouldn't excite me either, but it was more tedious than that. During "Man Gave Names to All the Animals," the actors sluggishly pranced around the stage in bear and sheep costumes. All I needed was a glass of milk and some choco-late-chip cookies to feel like I was at a kindergarten play. Classics like "Masters of War" and "Blowin' in the Wind" were forced into this pro-duction, even though their inclusion made no sense. With a few excep-tions, the audience was fed a steady diet of Dylan's greatest hits. Tharp's song selections were insipid. She squandered a golden opportunity to create something inspirational.

All the other pieces seemed to be in place for a triumphant musi-cal. The performances and song arrangements were better than I had expected. A five-piece band that sounded like they could back Dylan on tour performed on an elevated platform at balcony level. When they charged into a rocking version of "Everything Is Broken," I took a long look at the guitarist, and sure enough, it was John "J.J." Jackson, Dylan's lead guitarist from 1991-1997. Our old friend Mr. Jackson was in fine form all night. Jackson's contributions gave the show a Never Ending Tour meets Broadway feel. It was a nice touch.

The three leading cast members all delivered admirable vocal inter-pretations of Dylan's works. Lisa Brescia's singing was explosive all night. Her operatic voice shined on "Everything Is Broken" and "I Believe in You." Tom Sesma (Captain Ahrab) turned in several Dylanesque performances, including a reflective "Simple Twist of Fate." The most obscure number of the night was a lackluster offering of "Please Mrs. Henry." Other selections that didn't fall into the greatest hits designation included "On a Night Like This" and "Not Dark Yet."

Despite the lame fable that was presented at the Brooks Atkinson Theatre, I was entertained by the music, choreography, and lighting. If you're fond of Dylan's music, *The Times They Are A-Changin'* is a pleasant night out. Just don't expect to be intellectually stimulated. The circus is in town, but it won't be for long.

After a two-week run, the cast was informed that the show was canceled, effective immediately. I remember that day because the following day, I was bobbing for Dylan at the Cumberland County Civic Center in Portland, Maine.

On the morning of November 9, 2006, I rolled out of bed with the roosters, stuffed a backpack, put on a Sly & the Family t-shirt, and headed for the subway—a salmon swimming against the stream of normalcy. As everyday commuters made their way to work, I was working my way to Maine for a lobster dinner and a date with Dylan. My heart was pounding like the jack-hammers in the distance. Cabbies honked, truckers grinded gears, and buses sputtered along Second Avenue—a municipal symphony. The fantastic weather was also man-made. Thanks to global warming, it was already seventy degrees. The destruction of our environment and ecosystems is a horrific global event, but it's hard be angry with a summer's day in November.

The Acela express to Boston is heaven in motion—clean, comfortable cars with electricity to recharge your electronic devices as you watch the countryside blur by. I enjoyed lunch in Boston before bussing to Portland. I drifted in and out of dreamless sleep and listened to a CD that had a mixed bag of Beatles outtakes, everything from "She's a Woman" to "Yer Blues." "I feel so suicidal, just like Dylan's Mr. Jones."

It had to be to eighty degrees when I hopped off the bus in Portland. I was on a tight schedule, kind of like Henry Hill in *Goodfellas*. I went down to the Cumberland County Civic Center and checked my backpack into the Holiday Inn across the street. I didn't have a reservation at the hotel, but that was no reason not to indulge in their guest services. I was an old friend. I'd given them my business twenty-one years earlier when I saw the Grateful Dead on the "I quit smoking cigarettes tour." I was still tobacco-free and still marching to the beat of my crazy rock-and-roll dreams. I socked down a few cocktails in the lounge and made a few karaoke-related phone calls to my employees.

"Matt, I got your message. I heard you had some issues at Brother Jimmy's last night," I said.

"Catfish. Yo, man, hate to bother you with this. I know you're seeing Dylan tonight, but people wanted to kill me last night. Livin' on a Prayer skipped every time I played it," said Matt.

"Hang in there, my son." I said. "Take a napkin, put some vodka on it, and clean the disc."

"Cat, that didn't work," said Matt.

"Balls," said I. "Hang in there. I'll get you a new disc when I get back. Shabbat Shalom."

I found a place down by the waterfront docks called Dimillo's. I sensed that they served a mean lobster, so I went inside and strapped a bib around my neck. I don't drown my lobster in butter; I just spritz some lemon juice on it, and I'm ready to roll. I crave the rubbery texture of the lobster meat as it grinds between my teeth and unleashes a delicate oceanic spray upon my taste buds. I savor the process of fussing, fighting, and struggling with the main body of the lobster. I avoid the green goop in the middle, saving the lobster tail for last, reveling in that final rush of boiled crustacean.

Shipyard beers were only $3.21, and I met a terrific trio of business ladies who were treating me kindly, but I had to go. I missed the opening band, The Raconteurs. Oh rats. I would hear their racket on four other nights before Dylan on this tour. I was super-pumped for this show; it was my first opportunity to experience *Modern Times* live. Dylan's new album debuted at Number One on the Billboard Charts, a strong showing forty years after *Blonde on Blonde*.

Inspired by the thunderous rock of The Raconteurs, Dylan opened up a can of whoop-ass on Portland with "Cat's in the Well." I was touched, and a bit saddened, by the song. I had to put my oldest and most beloved cat to sleep at the end of the tour. I actually had to choose the date of her death, 11-21-06—one day after Dylan's tour was completed. Shagville, my furry companion, had enjoyed sixteen years of living in various apartments with me.

"I'm going back to New York City; I do believe I had enough," sang Dylan. It was the end of the second song, and with those words, I went to visit the young lady serving beers in front of the Coors Light banner that I coveted. That great souvenir might end up in a trash can if I didn't save it. She told me to return after the second song when beer sales were eighty-sixed. This banner was ambitious. Simultaneously, it welcomed Bob Dylan to Portland, and it explained the rules and procedures for purchasing beer.

The young lady rolled up my souvenir and said, "A few people asked me if they could have this, but I saved it for you. I had a feeling you'd be back."

I slipped her a twenty, which she kindly tried to refuse, and I returned to a seat by the side of the stage. It was a general admission hoedown—the floor of this hockey rink was packed. I was close to the back of Dylan's cowboy hat, and my ear drums were pounded by the sound. Dylan's voice rocketed straight into my brain, "You come to my eyes like a vision from the skies, and I'll be with you when the deal goes down." My first taste of *Modern Times* was sweet. Denny Freeman's jazzy guitar licks intensified the poignancy of this ballad. "When the Deal Goes Down" is the type of song Jerry Garcia would have loved to cover. Captain Trips would have brought this to a boil after letting it simmer and stew for fifteen minutes.

"Desolation Row" appeared towards the end of the stellar set. "They're selling post cards of the hanging," came from Dylan raw against the ringtones of his organ. The band kicked in on the second verse—the perfect texture for Dylan's voice. Each verse became more exciting than the last, a huge credit to the band's sensibility. Donnie Herron played cat and mouse with Denny Freeman. They chased each other around with licks that were reflective of Dylan's cadence. During instrumentals, Dylan tastefully added his organ licks into the collage. The unique improvisation accented the epic lyrics, and Dylan's rugged voice boomed—a masterpiece anew.

The GA floor swarmed like a massive mosh pit to a savage "Highway 61 Revisited." I had a great view of the scene as I stood there with my rolled-up poster, getting pummeled by the powerful sound system. With Dylan's haunting organ tones opening the path, his mates played this longer and louder than I'd ever heard it.

I was moved to tears when Dylan busted into "Thunder on the Mountain," the first encore. The spectacular opening riff of *Modern Times* sounded even thicker live. Dylan was off chasing Alicia Keyes through Tennessee, rounding up tough sons of bitches from the orphanages, and sucking the milk out of a 1,000 cows. "Thunder on the Mountain" was teamed with "Like a Rolling Stone" and "All Along the Watchtower." What a lethal triplet!

Cumberland County Civic Center, Portland, Maine

November 9, 2006

1. Cat's in the Well
2. Just Like Tom Thumb's Blues
3. Stuck Inside of Mobile with the Memphis Blues Again
4. High Water
5. Tangled Up in Blue
6. When the Deal Goes Down
7. It's Alright Ma (I'm Only Bleeding)
8. Watching the River Flow
9. Most Likely You Go Your Way (And I'll Go Mine)
10. Desolation Row
11. Highway 61 Revisited
12. Spirit on the Water
13. Summer Days
    (encore)
14. Thunder on the Mountain
15. Like a Rolling Stone
16. All Along the Watchtower

It was still Indian summer when we gyrated out of the arena. The crowd was exceptional—younger and rowdier than what Dylan usually draws. I penned my concert review in the Holiday Inn lobby and closed the bar. I had five hours to kill in Portland before catching my bus at 6:30 AM, and the town was shut down except for Denny's. I went there, drank java and ordered food which turned out to be inedible. With four hours to kill, I grabbed my overstuffed backpack and coiled banner and strutted into the Portland night singing *Modern Times*. When I left Manhattan, I could swear that the backpack weighed twenty pound less, but I staggered forward, propelled by the songs in my mind.

The lights were out, and the doors were locked at the bus station. Portland really shuts down after the midnight hour; there was just me and the imposter cook over at Denny's. The booze was wearing off. I wished I was tucked into a bed at the Holiday Inn. Instead, I was lugging a knapsack of lead and a telephone pole-sized banner around. With four more shows to go on this tour, not splurging on a hotel was part of my economic plan. I can't recall if the door was open, or if I picked a lock, but I found my way inside the bus station and landed on a cushioned seat. I closed my eyes and dozed off at a 90-degree angle until an agitated security guard found me at 5:30 AM.

The guard said, "Who are you, and how the hell did you get in here?"

These were fair questions. I told him the truth as I saw it. Luckily, I look like a detective. My behavior was most peculiar for a forty-three year-old man.

Now came the seven-hour journey home. There were two parts left to my quest: 1) I had to continue to protect that Dylan banner and get it on to my apartment wall in mint condition; 2) I had to feed my growling stomach, which had been neglected since my lobster feast. There was a place I vaguely remembered—a second-floor cafeteria in Boston that had a great breakfast buffet. On the ride from Portland to Boston, I craved that buffet—the fluffy pancakes, lightly fried hash browns, and the finest turkey sausage anywhere. Thanks to some kind of primitive animal instinct, I found that breakfast joint. The turkey sausage was more succulent than I had remembered.

Dylan and his Cowboy Band stand proud. Another job well done.
11-18-06 Philadelphia

SING ME BACK HOME

Seriously Discussing Dylan...The Time Out Of Mind Combo Platter...The pit and the palace... Rebel Mecca...Historic Homes of Hibbing...The Money Doesn't Talk, It Swears Exhibition...

In 2006, I'd done just about everything Dylan-related except visit his hometown.

Hibbing, here I come! I decided to attend the first Dylan Symposium at the University of Minnesota in March of 2007. Prior to the symposium, speakers and guests were invited to take a bus trip to Hibbing. It was a chance to stand inside Bob's shoes and actually experience the fabled town of his youth. This intrigued me. I didn't know anybody who had ever been to Hibbing. And, while I was in Minneapolis, I could visit Dinkytown, that magical vortex where Robert Allen Zimmerman disappeared and Bob Dylan emerged. The symposium consisted of three days of professors delivering papers on Dylan, but I only stayed for one day. That was about all the academic rag-a-ma-tag I could endure.

Lining up for the bus to Hibbing, I spotted Robert Polito from The New School. I had no idea that he was making this trip, or that he would be presenting a paper at the symposium. Robert's a few years older than me, and he looks a cross between Robin Williams and Michael Douglas. We had an engaging chat on the state of Dylan affairs before boarding the bus with forty other geniuses. Hibbing is way out there through the sticks and flatlands of Minnesota—mining and lumberjack country.

Polito was jotting down notes in his journal in the row in front of me. In between jotting down notes in my own black leather journal, I was shooting spitballs at the kids up front. Michael Grey, author of over a thousand brilliant pages on Dylan, was amongst us somewhere. Coleen Sheehy was the bus monitor and one of key organizers of the symposium. She was a kind woman who kept us occupied with Dylan DVDs and a few episodes of Theme Time Radio.

Global warming had been hounding me since Hurricane Katrina. It was unseasonably warm in Amsterdam and Portland, but it was 70 degrees when I arrived in Hibbing on March 24, 2007. That's flat out preposterous. Hibbing locals were telling me that it was twenty below zero just a month earlier. Our first stop was on Howard Street at a joint called Zimmy's.

In addition to local favorites like Porketta and Ribbon Sandwiches, Zimmy's lunch buffet menu had "Highway 61 Revisited" Pizza and the *Time Out Of Mind* Combo Appetizer. If you had a sweet tooth, you might get a rush out of Beatty Zimmerman's Banana Chocolate Loaf Bread, or Beatty's Fudge Bars.

If I were the chef at Zimmy's, I would have given that menu an overhaul: Ballad of a Thin Man Salad…Romance in Durango Clam Chowder…Gotta Serve Somebody Pot Pie…I Shall Be Free-Range Chicken…Freewheelin' Fajitas…Union Sundown Scallops…Tough Mama Meatball Parmesan…Bye and Bye Buffalo Wings…Handy Dandy Lamb Chops.

Abe Zimmerman's old house was only a few blocks from Zimmy's. Hibbing was a quaint town, frozen in time, appearing to be little more than what it was when it came of age at the dawn of the Twentieth Century. If one didn't attempt to flee, a lifetime could swiftly pass by in Hibbing. Bob's childhood home was a light blue house on the corner with a two-step stoop, cramped yard, and short driveway. The current owner, Craig, purchased the house for market value in the '80s. At the time, he wasn't much of a Dylan fan; he was just looking for a home. Things have changed. The music has infiltrated his mind. Craig commissioned an artist to paint the cover of *Blood on the Tracks* on his garage door.

The gracious owner of the old Zimmerman residence let us roam through the modest house in small groups. The ceilings were low, and the ghosts were on vacation. There wasn't much to ponder or feel, but I tried. Standing in Bob's bedroom, I imagined him listening to radio stations from the South. I recalled the tight living quarters from my past on Walton Avenue and Nassau Road in the Bronx and Yonkers, respectively. Beyond the constricting walls of our childhoods, people were digging ponies and drifting too far from shore. The road was inevitable for the two of us.

Our distinguished tour group bused over to old Hibbing, which was now the largest man-made pit in the world. The original town of Hibbing, houses and all, was literally moved to get at the iron ore treasures below. The pit appears endless, as wide as an ocean with nothing but clouds, sun, and sky on the other side. This vast pit helped fuel American triumphs in two World Wars. The mining companies who profited from the pit financed Hibbing High School, a reward for the uprooted community.

Hibbing High is a colossal structure—an architectural monument to education that cost the mining companies $4,000,000 to build in 1920s currency. Instinctively, the sight of a high school stirs negative associations in my brain; however, this building had charisma and the welcoming atmosphere of a historic palace or an ancient cathedral. The school was built in the heart of the community, not as an isolated complex. I was beginning to understand how Dylan had emerged from this town in the middle of nowhere. That pit and that school made Hibbing unlike any other small town in America. Even if you're not drawn there by Dylan, this small town's worth the visit.

Clarkstown Public Schools, my prison, was supposedly a sought after educational district. But, every step of the way, the buildings were cold, institutionalized. Hibbing High was a different beast; it wasn't a system, it was a place of learning. From the gold trimming, to the ornate interior molding, to the hand-painted murals on the walls, the building exceeded the needs of its students. It must be a privilege to teach there.

Additionally, the Beacon Theater was hidden in Hibbing High. The auditorium was magnificent—a place where Dylan undoubtedly performed in his fantasies. He actually made his rock and roll debut on piano on that stage during a school talent show. Bobby Zimmerman's dog and pony show was ahead of its time. Unfortunately, the students didn't care for his ruckus, and he was gonged by the principal. Everybody must get stoned. But people noticed. Either they liked his heart and soul, or they booed and hissed. Ain't it just like a Dylan?

My high school auditorium was a colorless room with a giant American flag hanging off a slanted pole to the right of the stage. It wasn't the type of platform that inspired artistic fantasies. If you imagine blasting a homer in the World Series, you'll be rounding the bases in Fenway, Wrigley, or the Ball Orchard in the Bronx. Hibbing High auditorium gave me chills. Our tour group stood in the orchestra in reverence. Bob Dylan emerging from Hibbing wasn't a myth anymore; like photosynthesis, it kind of made sense.

I never would have traded Hibbing for Nanuet. The hub of my hometown was the Nanuet Mall—a place where there was always something going on. Tapesville U.S.A. and Nathan's Famous stood proudly in front of the mall on Route 59. You couldn't ask for a more enticing suburban enclave in the '70s.

The shopping arcades surrounding the Nanuet Mall attracted teenagers, especially those with a rebellious streak. On Middletown Road, by the mall's side entrance, there was a stamp and coin store and a head shop side by side. Cash in your Presidential Series stamps and buy a two-foot U.S. bong, or pick up some roach-wired rolling papers with your loose change. Moving closer to the mall, there was a create-your-own t-shirt shop. This is where I got my first cool jean jacket—the one with the Grateful Dead skull on back.

Nanuet was an idyllic place with a cozy balance of commerce, technology, and nature. I was in no rush to escape. On the other hand, I couldn't imagine wanting to stay in a place like Hibbing. Once the iron ore was gone, Hibbing stopped in its tracks—a town past its prime with no reason or rhyme.

The next stop on our Magic Bus Tour brought us to the outskirts of Hibbing. Our guide said, "Now we're going to Echo's house." Everybody knew we were headed to the childhood home of Bob's first love, Echo Helstrom. He referred to Echo nonchalantly as if she was part of our family. I thought, *Why in the world are we going to Echo's?* It seemed a bit extreme as the bus rolled up in front of the Helstrom homestead. I half expected somebody to come out the house firing at us with a sawed-off shotgun. We just sat on the bus and looked at this house as if it would unlock the mystery of Bob Dylan. It didn't. I must confess that these candid observations are coming from a guy who purchased a pillow with Bob Dylan photos stitched on it while I was at Zimmy's. Honestly, I don't sleep on the thing; it's strictly memorabilia.

This day trip through Dylan's past ended up at Zimmy's. I found myself at a mini round table enjoying cocktails with the owners of Zimmy's, Ed and Linda, Craig, the owner of Dylan's house, and the webmaster of Boblinks.com, Bill Pagel, a Hibbing resident. I napped on the bus ride back, wishing we had spent the night in Hibbing.

Day one of the Dylan Symposium featured performances by renowned rock historian Greil Marcus and Beat poet, Anne Waldman. Greil was holier than usual, delivering a sermon linking "Ain't Talkin'" to Hibbing High. Greil could convince you of anything using his circular academic logic. With a cunning mix of scholarly authority and personal passion, he could convince you that the "Purina Cat Chow Theme" was a watershed moment for American culture.

After several papers and lectures on Dylan, I was glad I was splitting Minneapolis early, although I'd have liked to have seen Polito present his paper on day two. As Dylan sings in "Nettie Moore," "The world of research has gone berserk; too much paper work." Yet, it remained an undeniable fact: Dylan had made such an enormous impact on all our lives. We had to bask in it and try to explain it.

The traveling exhibition, *Bob Dylan's American Journey, 1956-1966,* was on view at the Weisman Art Museum on campus. I had seen this exhibition in Manhattan and was equally bored on that occasion. Museum exhibitions are dead meat unless there's a historical twist to the host building. The Stax Museum in Memphis works because that's where its music was born. The soul is alive in its natural habitat.

Across from the traveling exhibition, there was a mass book signing. The finest Dylan authors ever were assembled in one room, signing and selling their works. This was the "Money doesn't talk, it swears" exhibition. However, this was much more than a capitalistic or hedonistic romp in Minnesota for anyone in attendance. We all revered Dylan's music, and most of us were struggling and striving to paint our own masterpieces. If, somehow, a kid from Hibbing could make us feel more alive and connected to the world, this needed to be researched, discussed, and debated.

Once the captain turned off the "fasten your seat belt' signs, I turned on *Modern Times.* As we blazed through the sky, and I heard the dynamic prelude of "Thunder on the Mountain," I was in my element—music and motion.

Thunder on the mountain, fire on the moon; There's a ruckus in the alley, and the sun will be here soon; Today's the day I'm gonna grab my trombone and blow. There's hot stuff here, and it's everywhere I go.

An urge to bolt of my seat and dance a jig in the aisle seized me. The pleasure of spontaneously blowing one's trombone was an idea that I'd been chasing since 9-11. I was readying myself for a challenge I never saw coming. My future was a thing I'd skipped from the past.

That's me posing in front of the garage of Dylan's childhood home in Hibbing. The current owner had *Blood on the Tracks* painted on the door.

BORN IN TIME

Good Morning Little School Girl...Getting Jiggy Wit
It at the Mohegan Sun...On our way to Woodstock...
VIP Seating...Nobody messes with Catfish in Dylan's
House...Blind Willie Mc Tell in the Mystic Garden...
Sucking the milk out of 1,000 cows in Montreal...

There she was by the chalkboard—jade blouse, beige skirt, fair skin, divine legs—a brunette with the bluest eyes. Good morning, little schoolgirl. Looking like Andie Mc Dowell in *Groundhog Day*, she was the first to arrive. Let me talk to her, get to know her, before the rest of the swine arrive. *You sly son-of-a-bitch.* These were the rewards for going back to college at the age of forty-three.

I said, "Hi. Am I in the right place? Are you here for American Literature in Music 101?"

"You're in the right room. I'm you're teacher, Lauren. And you are?"

That's a good question. Who was I? Catfish, Howard, Howie, but, whoa, I never had a hot teacher before, and what a class!

The opening paragraph of the course description read:

> Was Elvis the King of Rock 'n' Roll, or as Alice Walker suggests in "1955," a native white teenager who made a fortune off of singing African-American music? Did Robert Johnson

sell his soul to the devil, or is the legend just a clever marketing ploy? Why was *On the Road* a "sacred text" for followers of the Grateful Dead?

Answers
1. Elvis is King
2. Yes to both parts.
3. *On the Road* was not a sacred text to Deadheads. Although we lived like the Beats, I never heard anyone mention Kerouac's name during the decade I was on the road. *On the Road* influenced the Grateful Dead and the Merry Pranksters, therefore making Deadheads Kerouac's grandchildren—grandchildren he would have disowned and cut out of his will.

Our curriculum included viewing the *Monterey Pop Festival* and *The Grateful Dead Movie*. If you're thinking this was an easy class, you're way wrong. There was a lot of required reading and writing, and Lauren graded us like we were Ivy Leaguers. She was an amazing teacher with a passion for the mechanics of writing. At any previous juncture of my life I would have dropped out of this class, or passively taken a failing grade by never showing up. I never had the impetus to produce a quality paper on a weekly basis—until now.

After researching my shabby academic past, I discovered I'd amassed eighty-four credits over ten years. I was thirty-six credits away from a Liberal Arts degree and a diploma that had little meaning to me. I was back in college to pursue an MFA in creative writing at The New School. Rationality is a horse I'd abandoned long ago. If I ever would have realized how tough it is to get into that program, especially with my academic pedigree, I would have forsaken that fantasy in its infancy.

I decided to wipe out twelve of those credits in one summer semester. When I told my academic advisor, Joe Salvatore, that I wanted to take twelve credits over the summer, he thought it might be wise if I took a lighter load. Joe said, "Four classes are three more than most people take over the summer."

But I'd been a slacker for too long. It was time to let my trombone blow.

My school surplus didn't interfere with Dylan pursuits. I started the 2007 summer tour off with a pair of shows at The Borgata. I hopped an Atlantic City casino bus, 100 feet from my Upper East Side apartment, which was now on 84th Street. The round trip was twenty-five bucks, and that included a free buffet comp at one of those eat-'til-you-pass-out joints. The food wasn't bad, but I got nauseous observing all the hefty people gulping down piles of slop. Fatlantic City has lost its charm. It's a Monopoly Board of lost souls flushing their dreams into the ocean.

Atlantic City did hold some sentimental value for me. After my parents married when I was eight, we took our family honeymoon on The Boardwalk. My mom was very pregnant with my brother Michael or my sister Michelle. On our first morning there, my Dad rented us bicycles. Under overcast skies, we pedaled side by side, rubber on plank, until The Boardwalk ended. The ride back was sad; we had to return the bikes. Dad cheered me up with salt water taffy. This reminded me of the cherry knishes that my father used to buy for me on the Boardwalk of Far Rockaway Beach. Dad and Grandma owned a ratty bungalow out there. Those fried knishes, packed with cherry and cheese make up the entirety of my positive memories from Far Rockaway. There was no music in the bungalow. My father's records were waiting for me in the Bronx.

The Borgata Casino Hotel & Spa was a couple of miles from The Boardwalk, cut-off from the schwag of Atlantic City. This chic resort employed voluptuous waitresses serving cocktails in low-cut designer dresses. The Borgata was bright and smoky, but it was a classy joint, in a Frank Sinatra Hoboken kind of way. I was slumming at a hotel on The Boardwalk, but I felt like ten-thousand bucks inside The Borgata.

A little weathered from five decades of performing, Dylan had to work the rust off on opening night at The Borgata. The following night,

6-23-07, he was firing on all cylinders. The women were swooning during "It Ain't Me Babe." Dylan was bustling with ideas; his creativity took on a physical dimension as he swiveled his hips and kicked his legs while chopping and slashing behind his organ. Welcome to the Performance Zone. The "Nettie Moore" from that night exceeded the mystical album version. Bob had the perfect rhythm, in time with the audience's heartbeat: "Lost John sitting on the railroad track…something's out of whack…."

What a great way to start—a solitary figure at the crossroads. "Nettie Moore" was instantly my favorite song from *Modern Times*. As Dylan continued to serenade the Borgata, it sounded autobiographical: "Travel the world; that's what I'm gonna do…I'm the oldest son of a crazy man, I'm in a cowboy band."

Dylan's perfectly pitched vocals peaked. "They say whiskey will kill you, but I don't think it will…I'm riding with you to the top of the hill." Intense inflection accompanied the second half of that phrase. *I'm staying with you all the way, babe*—ultimate loyalty. Crowds often roar to the first half of that line; slugging whiskey is a popular pastime. A copy of the 6-23-07 "Nettie Moore" is worth seeking out.

Over the next three days, I typed reviews for my blog, penned papers for four classes, finished recording a new episode of *Visions of Dylan* radio, and hosted a few karaoke nights in the city. Then I was off for another rendezvous with Mr. Phil Hyman at the Mohegan Sun—martinis and beer from dusk to dawn. Dylan's performance was solid, but nothing sparkled. After the show, Phil and I cleaned up to the tune of about $500 a piece at the blackjack tables. I'm rational when I take the gambling plunge. If I'm up $500, I pocket it and say, "Thank you; goodnight."

We stayed at a cheap hotel in Uncasville and continued drinking and listening to iTunes in my room. Then there was a wakeup call from the front desk. Will Smith was "Getting Jiggy Wit It" real loud. I was fully clothed and still fully inebriated. How did I sleep with that racket going all night? iTunes gone wild. At some point, Phil must have stumbled back to his room. The bus ride back to Manhattan was an excursion of pain—the severity of my headache intensified with every mile.

A few containers of Chinese cuisine revitalized me for the next gig at Robert Moses' playground, Jones Beach. The set list was all right, but an old nemesis was haunting me: too many shows. As I'd grown older, I've been able to tame my inner-critic, but not entirely. I always bring great expectations to Dylan shows—expectations that he'll find a new way to arrange his set, or play those rarities I crave, or just be flat-out awe-inspiring like he was the second night at The Borgata.

The morning after Jones Beach, I rode a Trailways bus to my old school, SUNY-New Paltz, where I met King and Blaise. King drove us through the snaky back roads of Sullivan County in his Volvo. Destination: Bethel Woods, site of the Original Woodstock Festival, the festival that Dylan avoided back in 1969 as if it were a gathering of the criminally insane. Old Yasgur's Farm was transformed into a state-of-the-art amphitheatre, and Dylan agreed to be part of the summer line-up christening the Bethel Woods Center for the Performing Arts in 2007.

On our way to Bethel Woods, King noticed a scenic reservoir and pulled off to the side of the road to spark a spliff. We stepped out the car and basked in the buzz of a lovely day that only the Lord can make. Our next pit stop was for beers at a grocery shack down the road, but that didn't work out. We were in a dreaded dry town. What gives any local municipality the right to repeal the repealing of the Prohibition Amendment?

Anyway, we scored six-packs on our way to Bethel and met up with King's sister, Mary, and their mother Joanne in the parking lot. King opened the back hatch of the Volvo, and everybody shuffled around and sang *Modern Times* with Dylan. On top of the music, I heard a familiar voice calling.

"Hey ah, Howie baby. What are you doing here?" said Stan the Man, behind the wheel of his Lexus with his wife by his side. "Keep the tunes cranking. Let me park this thing. Me and Betty will be here soon." Stan's laughter tailed off as he rolled down the dirt path."

Thanks to some well-timed strokes on my computer keyboard on the morning of the bobdylan.com presale, I landed a second row ticket, dead center, for Dylan's return to Bethel Woods. Dylan was already locked into a "Leopard Skin Pillbox" opener as I strutted down the aisle.

What a wonderful feeling it is to prance up to the second row knowing you belong. You're a VIP, nobody's getting in your way. Tonight's the night! Yes, You know it's special because Dylan's at Woodstock, but like an animal that can sense an impending earthquake, your sixth sense tells you that you're about to experience something more thrilling than rock history. Your body tenses and your blood begins to boil. The performance you've been dreaming of is at hand. This premonition is scary; you have the instincts of a wild beast, yet you're brain is churning, and your soul is yearning. You want to freeze time, you live for this crazed state of anticipation. But as time marches forward, you'll get everything you came for, and you'll leave with precious memories that fade. The ticket has been ripped. It's time to ride.

A floating gypsy in a white dress and flowers in her hair had the seat next to mine. Upon my arrival, she said, "I hope you're a dancer; please don't sit down."

"No chance," I said, as if I could twist like John Travolta in his prime.

"Awesome," she said. "All these uptight people behind me are yelling at me to sit down. One of them even threw a cup at me."

Apparently, there were some lowlifes behind us.

Dylan was now snarling "The Times They Are A-Changin'." Bob's face was wrinkled, and his eyes were almost completely shut. Dylan appeared stiff, almost in pain, as he played electric guitar for the first four songs, but when he moved to the organ, rejuvenation surged through his lean body. My situation was complex. I was two rows from my muse, yet my mind was partially on the cretins behind me. I heard them smattering and snickering, "Oh no. He's standing too…oh, the bald guy must belong to the same cult…Come on, you, we want to see…Hey man, sit down." I was backed into a corner. There was no way I'd abandon my little gypsy girl. I had to take a stand. I'm a hippie at heart, but I look like a Westie. Nobody pushes Howard "Catfish" Weiner around at a Dylan concert.

One of the infidels behind me tapped me on the arm and asked me to sit down. I scoffed at the suggestion. I almost settled into the show, but the same clown put his paw on my shoulder again and handed me a Post-It. He said, "That guy over there wanted me to give this to you. I agree."

The yellow Post-It yelled: "SIT DOWN!"

I don't have a violent bone in my body, but I paid $125 for this seat. This fiasco would end now.

I eyed the guy who handed it me the Post-It and said, "With all due respect, don't even think about touching me again." I then fixed a deadly stare upon the author of the note and put the Post-It in my back pocket. My lips widened into a fearless smile, and I laughed a demented laugh, like Robert DeNiro at the end of *Cape Fear*.

Mission accomplished.

By the way, who brings Post-Its to a rock-and-roll concert?

I understood that the folks behind me were crabby, cranky and old. Hell, I was part of their peer group, but for the love of God, we were in Bethel with Dylan! This wasn't the *Vagina Monologues*. Dylan's organization releases choice seating to fans so that there are lively bodies up front. Most of the fans beyond the tenth row were reelin' and rockin' and a-carryin' on. As Dylan popped the cork on "When the Levee Breaks," I fixated on the inspiration unfolding before me.

Donny Herron strummed a wicked banjo during "High Water." As the smoke cleared from the blues stomp, Herron still had his banjo in hand. This was a positive omen. Herron only played banjo on a few songs, and one of those tunes was my desire, "Blind Willie McTell." The silence screamed, "Blind Willie McTell." Fortunately, I was tuned into the same blues station as Dylan.

The Cowboy Band thundered into "Blind Willie McTell." I was airborne, leaping again and again, like Michael Jordan on horse tranquilizers. I pumped my fists into the air. I was the maestro leading the band to the Promised Land. Dylan may have ducked Woodstock in 1969, but he had the right stuff in 2007. Dylan now had twice the song arsenal at his command, and his band had IT going on. Freeman, Kimball, and Herron executed exquisite tag team instrumentals, as if they were schooled in the Miles Davis quartet.

The Bob Dylan eye logo banner came down from the heavens when the band rolled out the first encore, "Thunder on the Mountain." Dylan's vocal phrasing was consistently and deliberately off-step, creating a thick groove that triggered explosive jams. Before closing with "All Along the Watchtower," Dylan said,

"It's nice to be back here. Last time we played here we began to play at six in the morning. And it was a-raining, and the field was full of mud."

Obviously, Dylan hadn't played at Bethel Woods in '69, or any time since. Our hero was either going bomkers, or he was invoking the spirit of Jimi Hendrix who had played out in these muddy fields at 6 AM.

As I filed out with the crowd, the winds howled and a cold rain began to fall. Somehow, I didn't get soaked. The rain drops were so thick I could almost walk in between them—more magic to ponder as I left the Mystic Garden. King and Blaise were exhilarated by Dylan's performance as well. Stuck in a traffic jam on the only road out of town, we nibbled on almonds, drank Coronas, and patiently waited.

Oh Canada, here I come. A day after I saw Dylan at Woodstock, I jetted to Montreal for Jazzfest. For all my wanderlust, I'd never crossed the Canadian border before. It was Independence Day weekend, and the festival headliners were Van Morrison, Branford Marsalis, and Bob Dylan. There may have been others top acts at the festival, but those were the three cats I was focused upon. On July 4th, 2007, the festival organizers presented Dylan with the Montreal Jazz Festival Spirit Award. Bob definitely has the spirit.

This Jazzfest had a more cosmopolitan flavor than New Orleans. The downtown site was blocked off from vehicular traffic. Several outdoor stages were blended into the urban landscape to create an aesthetically pleasing environment. The people of Montreal flocked into the heart of it all, flooding the streets and the outdoor cafes. This might sound like a mind-blowing experience, but only those willing to shell out serious dough got to see the headliners. The top draws of Jazzfest were playing in nearby venues, and tickets averaged $100 per act.

I shelled out $175 to see Van Morrison at the Salle Wilfred-Pelletier. Van's an elusive rascal, probably more reclusive than Dylan. Casual Van fans expect trinkets like "Brown Eyed Girl," "Moondance," and "Gloria." Van coughs up a few hits for the crowd, but they are usually expedited. Van's primary concern is working his mojo, creating on his own terms with a heavy infusion of the blues. Like Dylan, he disappoints those who are seeking familiarity. Actually, Van's gruff demeanor makes Bob Dylan come off like Dick Clark.

Storming the stage in a snug suit that hugged his rotund body, the surly Belfast Balladeer shouted and sang viscerally, often echoing his own lines, his own lines, his own lines. This was my tenth Van show, and it was as suspenseful as my first. Van played "Raincheck," from *Days Like This*. I cut loose with a vigorous "Yee-hah!" The woman next to me swapped seats with her husband. She didn't care for my exuberance.

Van was good in Montreal, but he really kicked ass and took names at the Theatre at MSG on 4-29-07. That performance was worth the $175 admission. I was at that gig with Dr. Z and his girlfriend, Liz. Dr. Z. was one of my karaoke regulars, a cardiologist who made a name for himself with his freewheeling rendition of "Tupelo Honey" at 3:30 AM. As I watched him act out his rock star dreams, I'd imagine him at work the following day in his hospital gown, slicing up human heart tissue under the bright lights of the operating room. Before we watched Van preach, we dined on top-shelf cow and crab legs at Uncle Jack's Steakhouse by the Garden, and then we met up again after the show for more crab legs at Uncle Jack's. Van really had his mojo working that night. The good doctor had talked me into taking a road trip to Boston for a Van show the following night, but reality hit him in the morning. He had lives to save, and Liz was ready to disown him.

Hey now; let's get back to Montreal on July 4th. Waiting for Dylan, I was in the fourth row of the Salle Wilfred-Pelletier, a futuristic venue that looks like a space ship. The acoustics were brilliant. When a guy in front of me kicked over his cup, the sound of the plastic striking the cement floor was full bodied and crisp.

My trepidation that I'd reached a threshold where Dylan couldn't amaze me anymore was crushed in Woodstock and obliterated in Montreal. "Rollin' and Tumblin'," a *Modern Times* blues revamp set the night on fire. "Shelter From the Storm" sparkled. Dylan gives that song a different ride every time he plays it. Master of his domain, Dylan presented a breathtaking "Chimes of Freedom," a birthday salute for the United States of America. Sixteen years earlier, I thought Dylan was washed up after his July 4th disaster in Tanglewood—wrong again.

"Like a Rolling Stone" as the last number of the set was dramatic, a welcomed twist. Song placement is an underrated art, and Dylan knows how to juggle his compositions for maximum effect. The Montreal "Thunder on the Mountain" was extremely rowdy in the jam department. Dylan smirked wildly and raised his arms during the curtain call, a departure from his usually stoic last stance. Montreal received Dylan more enthusiastically than they had Van the night before.

A peculiar dream awoke me from a deep sleep in Montreal. "Thunder on the Mountain" was raging in my brain. The band was high-flying. As Bob growled, "I sucked the milk out of 1,000 cows," the music slowed to a grinding halt. There was a moment of silence before Bob and his Cowboy Band began to laugh hysterically. Dylan then turned to Tony and said, "Let's get out of this barn." I was observing this from the last row of the orchestra pit. Dylan and his band marched down the center aisle and headed towards the exit. Before splitting, Dylan turned around, raised his hands over his head, and yelled, "I am the greatest." I woke up amused on a Montreal motel mattress at 4:30 AM. I then went for a long stroll through the quiet streets and listened to *Desire* as the sun came around. I had delusions of leaving Montreal to follow the Cowboy Band to Ottawa, but it was too much of a hassle on short notice. Besides, I was booked for another night in Montreal.

Béla & the Flecktones and Branford Marsalis were my last entertainment flings at Jazzfest. The virtuosity of B &F was undeniable, but I failed to make an emotional connection to what they were doing. On the other hand, Branford was the bomb. If you crave depraved improvisation, check out Branford on the "Eyes of the World" from *Without a Net*, the Grateful Dead's live 1990 CD. Branford's first solo captures Jerry's essence without copying him. In Montreal, Branford played like a man possessed. His quartet covered a lot of territory, going from love ballads to furious arrangements that captured the sound and pulse of city life.

The collegiate lifestyle in Manhattan was treating me kindly. I had a new friend and writing ally in Lauren, and Robert Polito was the director of The New School Creative Writing Program. It didn't surprise me when I learned that Greil Marcus would be teaching at The New School for the first time in the fall of 2008. The class was called The Old Weird America. Of course, I enrolled in the course. America was weird, and my fate was stranger.

SEÑOR (TALES OF YANKEE POWER)

Pyramid Legs...Grunts, growls, and coyote barks...
Modern Times in Mexico City...Don't disturb a giant when
he's getting a shoeshine...Acapulco Gold...Revolution
in the Air...Mailman, don't bring me no more blues...
Fee fie fo fum, Muhammad Ali, here we come...

I broke a sweat as we hit the second tier of the pyramid. There was one more ledge before my sightseeing group ascended to the zenith of Teotihuacan civilization. This climb was child's play for a physically fit specimen like myself. Full of hubris, I turned to survey the terrain. I wondered if I could see Mexico City over the horizon. This is when sheer terror struck.

Jumping Jesus! How was I going to get down?

This gringo had gone too far. I'm terrified of heights. You fool! Why didn't you think about this before charging up the pyramid? I'd always avoided rock climbing and cliff diving, but I never considered the perils of scaling a pyramid. I was hoping for guard rails, an elevator, or some sort of tangible update from the past thousand years

What were my options? I had a cell phone. I wondered if the Federales might arrange a helicopter rescue. Sure. They were waiting for the call, eager to rescue a frightened bald-headed American on top of an ancient landmark. My rescue mission might provide the Federales with a breather from their life and death struggle with the dastardly drug cartels. All right, it wasn't much of an idea. What goes up, must come down; overcoming my phobia was inevitable. I marched upwards with my group, refusing to look down until I reached the peak of the Pyramid of the Sun.

There were no concession stands up there, no confidence building tequila poppers for the steep plunge down. The dirt row at the base was called the Avenue of the Dead, and I finally understood why. I copped a squat to reboot my legs and harness whatever spiritual energy emanated on top of this stone triangle in the sky. Others from my sightseeing posse were enjoying themselves, freely moving around and taking pictures.

It occurred to me that I wasn't going to die up here. Somehow I'd make it to the Dylan show that night, the first concert of his forty-seven year career in Mexico. This certainty eased my mind. As I began to descend with my group, I further bolstered the positive imagery in my mind by thinking of Eli Manning. The Giants had just pulled off one of the greatest Super Bowl shockers, a 17-14 victory over the previously undefeated New England Patriots. After taking a few heart-pounding steps, I conceded that the bricks were narrow, battered, and chipped, but all I needed to do was baby step my way down. Besides, if I slipped and fell, I could always latch on to the beefy Australian couple in front of me and sleigh ride my way to the bottom.

Pyramid of the Sun

Manuel, our tour guide, was waiting for us in the van. Our next stop was a guava shop a couple of miles down the road. There was no town, just a big ole hacienda surrounded by acres of guava, those wonderful plants from which we drain tequila. On the way back to Mexico City, I sat shotgun by our fearless leader. Manuel's movements were deliberate and dignified. He wore a white cowboy hat with a blue shirt beneath a brown vest. Manuel personified the timeless spirit of Mexico.

Observing me scribbling in my journal, Manuel said, "I hope you write good things about me. My name is Manuel."

I smiled and said, "I know who you are, señor."

Señor, Señor, Can you tell me where we're heading, Lincoln County Road or Armageddon. Seems like I've been down this way before. Is there any truth in that, Señor?"

This was a hardcore sightseeing tour. We had started at nine in the morning, and now it was 5:20 PM. I had prayed in every slanted church in Mexico City, and my prayers had yet to be answered. I had to beg Manuel for mercy. "Señor, I'm going to see a Cowboy Band tonight. Please take me back to my hotel soon."

I grabbed my ticket and hailed a taxi to Auditorio Nacional and almost triggered an international incident. Leaving the lime-colored cab, I handed the driver the fare, and what I thought was a healthy tip as I marched past a group of militia with automatic weapons. I speak and understand *poquito* Spanish; however, I could hear the taxi driver raging in the background. Apparently, I had a pesos comprehension problem. I paid a grand total of fifty cents on a seven-dollar fare, or something like that. I forked over the difference and gave him a quality tip this time, but he was still bitching to the militia. I rapidly ducked inside.

Auditorio Nacional was a strange indoor venue shaped like a pyramid. I'd purchased floor seats for the second night, but for the opening show, frugality got the best of me. I was in for a tedious hike up. By the time I got to my seat, three rows from the rafters, I'd developed a nasty case of pyramid legs.

This seat was unacceptable, even if I had purchased it due to frugality. I hadn't traveled to Mexico City to sit in the foothills of Guatemala while Dylan played. I knew the Dylan would be coming on any minute. I had to act swiftly. My pyramid legs almost gave out on me as I shuffled down to the ground floor and found the hospitality desk.

A Mexican beauty was in the hospitality booth. Her English was mellifluous, a rarity in this overcrowded mole hill. I smiled, engaged her eyes with mine, and improvised a heartfelt pitch.

"Hi, my name is Howard. I'm from New York City. I'm here to enjoy Mr. Dylan tonight," I said. I feel like I'm patronizing people if I start winging phrases like "Hola, señorita" and "Como estás?" I don't speak Spanish, and mixing seven words into my conversation will only magnify that point.

"Hola, Senor Howard," she said. "I'm Gabriela. How can I help you?"

Damn, she was gorgeous! Beautiful enough to disturb my thought process, but I was on a mission.

"Gabriela, I've come here to Mexico City to see Bob Dylan. I have a favor to ask of you. I made the mistake of buying some cheap tickets online. I'm a writer for USA Today. I was wondering if I could upgrade my ticket. Money is not an object. I have excellent seats for tomorrow night. Is there any way you can help me tonight?

"Señor Howard, there's a box office still selling tickets right outside."

"Yes, but the show's going to start any minute, and I don't know if I can get back in."

"Don't worry Señor Howard, you will get back in."

"Yes, but, I don't know if they have good seating left out there. Gabriela, I report Dylan's set lists to a site called Boblinks…I, ah, have to phone in a review after the show. A lot of people in America are waiting for me to dispense an accurate set list and report what happened. I need to be closer to the action."

Fighting off laughter, Gabriela said, "Excuse me. I'll check to see if we have anything in the back." After disappearing a minute for dramatic effect, she returned with a mischievous grin, and then waved the ticket at me. She said, "You're very lucky Señor Howard. Enjoy the concert."

Luck and fate are intertwined forces, but I spared Gabby the philosophical foray. On this occasion, "You're very lucky" meant she was handing me a third row ticket in the center balcony, about three zip codes closer to the stage than my original ticket. Gabriela is the goddess of hospitality.

Perched in my little overhang above the orchestra, I had the best seat in Mexico City, seating befitting the head of a drug cartel. The lights went out, and a familiar voice introduced Dylan, the same introduction that he's used since 2002.

Ladies and gentlemen please welcome the poet laureate of rock 'n' roll. The voice of the promise of the '60s counterculture. The guy who forced folk into bed with rock. Who donned makeup in the '70s and disappeared into a haze of substance abuse. Who emerged to find Jesus. Who was written off as a has-been by the end of the '80s, and who suddenly shifted gears, releasing some of the strongest music of his career beginning in the late '90s. Ladies and gentlemen, Columbia recording artist, Bob Dylan.

Dylan's visceral grunts, growls and coyote barks filled the Mexican night. It was 2-26-08, the opening night of his tour across the border, which was eventually dipping below the equator into South America. Dylan sacrificed the first three songs of the night, tossing them away, biding his time until he hit his stride.

"When the Levee Breaks" set the tone for the night. Bob bounced around by his organ as Denny Freeman took flight on his guitar solos. Six minutes of gritty American blues ended with Dylan proclaiming, "This is a day only the Lord can make." Amen.

Dylan's performances usually reflect upon the American experience, but on this night, Bob's art embraced the entire North American continent—borders erased. "Come, you masters of war; you build the death planes," Bob sang solemnly. "Masters of War" wasn't a protest song on this night; it was a mournful prayer. Centuries of endless conflict had worn Mexico out. From the dynasties who ruled Mexico to the drug lords who raped it, Mexico was war weary. In "High Water," when Bob sang about the shacks sliding down, I thought of those poverty-stricken shacks I had seen on the hills leading into Mexico City—cinder brick walls with tin roofs tenuously strung across.

Modern Times dominated this show in ancient lands. "Workingman's Blues # 2" was delivered with tenderness. The world of labor has gone berserk—too much work. When Bob sang about living on rice and beans in Mexico, it hit the sweet spot in my gut. Rice and beans is economical Mexican cuisine, but as long as the beans are black and the rice is brown, I'm satisfied. Throw in some steamed broccoli and red salsa, and I'll declare that dish a culinary masterpiece.

Hearing Dylan's band ramble and shift gears through "Highway 61 Revisited," I was reminded of my afternoon rattling down Highway 85 in Manuel's tour van. Highway 85 slices through the gut of Mexico east to west like Highway 61 cuts through the heart of the United States north to south. I was overwhelmed by emotion when Dylan stomped into "Nettie Moore." It was a rare occurrence to hear this in the same show as his other fabulous *Modern Times* ballad, "Working Man Blue's #2." Dylan was in the zone for his Mexican debut, and once again my wanderlust and dedication had paid unforeseen dividends. It was validation of my trip to Mexico City—living by my instincts, I was in the right place at the right time.

The huge crowd politely received Dylan's show, but they really came to life as Recile slammed down the opening drumbeat of "Like a Rolling Stone," the final tune of the fifteen-song set. Waiting for the encores, Mexico chanted: "Dil-awn! Dil-awn! Dil-awn! Dil-awn!"

I lodged at a dive around the block from the American Embassy. The banner in front read: Hotel del Angel—ABIERTO. The battered condition of the door to my room led me to believe that the door had been kicked an average of ten times a month for the past twenty years. It was obvious that the carpet hadn't been cleaned since the 1968 Olympics in Mexico City, although my only concern was getting a solid night's sleep. I hopped into bed and bruised my shoulder against the mattress, which had the comfort level of a Formica slate. I drifted in and out of dreamless sleep until dawn. When I awoke, my pyramid legs felt like they'd been climbing all night. My quads were burning, and my calves were tighter than a bongo.

In the Starbucks around the corner, I scored a venti iced coffee with vanilla syrup and a slice of chocolate chip banana cake. For a touch of Mexico City, I bought their local paper, *Reforma*. There was a color picture of Dylan on the front page—something you would never see on a New York City tabloid after a Dylan show. The headline read "Gracias, Dylan!"

As I wrote my review of the show, a guard with an automatic weapon was standing at the Starbucks entrance. The threat of violence lurked everywhere. American businesses were protected with armed warriors at their doors. Aside from men in business suits, I didn't notice any other Americans; that is, until I passed a hotel and saw a big old cowboy getting a shoeshine. It was Stu Kimball, the acoustic, and some time lead, guitarist of Dylan's band. I probably should have engaged him in some banter, but I was out of my mind from lack of sleep. Besides, disturbing a six foot-six giant while he's enjoying a shoeshine isn't prudent. I just gave him an enthusiastic thumbs-up. Stu acknowledged me with a smile and a friendly one-hand salute.

My biggest fear in Mexico City was the very real threat of Montezuma's Revenge. Back in 1985, when Acapulco was the hot tourist destination of Mexico, I was put out of commission by Montezuma's. I had a toilet bowl strapped to my ass for forty-eight hours. Outside of that awful conclusion to my family vacation, I had a grand time in Acapulco. I recall wearing a Phil Simms jersey while watching the Giants beat San Francisco, 17-3, in a playoff game and then celebrating by buying a half-ounce of Acapulco Gold on the beach. I was actually dumb enough to smuggle a few joints back on the flight to New York. Those were the golden days for tourism in Acapulco, but things have changed for the worse, thanks to the drug wars.

O. K. I've digressed a bit. To protect my digestive system while in Mexico City, I avoided any fluids besides Starbucks, bottled beer and bottled water, and I only dined at places where the business elite go. There was a deli-styled restaurant with a bar right next to the American Embassy. Their buffet display looked sanitary. I feasted on the bagels, turkey slices, and lox during my three day stay. This diplomat's hangout was connected to the lobby of the adjacent hotel. I tuned-up for the second Dylan show on three-dollar margaritas during happy hour at this fine establishment. Across the street, a small group gathered. I thought it might be the start of a soccer parade, but I realized this was a spirited protest rapidly morphing into an angry mob.

A barricade and a thirty-foot fence stood between me and the rebels, just in case they wanted to start tossing foreign objects at the American Embassy, or the deli. There was, and always will be, unrest in Mexico

City; it's too hot, and there're too many people. The homeless beggars of Manhattan are fat cats in comparison to the homeless of Mexico City. I saw the soul of despair in the eyes of Mexican street beggars—despair that no handout could ever cure. Revolution was permanently in the air.

Protest leaders with red flags and brightly colored signs started rallying the crowd. The big cheese had a black scarf wrapped around his head and a bullhorn in his hand. The crowd of rebels multiplied on the west side of Paseo de la Reforma, the longest-running avenue in Mexico City. The Mexican Fidel yelled, and the rebels cheered their demagogue's rhetoric. I was curious to find out who they were mad at and why. I asked the bartender what was happening. He replied, "Don't worry...this happens all the time," with a dismissive hand wave. As I sipped margaritas, I felt as if there was a giant bull's eye on my forehead. I wished I was on the other side of the fence—Masked and Anonymous.

Dylan would probably take the stage around eight. It was six-thirty, and I needed some more margarita-induced confidence to step outside. I could have snuck out the side door, through the hotel lobby, but curiosity got the best of this Cat, and I always like to leave the way I came. The rebels lined up and began marching down the avenue, following their leader beneath the setting sun. I walked out the door and pumped my fist in solidarity towards the crowd. I really did feel a strange connection to them, but I was headed the other way—off to see my leader and his Cowboy Band.

I felt anxious around 2:30 PM every day after my trip to Mexico. That was the time the mailman would make his appearance in the hallway of my building on East 84th Street. Hearing the turning of the key, I'd jump to my feet and salivate until I heard the box slam. Then, I'd charge out into the hall, barefooted, and pounce on the mail. Would I be accepted into the MFA Creative Writing program at The New School? Would my twenty-six page writing sample cut the nut? It was a long-winded rant on how the Grateful Dead influenced Dylan.

The letter arrived on March 17, 2008. I pulled it from the box and calmly walked into my apartment. With one manic motion, I ripped the letter out. It read:

Dear Mr. Weiner,

It is my pleasure to notify you of your admission to The New School's Master of Fine Arts in Creative Writing beginning in the Fall 2008 Semester. You have been selected for the concentration in Nonfiction. You must submit your final official transcript, indicating degree completion, prior to the start of your first semester.

I hopped around my apartment in circles before flopping to the floor. I thought about how proud my father would have been. I called my mom, sent out emails, and then went to Mustang Grill for several celebratory pops. I'd composed most of my Dead/ Dylan screed during happy hour at Mustang on the corner of 85th Street and Second Avenue. The successful paper was titled: *Busy Being Born: Tales of American Spirit.* I completely rolled the dice on getting into The New School. I didn't have a back-up plan.

I joined the cap and gown ceremony for The New School graduates at the Theatre at Madison Square Garden on May 16, 2008. I had earned my first college degree! A news crew or two should have been there to cover the story. I had extended a four-year education into a twenty-eight year odyssey. My mom treated the family to a scrumptious meal at Uncle Jack's Steakhouse to commemorate the occasion. I was one of the worst college students in the annals of American academics, but I returned to complete my final thirty-six credits and was accepted into an elite MFA program in less than one year, and I did it my way, without missing a beat from the Cowboy Band.

The day after graduation, I continued my wicked touring rampage. I rode an early morning train to Boston, where I transferred on to a bus headed for Maine—Lewiston, that is. I claimed my hotel room and snapped-off a twin lobster dinner before heading over to the gymnasium, where Ali shook up the world again with a phantom punch. The Big Bear, Sonny Liston, knocked out loaded on the canvas. Forty-three years later, the lights went out in that same gymnasium. Dylan took the stage, and I went shuffling in Ali's footsteps.

WHEN I PAINT MY MASTERPIECE

Together Through Life and Pig Flu Fever...Struggling waiters pitted against hungry writers...Caught between heaven and hell on a Greyhound to Allentown...Dylan in the land of Coca Cola...The Village Beasts of Lakeland...The Red Rocks of Sedona...When you're a Jet, you're a Jet all the way...

The stock market crashed on cue when *Tell Tale Signs* hit store shelves in September of 2008. Volume 8 of Dylan's Bootleg Series arrived as the American economy began to freefall into recession. Six weeks later, I went to see Dylan in Minneapolis on my 45th birthday, on the day Obama was elected President. Four months later, Dylan's new CD, *Together through Life,* was released. With it, came the Swine Flu. People were walking around Manhattan with hospital masks as I emerged from the subway listening to "Beyond Here Lies Nothing." A public panic had now accompanied the release of four Dylan albums in the Twenty-First Century.

Somehow we keep marching on. Dylan's music is a source of continuity, a healing salve in a world gone wrong. Jack Fate. That was Dylan's character Dylan in *Masked and Anonymous.* I don't believe Dylan's a prophet, but he has always been in the right place, singing all the right songs—*I can't help it if I'm lucky.* Remember, Bob's pseudonym as a member of the Traveling Wilburys was Lucky Wilbury.

Tell Tale Signs confirmed that Dylan's leftover scraps are immense. Everything counts, even when he's winging it in the studio. This junkyard collection introduced "The Girl from the Red River Shore," an outtake from the *Time Out Of Mind* sessions, a ballad of yearning for love that's just out of reach—similar in spirit to "Nettie Moore." *"I been to the east, and I been to the west, and I been out where the black winds roar; but I never did get that far with the girl from the Red River Shore."*

David Gates, the journalist who interviewed Dylan for a 1997 *Newsweek* cover story, was the professor for my first literature seminar in grad school. Gates was a soft-spoken literary genius delivering lectures in a hooded green sweatshirt. Between Gates, Marcus, and Polito, I had the finest education any aspiring Dylan writer could have. Jonathan Ames was my writing workshop professor. Jonathan appeared just like I'd pictured him: seersucker jacket, tan beret, and slightly uncomfortable in front of the class. His aloof aura gave off an air of indifference, but nothing could have been further from the truth.

My second year classmates expected formal writing instruction from Ames, author of *Extra Man* and *Wake Up Sir,* a pair of witty novels. I had no expectations; I couldn't believe I was in an MFA program. I thought it was a tremendous class, and my education continued at our post-class drinking sessions with Ames at Café Loop, an upscale dive on 13th Street, close to Sixth Ave. Observing the writer as he observes his environment is more valuable than any preconceived lessons.

Ames liked my underdeveloped pieces, even though he wasn't a music enthusiast. After reading about my *Blood on The Tracks* revelation, he picked up the album to see if he could connect. This was a small step for me as a writer, but I don't think Dylan picked up a new admirer in Jonathan Ames.

During the three-hour workshops on Monday nights, the class critiqued tales of anorexia, bulimia, homosexual romps, S&M mistresses,

Fidel Castro, and Holocaust survivors. Somehow, in this funky shuffle, my road tales were well-received. After our therapy session, we'd grab a long table and hang out with Jonathan and his girlfriend, Fiona Apple. At the time, Ames was heavily involved in shooting a pilot that he wrote for HBO, *Bored to Death*. His pilot became a series on Sunday nights. With his HBO money, Ames usually picked up the tab for us, but his real generosity was giving us a glimpse into the life of a successful writer. Most writers are convinced they will be living like paupers, and that's a prophecy that will fulfill itself until the writer changes his or her way of thinking.

Most of my fellow students lived like struggling artists, and they were young enough to be my forsaken children. The wait staff at Café Loop cringed at the sight of us. They reluctantly brought us bread and water. Inmates get better service. The famished writers would snatch at the bread before it hit the table. Occasionally, someone would order French fries, and the staff was lucky to get a dollar per person—unless, of course, they were waiting on the Jonathan Ames table. I loved the tension: a struggling wait staff of wannabe stars pitted against hungry writers in a snooty French café. Priceless.

Free meatballs and fried potato things blotched in hot sauce were the attraction at Spain, a stone cold dump one door down from Café Loop. The graduate school writers embraced Spain in spite of the seven-foot ceilings and the gruff staff of elderly gentlemen serving up drinks and free "food." Sometimes they served chicken wings—nothing but skin and bone. I was often hungry after class, but I could never summon the courage to eat their free offerings. I often closed the place, pounding Dos Equis with my attractive classmates Erin, Kim, and Brittney. Erin and Kim were working for literary agencies. I was a Mattress Professional for Sleepy's.

In *Post Office*, Charles Bukowsi's opening line reads:

"It began as a mistake."

You too, Mr. Bukowski? My year at Sleepy's was a God-awful gaffe. After nine years as the Karaoke Godfather of the Upper East Side, I quit while I was on top. I said "No thanks" to dragging home speakers at five in the morning, and if I heard one more yuppie sing Bon Jovi, I was going to go postal. I returned to sales, and a nine-to-five job, at Sleepy's. Before I knew what happened, nine-to-five became an eleven-hour shift five times a week, and I kissed my weekends goodbye. Welcome to Retail Hell, old sport.

I pictured myself going off on wild writing tangents during my down time at Sleepy's; however, the mattress showroom sucked my brain dry. I didn't have three creative thoughts while I was there. The place was a morgue driven by the heartless corporate beast. At least I earned decent dough during tough economic times—enough dough to follow Dylan to Atlantic City, Amsterdam, Allentown, Lakeland, Phoenix and Las Vegas.

Commuters poured into the Port Authority through every pore on Tuesday morning, July 14th, 2009. Supreme Court nominee Sonia Sotomayor was being grilled by the Senate during her confirmation hearings. I was reading David Foster Wallace's *Consider the Lobster* and sipping white wine in a self-service cafeteria at 9:30 AM. This is how abnormal people live. I was the only person on the planet busing from New York City to Allentown for a Dylan show. Fabulous. Maybe I was the one who should be getting grilled by the Senate suits. After further deliberation, I considered the lobster and boarded a Greyhound.

An hour into my journey, I heard a bizarre noise behind me—psssst...psssst. It sounded like a punctured tire slowly leaking. I jerked my head around. Two rows behind me was a suspicious looking dude in shades sporting a Rick James Jheri Curl and a tan fedora. The beast was spraying a powdery silver substance from an aerosol can against some kind of plastic contraption. Say what? I know what I just said, and what I saw, yet I can't explain what he was doing. This malcontent even scared away a couple of gangsters who moved from the back of the bus to the front. Things simmered-down for a brief spell, then there was that noise again—psssst...psssst. A toxic odor filled the bus. Now the Greyhound smelled like Red Bull meeting Aqua Velva in a pizza oven.

I began to worry about the air quality. I didn't want to die on my way to a show. If I have to meet an untimely death, I'd rather it happen during the encore or on the return trip. I can't believe the driver didn't pull the bus over to evict the whacko in the tan fedora, but like everybody else, he must have been terrorized, I suppose. Talking on cell phones was prohibited during the ride, but apparently there was no ban on the spraying and inhaling toxic fumes.

Somewhere past Easton, home of former Heavyweight Champion Larry Holmes, strange got stranger. Two sexy girls, exchange students from Romania, struck up a conversation with me in arousing, yet imperfect English, asking me 99 questions about America. For some reason they were headed to Harrisburg, the state capital of Pennsylvania. If they really wanted to dig America, I suggested they should join me, Willie Nelson, John Cougar Mellencamp, and Dylan at Coca-Cola Ballpark. Alas, they knew nothing of baseball or Dylan—they were really hoping I could explain the Jerri curled nightmare behind me. As we continued to chat, the mystery vagabond started laughing and farting until he subdued himself by lying perpendicular in the backseat. A few miles from Allentown, I could see the finish line to this madness. I had two Romanian angels in front of me and a hallucinating hell cat behind me. Ain't that America?

The heart of Allentown was long gone—the American Dream, dead. The old factories and mills appeared like abandoned honey combs, and the old train junction was sprouting wild weeds. There were gorgeous mountains in the distance and a picturesque waterfall just up the road, but nobody wanted to reclaim this section of town. I grabbed a cab to the Red Roof Inn and, much to my horror, a Sleepy's was across the way, in the same shopping center. It makes a fella proud to be a Mattress Professional. Oh, balls!

My sanity was on trial as I walked to Coca-Cola Park, past an imposing graveyard smack in the middle of Allentown. I should have hailed a cab from the Red Roof Inn because there was no path for a man to walk, even in an old-time American haunt like Allentown. It was a perilous three-mile stroll in a stream of scorching heat. Motorists looked at me in awe. Who was this strange, bald-headed straggler with the backpack walking roadside? Where the hell is your car, Buddy? This is why I love New York City. Foot marching pedestrians whizz by stalled motorists and ponder the sanity of those who drive.

Coca-Cola Park was a wondrous vision. That Coke bottle shooting out of the centerfield scoreboard was quite an erection. Corporate America covered every parcel of ballpark, even if China was fronting the money. I rested my beer in a News 69 cup holder and stretched out in the Empire Blues Shield on-deck circle. I stood by home plate and wondered if my forty-five-year-old body could still pull one down the line, just below the clouds and above the left-field fence 350 feet away. Keep dreaming.

After enjoying Willie Nellson, and observing the crowd rock out to Mellencamp, I stepped up to the left-field fence as the skies darkened over the Lehigh Valley. It was 9:10 PM. Does anyone know where Bob Dylan is? And, suddenly, there he was—all one hundred and thirty pounds of him, loping towards the stage behind his Cowboy Band. If he didn't play a song, hot shit, this was already a great night. There was something thrilling about watching Dylan skip across the outfield grass like a marionette. His gait was extraordinary—kind of like "The Mick" limping around the bases.

Dylan looked like the Jack of Hearts standing there with his electric guitar slung around his slender torso during the "Leopard Skin Pillbox Hat" opener. A phenomenal version of "Don't Think Twice It's Alright" followed with three biting solos. I never heard Dylan express himself so lyrically on electric guitar before. Either that, or the Lehigh Valley was playing tricks on my mind. The sound dynamics of the Valley were astounding. Some spaces are alive with a magical vibe. The Lehigh Valley is one of those inspirational hotspots for music. It reminded me of Sullivan County.

The next day, the only bus rummaging through Allentown was picking up passengers at 7 PM. I assumed there would be an earlier bus to New York—now I had a day to kill in Allentown. I checked out of the Red Roof Inn with my stuffed backpack and spent the afternoon listening to *Modern Times* underneath a wooden pavilion, ducking the sun with a peaceful hive of bees. If I had known it was going to be 100 degrees, and I wouldn't be able to escape this hog-eyed town until nightfall, I might have called the whole thing off. Happy Hour at the Jack Creek Steakhouse made the final hours bearable. Sam Adams Summer Ales were discounted down to a dollar.

The Greyhound back to New York was no picnic, either. The main culprit of despair during this leg of the journey was the toilet bowl that hadn't been flushed since Louisville. My kidneys clinched tight for two hours. I was the only Caucasian on the packed bus, and these cats around me talked up a storm. Hilarious cats. I eavesdropped on their incredible tales—back of the bus blues.

A week after Allentown, I talked Stan into another Ballpark Extravaganza. Pulling out of Manhattan, Stan had satellite radio blasting in the Lexus. We listened to BB King's Bluesville, and then switched to *Together through Life*. It took me a few months to love that album, but I was eventually swayed by the accordion-dominated sound and lyrics which clung to my heart more with each listen. *The next time I leave here, will be the way that I came, I gotta restless fever, burning in my brain...I'll run this race until my earthly death; I'll defend this place with my dying breath*

Into the rain and the clouds and the Garden State we drove. It drizzled steady as we pulled into a vacant lot of an office complex near Blue Claw Stadium in Lakeland. This was the place to be. Stan had a couple of yellow rain jackets in the back of his trunk. We heard Willie playing, but we were having too much fun singing to Dylan CDs in the rain. Stan lit a cigar and said, "Hey, Howie, you want to check out Mellencamp?"

I said, "Screw Mellencamp; let's listen to *Together through Life Again*."

It was a strange day in Dylanville. Unbeknownst to us, Dylan was picked up in the afternoon by local police. Mr. Dylan, AKA Robert Zimmerman, had been roaming around Lakeland, just checking out the real estate, on foot, when he was pulled in for questioning. I wonder if he was wearing a rain jacket or a hooded poncho. Maybe he was out there, peering in on everyday people, imagining what it was like to be one of us.

Completing our pre-show festivities with "I Feel A-Change Comin' On," Stan and I fixated on our favorite line: *I see my baby coming; she's walking with the village priest.* Stan told me that Perry thought Dylan was singing "Village Beast" when he first heard it. Now that's a great line. Why can't Dylan come up with stuff like that? You can see the Village Beast, can't you? Our suspect stands about six-foot-three, ZZ Top beard dangling down by his extended mid-section, torn jeans sliding south, checkered green flannel, red beret, thick-rimmed shades, and several species of insects buzzing around. Hide the women and children; here comes the Village Beast.

Bob was extra-fidgety on stage in his dazzling lavender suit and white top hat, a tell-tale sign that we were in for a sensational night. Stan noted that Dylan looked like The Joker, as played by Cesar Romero. After a radical "Tweedle Dee & Tweedle Dum," we were blessed by "A Hard Rain's A-Gonna Fall." Sweet destiny! Although the rain had stopped, the lavender bard howled out the mystical words against a funky arrangement. All old things became new again. And, as a laborer toiling over fifty hours a week, I was touched by "Workingman's Blues #2." Dylan's vocals were tender and his harp solos were plush—you could feel the everyday grind of the American worker.

"Ain't Talkin,'" the masterful last sermon on *Modern Times* was marvelous in Allentown, and it ricocheted back to the dramatic beginning of the album with "Thunder on the Mountain," a fabulous loop-de-loop. *Modern Times* was still the carbs fueling Bob's creativity.

Ninety minutes from New York City, Stan and I were in no rush to split. *The same way I'm leaving; Will be the way I came; I got a restless fever burning in my brain.* If we hung around long enough, we might have bumped into Dylan prowling around the hood, looking for a place where there was still something going on. Instead, we met Joey D.

Joey D, a bulky Jersey type of guy, joined us for a brew and a jig. His befuddled date watched in horror as we danced in the dark to Dylan. Joey was also into Jerry. I pulled an '83 JGB Roseland CD out of my traveling bag to extend the night. Eventually Joey D. and his date spilt. Stan and I headed for Chinatown. Wo Hop beckoned.

"Stan, Catfish. Good to see you guys. Where have you been?" asked the blue-smocked waiter.

"Where have you been, my blue-eyed son? You look beautiful. We were in Jersey tonight with the Jokerman," exclaimed Stan.

"You guys want a table for two?"

"Better make that three," I said. "The Village Beast is on his way."

Before I knew what happened, three semesters of grad school disappeared. The time for my thesis had arrived. I was ready, but I decided to clear my head with one more rendezvous prior to scribbling my epic story. I headed west to see gigs in Phoenix and Las Vegas—my 99th and 100th Dylan shows.

After a noon arrival in Phoenix, I bolted north in a shuttle van with six strangers. Destination: the Red Rocks of Sedona, Arizona. The driver of the van had a list of passenger names. For some reason, he kept calling me Conrad. I enjoyed being Conrad for an afternoon. Our ninety-five minute jaunt north featured nothing but cactus and tumbleweed and tumbleweed and cactus. Some of the cacti were enormous and phallic; other cactus plants grew in groups. Some sprouted two enormous arms; others were multi-armed genetic misfits.

We blew by Carefree Highway, and then passed a town called Bumble Bee on our way over Mingus Mountain, elevation 4000 feet. Freefalling down the backside of Mingus, somewhere near Cottonwood, the Red Rocks of Sedona shimmered on the horizon. The Red Rocks were also purple, lavender, and bright orange as the rays of the sun lambasted the ancient mesas—another day, just as it has been since the dinosaurs thundered through the valley. I haven't validated the dinosaur thing, but Sedona is a vortex of hallucination.

Doug Schmell called when I was in Sedona. He had come into New York to see the Yankees and the Los Angeles Angels in the American League Championship Series. 2009 was a very good year for Yankee Baseball. We won it all. Doug was doing fine, living in a cushy house on the west coast of Florida. He abandoned his law practice before it ever trapped him. Doug was well-off, thanks to his comic book business. His wife, two kids, and his dog Goliath, all manage to share him with Jerry. Doug still loves Garcia with purer enthusiasm than anybody I've ever met. And he still loves it loud.

I decompressed in Sedona for a few days before joining the Kerr clan in their new Phoenix home. Jim and Suzie had their first child, an adorable seven-month-old girl named Ava. Jim wanted to name her Althea or Peggio, but that notion was vetoed. Jim was building his own recording studio in back of his house, a sacred shack where the Sirius Grateful Dead channel played all day. I'm not sure if this studio was for other bands, Jim's own musical dreams, or if it was just a shrine to the music gods.

Extreme weather was nipping at my heels again. It was 102 record-breaking degrees in Phoenix on October 17, 2009. Jim took me to the Phoenix Botanical Garden, a place where only the cacti were content. Fortunately, the traveling butterfly exhibit provided us some shelter from the scorching sun. I admired these remarkable creatures and basked in the cooling mist being pumped into the tent for their comfort.

Suzie despised Dylan's voice, but she joined us for "The Bob Dylan Show" at the Arizona State Fairgrounds. Most folks love a busy week-end carnival. I don't. This carnival featured the standard hoopla: Ferris Wheel, freaks, midgets, clowns, barkers, neon lights, octopus and tea-pot rides, candy apples, snow cones, Polish sausage, Cajun corn dogs, Indian fry bread. For those who craved something more innovative and risqué, deep fried scorpions and lizards on a stick were also available.

Charlie Sexton, a Kevin Bacon clone, who was last seen in Bob's band back in 2002, had returned, replacing the irreplaceable Denny Freeman. I was sad to see Denny go. He bended notes with feeling, an old-timey touch that suited the band. If Denny was out, Charlie was an adequate replacement. For three songs, Dylan chose to stand and deliver vocals as if he were center stage on Broadway. In his right hand he carried a harp and a wireless mic shaped like a turkey drumstick. The cowboy/ caveman disturbed the peace with long emphatic harp solos. More than ever, this was the Bob Dylan Show. Suzie loved Dylan's stage routine, and she developed a crush on The Maestro. Jim had a great time, but he was a Jerry Garcia devotee all the way.

After the show, we got pretty ripped on Sierra Nevada ale at a place called The Loose Leaf. Eventually, we had to go back to Jim's place. Rick was waiting for me. Bad Boy Rick, Jim's twenty-nine-pond pussy-cat, made me feel like an intruder at the Kerr house since I showed up. I said, "Jim, what's up with Rick? He's been giving me the evil eye since I've been here."

"Yeah, Catfish. Rick's got a bit of an attitude; he's territorial. He's attacked a few of our guests. He scratched Suzie's sister pretty bad, and he recently gave the babysitter a black eye."

Whacked from several pints, I raided Jim's pantry. I found the cat treats, tiny canisters of shrimp and chicken flavored Pounce. I cautiously fed Rick treats until he started to purr. We passed out together in Ava's room.

My cell phone alarm awoke me at 6:30 AM. Jim delivered me to the airport, and I landed in Las Vegas by nine. I dropped my bags off at my room in Hooter's Hotel and then rolled down to The Mirage to place bets on NFL games. While I was there, I spent a few hours grazing at the Champagne Buffet Brunch at Cravings. Old times; good times. My next stop was the Las Vegas Hard Rock Café Hotel & Casino. Dylan was playing inside at a venue called The Joint.

Las Vegas has been, and may always be, the ultimate delusion—a hedonistic hustle, a diversion in the desert, a pressure-packed opportunity to feel the heat of humanity. What happens in Vegas stays in Vegas. But what really happens? You gamble, you gorge, you drink, you gamble, you walk the Strip, you see a few shows, you eat a few matzo balls, you gamble, you have an orgasm or two, and you feel a connection to others aimlessly roaming around the desert. When it's all said and done, you get the bill. That's why what happens in Vegas stays in Vegas.

This was the ideal place for my 100th show—I'd reached a milestone of weirdness without ever targeting it. I believe seeing Garcia 200 times, and Dylan 100 times, is an accomplishment to be proud of. It wasn't easy, but manifesting your destiny never is.

What are Milestones? Well, Miles had a sensational album called *Milestones*, but besides being landmark numbers, what do they represent? For one thing, milestones tell us about ourselves; who we are, where we've been, and where we're likely to go. I've always followed the songs in my mind. They've been my inspirational compasses. After 300 nights with Dylan and Garcia, and grad school nearly completed, the vision for my book was finally clear.

On my own for the show, I had a Heineken in my left hand and a journal in my right. I took my place amongst the beautiful people waiting for Dylan in The Joint. My 100th show would be a confirmation more than a celebration—a continuum of my existence. *I love the life I live, and I'm gonna live the life I love.* The lights went out and Dylan appeared on stage. When you're a Jet, you're a Jet all the way…Selah!

Made in the USA
Charleston, SC
05 July 2012